The Underwriter's Bedside Book

Edited by
JONATHAN S. IGNARSKI

|L|L|P|

Lloyd's of London Press Ltd
Sheepen Place
Colchester, Essex CO3 3LP

USA AND CANADA
Lloyd's of London Press Inc
Suite 523, 611 Broadway
New York, NY 10012, USA

GERMANY
Lloyd's of London Press
PO Box 11 23 47
Deichstrasse 41, 2000 Hamburg 11
West Germany

SOUTH EAST ASIA
Lloyd's of London Press (Far East) Ltd
903 Chung Nam Building
1 Lockhart Road, Wanchai
Hong Kong

First published 1987

British Library Cataloguing in Publication Data

The underwriter's bedside book
1. Insurance
I. Ignarski, Jonathan S.
368'.012 HG8051

ISBN 1–85044–133–2

Jacket design and illustration
Alan Mauro, Artform
Text set in 10 on 11pt Garamond by
Wessex Typesetters, Frome, Somerset
Printed in Great Britain by
WBC Print Ltd, Bristol

For Mary and Sophie

Acknowledgements

Part of the pleasure of compiling an anthology lies in the many ideas and suggestions of third parties. I am obliged for the kind assistance afforded by: David Scully and Tom Denniston of Thomas J. Bradshaw and Associates; Leslie Blake of the South Bank Polytechnic; Ian Hay Davidson of *The Independent*; Manfred Schaefer of Securitas-Gilde; Simon Gutteridge of Shaw & Sons; Brian Richardson of Gibbs Hartley Cooper; Richard Horsey of the Mercantile and General; Barry Coulson of C. E. Heath; and John Tilley, Phil Nicols, Philip Bennett, Nicholas Sanson and the Hon. Michael Summerskill, all of Thomas Miller & Co; and finally Ake Nilson and Ivor Gibson of Atlantica Continental.

My thanks also go to the keepers of the bibliographic flame at the London Library (Mr Douglas Matthews), the Corporation of Lloyd's (Mr John Curtis) and the Chartered Insurance Institute (Mr Robert L. Cunnew – particularly in respect of material supplied on Cornelius Walford).

It would be base ingratitude not to single out at Lloyd's of London Press Mrs Pat Morris for her valued help in obtaining copyright permissions and Ted Martin for his matchless print and design expertise. I must also mention Alan Mauro for his conception of the sleeping underwriter and the jacket design. Not for the last time, I am sure, I am also obliged to Laura Tatham of Wordpro Business Services.

Needless to say, any errors in selection and lapses in editing are all mine.

The drawings, based on various aspects of the new Lloyd's Building, are by Andrew Ignarski.

We are grateful to the following for permissions granted in respect of copyright: Macmillan & Co Ltd: D. E. W. Gibb, *Lloyd's of London* (1957); Charles Wright & C. Ernest Fayle, *A History of Lloyd's* (1878); Tony Waltham, *Catastrophe – The Violent Earth* (1978); Cambridge University Press: Frank C. Spooner, *Risks at Sea* (1983); Robert Hale Ltd: Frank Ledwith, *Ships that go Bump in the Night* (1974); Frank Ledwith, *Ships Afloat in the City* (1977); James M. Cain, *Double Indemnity* (1936); The Bodley Head: David Keir, *The Bowring Story* (1962); L. T. C. Rolt, *Red for Danger* (1955); Hodder & Stoughton Ltd: Rudyard Kipling, 'The Ballad of the "Bolivar"' (1890); Jon Connell & Douglas Sutherland, *Fraud – The Amazing Career of Dr Savundra* (1978); University of Chicago Press: A. W. Brian Simpson, *Cannibalism and the Common Law* (1984); Stevens & Sons Ltd: R. E. Megarry, *A Second Miscellany-at-Law* (1973); Messrs William Charles Crocker: William Charles Crocker, *Far from Humdrum* (1967); *Police Review*: Insurance claims statements from 'Spare A Copper'; Macdonald &

Jane's: J. M. Ramsden, *The Safe Airline* (1979); John Murray Ltd: John E. N. Hearsey, *London and the Great Fire* (1965); The Harpur Trust: M. E. Barlen, M. P. Stambach & D. P. C. Stileman, *Bedford School and the Great Fire* (1984); Routledge & Kegan Paul: Stephen Pile, *The Book of Heroic Failures* (1979); Lionel Rose, *The Massacre of the Innocents* (1986); Paul Zsolnay Verlag, Vienna & Hamburg: Alexander Roda Roda, *Die Versicherung* (1905); Eyre Methuen Ltd: A. P. Herbert, *Uncommon Law* (1935); Lawrence Pollinger Ltd: Erskine Caldwell, *The Complete Stories of Erskine Caldwell*; The Baynard Press: E. P. Leigh-Bennett, *On This Evidence* (1936); McGraw Hill: William H. A. Carr, *Perils Named and Unnamed* (1967); Sampson Low, Marston & Co Ltd: F. J. Maclean, *The Human Side of Insurance* (1931); Dennis Dobson Ltd: William Bolitho, *Murder for Profit* (1953); Lloyd's Log: Marcel Berlins, 'Who Owns the *Titanic*?'; William Kimber & Co: Edward Cowan, *Oil and Water* (1968); David & Charles: Antony Brown, *Cuthbert Heath* (1980); Penguin Books in association with Michael Joseph: E. S. Turner, *Roads to Ruin* (1966); Guardian Royal Exchange: Alan Chalkley, *Adventures and Perils* (1985); *The Review*: Anne Swain, 'The Secret Diary of Frederick Hole, Aged about 39', Secker & Warburg: Max Brod, *The Biography of Franz Kafka* (1947).

Every effort has been made to obtain consent from the respective holders of copyright. We will gladly rectify any errors and/or omissions made inadvertently.

J.S.I.

Foreword

This is a marvellous miscellany for anybody connected with Lloyd's, in particular, or insurance in general. It brings together the works of some first-rate writers on the subject, pokes some gentle fun, and is very enlightening in some of its historical text.

I recommend this book to anybody during sleepless nights or any other occasion when one wants a gentle and pleasant distraction.

PETER N. MILLER
Chairman, Lloyd's of London

Preface

The life of an underwriter can be hard and full of unpleasant surprises: sometimes risks slumber for decades, grumbling occasionally, but giving no real trouble. Other risks, once underwritten, fly up like hornets and sting very badly those who have had the temerity to disturb them. The worst risks are uncomfortably like the train about to leave Thorpe station (p. 33). You initial the broker's slip and almost immediately (though not almost enough), you are oppressed by a feeling of certain disaster. It is not, in any event, a boring life.

Given the nature of the business, underwriters need to know something of a great many things. In addition to exhibiting the usual professional virtues of sound judgement and commercial instinct, an underwriter has also to find time to read the publications of his trade, such as *Lloyd's List*, insurance journals, and many other informative or legalistic publications which in some way or other bear dryly upon the business of insurance.

Yet, at the end of a day, there may be a need for something less unremittingly utilitarian. The world of letters has many references to the underwriter's world. Sometimes these are in terms of a loss suffered, or some individual's attempt to enrich himself unjustly at the underwriter's expense. Other, and rarer, passages shed light on the underwriter's past and present way of life. Such writings deserve to be lifted out of context and brought to the attention of interested readers.

The undersigned can make no large claim for the selection of passages in this anthology. The criteria used for selection were simple: any passage which seemed interesting, well written or amusing was selected. Passages which were none of these things were excluded. Inevitably the compiler's prejudices are reflected in the number of maritime and historical passages included.

The modest intent of this collection of extracts is simply to provide a selection of reading which might cater for the variable moods of such readers who return home each day after long hours spent at least in the contemplation of risk, if not insurance.

June 1987 JONATHAN S. IGNARSKI

Contents

I
Early Days

1 *In London*

England owes the introduction of coffee to Archbishop Laud. He was interested in the welfare of Christian refugees who sometimes came here escaping from Mohammedan rule in the Eastern Mediterranean. One of his protégés was a Cretan scholar named Canopis who was brought by the Archbishop to Balliol College, Oxford, and there 'desseminated his grave learning and amused his colleagues' by brewing 'a drink of a soote colour dryed in a furnace and that they drink as hot as can be endured'. He seems to have communicated the taste quickly to a number of people both in Oxford and in Cambridge. An apothecary started selling coffee publicly in his house 'against All Soules College', and within a few years undergraduates in both Universities were spending so much time in the coffee-houses that the practice was denounced by some of the more serious-minded dons. In our own day the head of an Oxford College once spoke regretfully of the 'time-wasting habit of morning coffee' and in saying that (whether he knew it or not) he was only repeating the complaint of a Cambridge don nearly three centuries before him. 'Why', cried the Cambridge don in 1677 'why doth solid and serious learning decline and few or none now follow it in the University? Answer: because of coffee-houses where they spend all their time.'

London kept pace with the University towns and in 1652 an English merchant in the Levantine trade, who had acquired the habit abroad, began making coffee in his English home. Immediately he found that he was a far more popular person than he had ever before realized. Friends and acquaintances gathered at his house every morning to enjoy his conversation, until they became an unbearable nuisance and he a most reluctant host. Suspecting at last that the attraction lay less in his personality than in the 'new kind of black liquor his servant was in the habit of preparing every morning', he suggested to his servant that he should set up professionally as a coffee-man in St Michael's Alley, Cornhill. The servant agreed and the first of London's coffee-houses was opened.

The earliest advertisements put out by this servant made the most remarkable claims for coffee, emphasizing rather its medical than its social advantages, and putting it forward almost as a panacea for the maladies of mankind. 'It so incloseth', the servant's advertisement ran,

> the orifice of the stomach, and fortifies the heat within, that it is very good to help digestion; and therefore of great use to be taken about three or four o'clock afternoon

as well as in the morning. It much quickens the spirits and makes the heart lightsome; it is good against sore eyes and the better if you can hold your head over it and take in the steam that way. It suppresseth the fumes exceedingly and therefore it is good against the headache and will very much stop any deflexion of rheums, that distill from the head upon the stomach, and so prevent and help consumptions and the cough of the lungs. It is excellent to prevent and cure the dropsy, gout and scurvy. It is known by experience to be better than any other drying drink for people in years or children that have any running tumours upon them, as the King's Evil, etc. It is a most excellent remedy against the spleen, hypochondriac winds and the like. . . . It is neither laxative nor restringent.[1]

That was a telling advertisement; but when the public had once tasted the black drink it was not its therapeutic value that drew them back to it. It was the new delicious flavour of it and the social pleasure of sipping it in company with one's friends, the charm of friendly conversation in familiar surroundings, the break in the monotonous routine of the daily round.

It is significant, perhaps, that the habit started between 1650 and 1660, the heyday of the Puritans, when Englishmen were living under strange new conditions, cut off from many of the pleasures with which they had been accustomed to fill their leisure time. Whether he liked it or not the citizen of London had at that time to subordinate his habits to the Puritan way of life. His pastimes must conform to the Puritan doctrine and pass the Puritan tests of conduct and morality. He might no longer pay for a seat in the theatre or go bear-baiting in the environs of the town. The stages were closed and bear-baiting prohibited – 'not', as Macaulay said, 'because it gave pain to the bear, but because it gave pleasure to the spectators'. Cockfighting and dancing were taboo; May-day festivities round that 'stynking idoll' the maypole were suppressed; and the Christmas dinner itself was robbed by law of all the things that made it a Christmas dinner. To the gay cheery sociable type of man, whatever his politics, life in the 1650's must have been abominably drab and austere; and he had to bear the austerity, not for economic reasons which he might have respected, but in the cause of a theology with which he did not necessarily agree.

To such a man the coffee-house, indifferent substitute though he might think it for the theatre and the bear pit, could still do something to pierce the gloom. He could at least go to his club, and what club could be cheaper or more handy than a neighbouring coffee-house where for three halfpence he could meet his friends and dawdle away an hour or two in talk? So the club-habit fastened itself on London, and when the Puritan rule collapsed the habit was passed on to the livelier existence of the Restoration, which adopted and fostered it till it grew so strong as to leave its mark on English commerce and English politics up to our own day.

Indeed Green in his *History of the English People* saw in those early coffee-houses the birthplace of modern English prose. It was in them that men learnt 'the new-found pleasure of talk'; and the habit of conversation they encouraged led to the natural easy style of the eighteenth-century essayists, which fixed for two centuries and more the standard of writing in English

1. Warren R. Dawson, FRSI, *The London Coffee-Houses and the Beginnings of Lloyd's*.

books and English newspapers. If that theory of Green's is correct, then every book and article written today owes something of its shape and form to the coffee-houses of the seventeenth century; and we may claim that Lloyd's and the modern English language have a common ancestor in the London of William and Mary.

How many of these coffee-houses there were in the City we do not know; but in 1708 the number was guessed by contemporaries as three thousand. That must be a gross exaggeration, but, in a contemporary picture of the life our forerunners lived, even a gross exaggeration may have some value for us as we try to reconstruct the scene. And the figure of three thousand could never have been suggested unless there was a coffee-house or two in every street and the houses had in fact become one of the chief features of the City. So we may assume that from 1700 onwards these places had a very important niche in the Londoner's life; that City men passed much of their time in them; and that many hours which might have been given to industrious toil were spent there in idle desultory conversation. How sharp is the contrast between that daily routine of 1700 and its counterpart in the City of 1956.

Of those old coffee-houses the greater part died long ago and are finished as though they had never been, leaving no memorial. But one or two of them laid an egg before they died, and so their stock was carried on to later generations, the line surviving (though in barely recognizable form) until today. The present Stock Exchange is the lineal descendant of Jonathan's, and the Shipping Exchange of the Baltic Coffee-House; while Lloyd's (internationally perhaps the best known of them all) still bears the surname of the man who started the house and for more than twenty years owned and controlled it. He was Edward Lloyd, and his shop was situated in Tower Street at the eastern end of the City. He himself was certainly an able, industrious and enterprising man and within his own sphere he achieved a certain amount of distinction.

But although many hours have been spent by antiquarians in poring over parish registers, rating books, old newspapers and other City records, and in searching out every crumb of information to be found about his origin, life and death, no one has been able to collect information enough even for a brief biography. We are told that he was born in or about 1648; that he was three times married; that he was a member of the Framework Knitters' Company; that he opened his first coffee-house not later than 1688–9; that within a few years his business was large enough to support a staff of two men and three maids; that he was a Churchwarden; that he tried to run a newspaper which did not prosper though his coffee-house did; that he left his business to a son-in-law; that his clientèle probably included (as well it might in Tower Street) a number of shipowners and captains; that he was about sixty-five when he died; that he was buried in St Mary Woolnoth's in Lombard Street; that his remains were dug up and reburied; that there is no separate tombstone to mark the place of his burial. Beyond these facts we really know very little about him. . . .

Where exactly in Tower Street the coffee-house stood has long been a matter of debate, but it seems certain that the official address was Salutation Precinct and is now identified with a small area at the western end of Great

Tower Street. But wherever it was, Lloyd was not there very long. In 1691 – only three years after the *Gazette* had printed the stray advertisement which proves his occupancy – he left the house and went to a place in Lombard Street in which he and his successors plied their trade for the next eighty years.

It has always been assumed – and there is no reason to doubt the assumption – that Lloyd took with him from Tower Street to Lombard Street a connection among shipping men; and it is possible that this connection was the mainstay of his business, bringing him the prosperity that justified a move to the larger premises in 1691. Anyhow, it is beyond doubt that a year after the move he was beginning (as they say of rising young barristers in the Temple) to get into the heavy commercial work. When some shipowner or auctioneer had three boats to sell down at 'Plimouth' and wanted to give London owners the chance of buying them, he sent an inventory to Lloyd's and published an advertisement telling prospective buyers to go to 'Lloyd's Coffee House in Lombard Street London' where full particulars could be had. The place was clearly frequented already by shipping and commercial people, and Lloyd was cutting into the business of his older competitors in the better class of City trade.

Fifteen years later, but still during the lifetime of Lloyd, a queer person called Ned Ward was dividing his time between keeping a public house and writing a vast number of racy books under such titles as *The Northern Cuckold or the Garden House Intrigue*, exporting (as Pope said of him) vile rhymes to the Colonies in exchange for bad tobacco. This author published among his many books a work called *The Wealthy Shopkeeper* which described a normal working day in an active merchant's life. And Lloyd comes into the description. The shopkeeper worked in his counting-house till 8 a.m.; breakfasted on toast and Cheshire cheese; spent two hours in his shop; went to a coffee-house for news; dined on a thundering joint; looked in on 'change; went to Lloyd's Coffee-House for business; moved on to a different coffee-house for recreation, and then to a sack-shop to drink with acquaintances. From this summary of a City man's routine it is clear that Edward Lloyd had now got what he was after – a solid connection among business men who came to him when they wanted to work, and went elsewhere to frivol, drink, and make merry. How Lloyd prospered and made money out of it all is something of a mystery, for his customers seem to have reserved their serious drinking for other places and (as one would imagine) drank but little in his shop. But prosper he did, and when he died in 1713 he left a substantial estate to his family and dependants.

D. E. W. GIBB
Lloyd's of London
(1957), pp. 1–7

2 *In Amsterdam*

The growth of mercantilist Europe made huge demands on navigation, but the prizes lay in the territorial and commercial opportunities of empire. The mastery of entry into harbours and estuaries gave access to the great river systems and their hinterlands of continental resources or colonial plantations. In consequence, cost-effective coastal shipping had to contend with a variety of conditions. All too often it was not a question of tying up to wharves and quays, but of anchoring in the fairway, or allowing the ship to settle on the beach when the tide was out. Apart from transport on land, there was often the intermediate stage of carrying the cargo to the ship, before it could be said to be laden. Little surprise then that the typical Amsterdam policy – as indeed the earlier formula of Antwerp – took account of this and gave insurance on cargo from the hour and day the goods arrived on the quay.

The navigation of The Netherlands took to the task in the manner born. The golden age of the early seventeenth century showed the adoption of 'best-practice techniques' in navigation, notable innovations both in design and freight capacity. Received opinion on the evolution of the *fluit* assigns it to Pieter Jansz. Liorne of Hoorn in 1595. Its striking characteristics in design made it a work-horse of maritime trade. It had greater length (a length/beam ratio of 1 to 5 or even 1 to 6), a rounder stern, and sharp 'tumble-home' (to minimise the dues at the Sound, at least until about 1700). It had marked rubbing strakes for tying up at wharves or mooring together in fairways; and the bottom was noticeably flat, an advantage in settling on a hard or negotiating shallow waters in difficult channels. It handled well in changing weather conditions; but its blunt, rounded design was less content with the rollers of the Atlantic.

The design adapted to different routes and destinations. The 'great' *fluit*, often used far afield, even in Asian waters, could be 130 voet in length with a draught/length ratio of 1 to 9.56. Small *fluits* for Norway could be 100 voet and 1 to 9.09 respectively; while the preferred *fluit* for the Baltic could be 100 voet and 1 to 11.11. The difference in the last version, no doubt to handle bulky cargoes through the difficult channels of the Sound, gave the navigation of The Netherlands a special edge in competition. The emergence of the *katschip*, a type of *fluit*, was a further facility for moving heavy cargoes.

Such innovatory drive tended to diminish after 1630, certainly after 1670. The cargo-carriers of the eighteenth century reached full development with 'Atlantic' versions combining both square and fore and aft rigged, in place of the reliance on lateen sails so often employed in the Mediterranean. Naturally there were variations in size, ranging from the great East Indiamen of some 1,000–2,000 tons to the 200–300 tonner for the heavy trade of Europe, and to the smaller versions adapted for local coastal waters. The size of ship was related both to the type of trade and to ship-building costs. The rising cost of masts and naval timbers, for example, tended in the inflation of the eighteenth century to make the ship of some 200–300 tons a preferred best-practice cargo-carrier.

Ocean-sailing and increased carrying capacity, then, required deeper draught and a high ratio of length to beam. This presented no few problems in entering and leaving many of the older ports of Europe. In some cases, they were no longer equal to the task, not least when they contended with the old problem of silting. It had undermined the prosperity of Bruges. And other ports were not exempt. Venice found itself hampered by difficult access to the basin of San Marco: a plan of 1667 to join Malamocco to Venice dragged on, but came to life again in 1725 with a channel 15 kilometres long, some 2 metres deep, and 12 wide. Genoa, too, had its problems, which the Serenissima did its best to solve. The *molo* to protect the port after the great storms of 1592, 1613, and 1636 was a notable achievement; but was constructed on the east side, to the *levante*. This breakwater hindered the disposal of debris and indeed increased silting. In consequence, the Republic, in order to maintain its maritime facilities, was saddled with elaborate and costly operations to clear the Darsena: the famous manoeuvre of the 'dispaccio' using special flat-bottomed boats, cofferdams, a forest of bucket-hoists, and swarms of labourers to empty the water and dig out the accumulated refuse. Such exercises continued into the eighteenth century. Further along the coast, the old port of Sète was subject to heavy silting and could admit only galleys and small boats; the province of Languedoc contributed heavily to the cost of keeping it open. On the western coast of France, according to complaints in 1724, sand blocked the harbour of St Valéry, one of the privileged ports for importing into north-western France. At the other end of Europe, access to St Petersburg was hindered by the silt of the Neva. Danzig found similar problems in the scour of the Vistula: to such an extent that a canal was projected in 1717 to remedy the difficulties. And Hamburg was not spared. In 1775, the city faced costs of dredging the outlet to the Elbe, but the awkward question remained: who should foot the bill? The *Commerzdeputation* finally agreed to make a small contribution but only with marked reluctance.

As for Amsterdam, the problem reached classic proportions. In the eighteenth century, it remained the premier port of The Netherlands – but at a price. Severe silting became a major concern in the commercial life of the Dam not only for the harbour but also for the intricate network of canals to the warehouses, lofts, and counting houses of the city. In 1778, five dredgers were at work, served by 150 barges. In the period 1778–93, f.1,598,000 was spent on improvements for depth.

However, the harbour was one thing, the channels of access another. Amsterdam probably suffered more from sandbanks than Rotterdam. The channel winding through the Zuiderzee to the outports of Den Helder, Texel, and Vlieland – the *stroom* or *rivier* – had special snags and hazards. At the start of the voyage, there was *Het Pampus*, a sandbank at the entrance to the IJ. If the prevailing south or south-westerly winds were strong, then the IJ could be dry before the city. Sailing tugs were on hand to help ships over the *Pampus*. Take, for example, the plight of the ship *De vrouw Alida*. She sailed from Málaga with a cargo of raisins, wine, and fruit on 4 October 1775. She managed to reach Texel on 17 November, and leave for Amsterdam, but with the ice ran aground and stuck fast on the *Pampus*, arriving at Amsterdam only at the end of December. Captains often unloaded part of the cargo to lighten the ships before negotiating the passage. And the delays encouraged passengers to tranship to smaller craft. When Gerrit Metzou arrived at Den Helder, returning after two years and seven months capture in Algiers, he disembarked into a *vaartuig* which came alongside to carry the passengers to Amsterdam.

Yet, the snags of the Zuiderzee were not all on the debit side. They spelled prosperity for the repair-yards and ship-chandlers of Medemblik. There was the *Maxiliannse Vriendschap*, sailing from Málaga on 7 March 1774. She passed Den Helder on 15 November, and with a Texel pilot on board, ran into a storm in the Vlieter channel, encountered ice, and sprang a leak. And so the master put into Medemblik for repairs but was unable to sail again until 9 January 1775, to arrive at Amsterdam a week later.

As the years passed, access to the Zuiderzee became beset with difficulties and in consequence underwent changes. The deterioration of the shore at Texel proved to be the fortune of Den Helder. When Brandligt published his chart (1780, but no doubt drawn about 1776) there were two channels of access – at the north entrance to the *Nieuwe Gat Stroom* (18 feet deep); and the *Drempel*, a sandbank between the *Zuider Haaks* and *Helder* (marked 17 to 18 feet deep). The latter, a preferred egress, was clearly an obstacle and the use of camels was a regular feature. Such was the case of the *Indien*, *a flute fregattée* built in Amsterdam for France, the finance being arranged through Horneca, Fizeaux en Compagnie on the Dam and Grand et Compagnie in Paris. Ready in 1778, the decision was finally taken in November to put off her maiden voyage until March in view of the weather conditions. In the end, it was necessary to unload the armament to pass the sandbanks. All such manoeuvres were expensive, but they were part of the cost of keeping the established market of Amsterdam in the competition of maritime trade.

Certainly, in the end, Den Helder gained. The report of 1772, the commission of enquiry of 1774, and the serious storm damage in 1775 and 1776 brought new initiatives. In two decades, f.2.5 millions worth of stone was dumped in the water to consolidate the channel and create the Nieuwediep. But access to the Zuiderzee remained a hazard; and a profession. There were important series of orders concerning this pilotage by the States of Holland, for example, in 1772. The pilots of Texel and Vlieland formed a sworn guild. At Petten, in 1777, there were 66 pilots in the village and its neighbourhood. In Den Helder/Huisduinen there were 89. Not always with successful results. The *Rebecka Gosvina* sailed from Bordeaux on 2 February 1774 with a cargo of sugar, wine, coffee, and prunes valued at f.30,775. She left the port of Texel on 2 March but the pilot managed to strand and then refloat her, to arrive at Amsterdam two days later. Or *De Polly*, sailing the same year on 15 July from New York bound for Amsterdam with a cargo of sarsaparilla, campeche wood, rice, and *reales de a ocho*: on 16 August a Texel pilot came aboard and at once stranded the ship, but she refloated and reached port two days later. . . .

What related to Amsterdam was shared by other ports in The Netherlands, particularly in the Delta with the scour from the Rhine, Meuse, and Scheldt. The Goeree-Dordtsche Kil-Meuse access to Rotterdam became a serious problem. So much so that in 1770, a deputation of some fifty from Rotterdam went to the States of Holland with the submission that the Krabbegat had only twelve to thirteen feet of water and craft could hardly pass. The bigger ships had to unload some of their cargo at 's-Gravendeel. In spite of some remedy, another deputation made virtually the same approach to the States in 1778.

Across Europe, along its coasts, ports contended with the combined problems of silt, debris and growth. The changing technology of shipping reclassified their facilities, and some admittedly were unable to cope. The bigger cargo-carriers often found themselves obliged to discharge in the estuary, with small craft making the final trip to reach the old-established city. For ports listed in the *prijscouranten* the evidence is mixed. Reval, for example, had a good port but a poor commercial performance – it was apparently the only outlet of Baltic Russia with an adverse balance of trade. At Königsberg, the big ships used Pillau, from which lighters made their way to the city. For Stettin on the Oder the big ships anchored in the estuary at the out-port of Swinemünde. Stralsund, a fine city lavishly provided with five bridges, nevertheless offered harbour access only to ships drawing 10 to 11 feet of water, hardly enough for a small *fluit*; others found it safer to discharge their cargoes at the bar. Rostock relied on the out-port of Warnemünde. However, all was not on the debit side of the account. A new generation of ports came to the fore, with either new locations, or refurbished facilities. Some invested in important improvements, such as the canal from Ostend to Ghent: the famous *coupure*, dug by cohorts of labourers, was declared open to sea-going ships in December 1753. The first vessel, the *Concordia*, made the trip carrying a cargo of wine and chestnuts from Nantes, and received a spirited welcome from the jubilant citizens with fireworks and festivities. By the eighteenth century, Hamburg, Altona, Glückstadt, Bremen, Emden, Lübeck, Memel, and Wismar, grew in activity as other older names slipped down the scale and slumbered in past achievements. So in southern France where Marseilles thrived in opposition to Sète. In Spain, the bay of Cádiz dominated Seville, hampered by the bar at Sanlúcar, a serious hazard during the dry months of summer. Appropriately, building of the great Customs House overlooking the bay began in 1764. In England, Liverpool succeeded against Chester; Deal and Dover against Sandwich; Hull against Boston. As for London, a capital city and focal port, it forged ahead, enjoying at the Customs House the tidal limit and virtually fresh water. Every port had advantages and disadvantages but growth was selective and some prospered more than others.

Access to markets or to the great river estuaries which penetrated the continent was a prime consideration. The manoeuvre often carried a special supplement of costs and perils. Part of the outlay for protection was carried by governments avid to claim national or territorial waters. Pilotage and aids to navigation grew in favour: lighthouses appeared early at Scheveningen, Huisduinen, Vlieland, Terschelling, Urk, and in the Channel. Authorities placed beacons, as for example in the estuary of the Meuse, or Schouwen, just as further north the same precautions appeared on the Elbe, at Skagen and Anholt in Denmark, at Örskär in Sweden, at North Shields and Caister in Britain. In the second half of the eighteenth century the improvements with the flat-wick and the patent lamp of Argand (1783) gave lighthouses added efficiency, but there were still fees and costs to be met.

A great deal of the navigation to the destinations around the coasts of Europe to the ports listed in the *prijscouranten* was 'in soundings' and often in sight of land. A large part of the southern section of the North Sea was at less than 50 metres deep, sometimes less than 25. The problems were summed up in the vignette on the title page of Klaas de Vries, *Schat-Kamer ofte Konst der Stierlieden* (eleven editions between 1702 and 1818) which featured the seaman with a lead and line. Jan Abrams Nanninga was clear enough on the dangers of neglecting the use of the deep-lead in heavy weather, all too often resulting in disaster at sea. The hand-lead recovered from the VOC ship *Hollandia* wrecked off the Scillies in 1743 weighed twelve Amsterdam ponden (about 5.9 kg). The quartermaster's stores of the *Haast U Langzaam* (1764) listed one deep-lead of 24–26 ponden (about 12.8–11.8 kg), one of 16 ponden (7.9 kg), and two of 5 ponden (2.5 kg): this was the provision for a trading frigate. It was *de rigueur* when sailing inshore. Not least when it is recalled that reliable maps of the coastal waters and estuaries of The Netherlands had to wait for the work of Beautemps-Beaupré and his remarkable chart of 1798–99.

Few will doubt the substantial contribution made by The Netherlands to the technology of shipping and navigation. As for the cargo-carriers they were often of moderate tonnage, bulging and manoeuvrable, with small crew, few guns, and minimal draught. Such equipment was admirably suited to cope with poor port facilities, the vagaries of bad weather, and the hazards of ice. However, shallow draught was vintage technology of the oceans, especially when French and English design favoured deep-draughted ships for the Atlantic. Ship-design probably affected insurance premiums quoted in Amsterdam, although it is difficult to find accurate information on this. The Netherlands remained largely committed to Europe – the groups of destinations quoted in the *prijscouranten* were an indicator – and less to the Atlantic than some of her competitors. Overall, there remained the dichotomy of harbours and high seas. Once clear of port, it seems that risks attained to linearity, the continuity of distance, and conditions of equilibrium.

Some perils of the sea

For sailing ships, the perils of the sea were legion. And no survey of navigation would be complete without a few indications of this intricate scenario in the second half of the eighteenth century. There were, of course, collisions: the crowded channel of the Sound at the height of the season turned in numerous cases of actual physical contact. The *Jonkvrouw Catharina*, for example, which left Arensburg for Amsterdam on 25 September 1774 with a cargo of rye: after colliding in the Sound and then battling against adverse winds, she returned to Sound and finally made her destination on 17 November. And the same year the *Vrouw Anna Catharina*, sailing from Kronstadt for Barcelona this time with a cargo of wheat: a collision in the Sound obliged her to put back to Copenhagen for repairs. She was able to sail again only on 19 April the following year having 'overwintered', and reached her destination on 11 June.

There was fire. We can look at the claim on *De 2 Gebroeders* sailing from Gothenburg on 29 September 1775. Her cargo, valued at f.94,000, was composed almost entirely of tea for shippers who included Jean Fizeaux en Zoonen and Horneca, Fizeaux en Compagnie. After receiving storm damage, fire broke out on board; she arrived finally at Amsterdam on 4 November.

And a master hazarding his ship, although this delinquency emerged clearly only when he was a servant of a company. As in the case of the VOC ship *Leijmuijden* (Amsterdam Chamber) sailing from the Texel on 29 December 1769 en route for Ceylon with a quarter of a million guilders in bullion and specie, mainly gold. She took the ground on 25 January 1770 and was wrecked near the island of Bonavista. Only a trifling 16 bars and 13 coins were salvaged. The master, Jan Hermanus Kinsbergen, and his navigator, Barend Wedelink, were dismissed their ship 'never again to be employed in any position in the service of the Company'.

As for stranding, a ship even under pilot was not always safe. Wreckers were waiting, apparently swarming the coasts, ready to carry out an impromptu salvage, little more than looting. The States of Holland set out the conditions of rescue in the *ordonnantie* of 12 January 1769: Article I stated that no-one could board a ship without permission from the master or crew; and Article 18 that no-one could prowl the beaches at night or during storms with axes, hammers, and saws. Such legislation did not save *De Helena* returning from Bordeaux on 15 November 1772 bound for Amsterdam with a cargo valued at f.27,100 (coffee for f.400 and barrels of red and white wine for f.26,700). In heavy weather in the Channel, she sprang a leak and ran ashore on the Sussex coast near Shoreham. The English locals were ready for the occasion and lost no time in going aboard to pilfer. The hull stripped of everything went for f.1,425 at a subsequent auction.

Then, since, the commitment of the navigation of The Netherlands was to co-ordinate flows of trade between regions of the north and south of Europe, there remained the huge problem of ice. Sailings out of the optimal season in the Baltic, Scandinavian waters, on the White Sea were at risk. The *Handelaar* leaving St Petersburg late on 15 October 1773 ran into storms and returned to Kronstadt for repairs. Although ready on 5 December, she was caught in the freeze. She sailed the following year on 6 May and arrived in Amsterdam on 2 June. And *De twee Gezusters* sailing from Gothenburg on 2 December 1767 with a cargo partly from the Swedish East India Company (1731) – tea, with some silk, porcelain and drugs; and partly from the hinterland – 986 bars of iron. Once out of port, normally classed as ice-free, she ran into ice and suffered heavy damage, surely a penalty for late-season navigation.

And no brief survey of damage received should pass without reference to bad or unusual weather around the coasts of Europe. The factor of event uncertainties included in the model would not be complete without some indication of such vagaries. Three particular instances arose in the 1770s: the unusual winds from July to November 1773 said to have kept some 500 vessels idling at their moorings for five months at Texel, holding up the flows of colonial goods and wines to the north, and of iron, hemp, and masts to the south, matters of concern to governments. It was said at the time that the delays allowed ships from North America to steal the market. There is another example from St Petersburg: in the spring of 1777 the port suffered from persistent westerly winds meeting ice-floes coming down from Lake

Ladoga. The River Neva rose more than three metres and the extensive floods were not experienced again until the nineteenth century. At that time, the evidence of winds at Deal shows an unusual 112 out of 365 daily reports were for winds from the south-west.

Then came the great gale of 13–15 November 1775, without equal in living memory, worse even, so it was said, than that of 1717. With destructive force, it lashed the dykes of the Hook of Holland, flooded warehouses in Rotterdam, put the Amsterdam–Harleem road under water, and at Delfshaven demolished the old sluice-gates built 180 years before. Many a building and warehouse lived to bear a tell-tale plaque on its walls marking the height of the flood waters. A few more inches, according to the English ambassador, would have delivered the *coup de grâce* and rendered his embassy redundant. But the Dutch nation rose to the occasion: the storm turned them, the French ambassador reported, into 'a colony of beavers swarming to plug the holes'. For shipping, it nevertheless left a trail of disaster: some 145 ships, it was said, were wrecked on the coasts of Holland, left strewn with debris. One of them, *De jonge Pieter* sailed from Cádiz on 30 September 1775 with salt, hides, and a special cargo of 50,000 pieces of eight from Carlos III to his agent in Amsterdam for payment to Cornelia Anna van der Wall; and, it was rumoured, another 30 sacks for merchants in Amsterdam sent in contraband. She lost her masts and ran aground near Egmond. Claims later submitted to the Kamer van Assurantie proved the rumour to be correct for the cargo was salvaged. The hull and cargo were valued at f.76,075; this included 4,300 *mexicanen* for Raymond and Theodor de Smeth and five lots of specie for Hope and Company. Another ship, *De Vriendschap*, sailing from Cádiz on 29 September met the storm off Dover and sprang a leak. She carried a large consignment of wool but shared the same consignment to Cornelia Anna van der Wall in the cargo value of f.252,925 and included tobacco (f.17,770) for Horneca, Fizeaux and Company; *mexicanen* for Muilman en Zoonen (f.2,525), specie for Hope and Company (f.13,150), and silver, gold and *mexicanen* for Raymond and Theodor de Smeth (f.16,700). These were the commissioners' adjustments, reducing service values to the conventional rates in the Wisselbank. Such salvage concealed high losses in insurance generally – in London 300 wrecks were listed – and in Amsterdam in particular. The fate of underwriting business was still pending when the New Year opened in 1776, another year of heavy floods and equinoxial gales. The premiums quoted in the market showed little response; it was for the individual dealer to receive the full weight of disaster. And the Amsterdam market, as we have seen, relied heavily on the private underwriter.

FRANK C. SPOONER
Risks at Sea
(1983), pp. 132–142

3 Gambling Fever at Lloyd's

At the accession of George III there were only 174 British peers (of whom twelve, being Catholics, could not sit in the House of Lords). These men, their friends and dependants, governed the land. They had been brought up to do so. But for all this, many of them lived empty, frivolous lives. 'It is a gaudy, thoughtless age' wrote Richard Cumberland, 'and they who live up to the fashion of it, live in a continual display of scenery, their pleasures are all pantomimes, their dinners steam along the columns of every Daily paper, and their suppers and assembleys dazzle the guests with tawdry lights and suffocate them with suspicious odours.' The great families tended to live in the country and to come to London for the Season; they had their Town houses in Mayfair and indulged in a hectic social schedule, if Horace Walpole is anything to go by. 'I had been' he wrote to a friend 'at the Duke of Cumberland's levy, then at the Princess Amelia's drawing-room, from thence, to a crowded House of Commons, to dine at your brother's, to the Opera, to Madam Ceilian's, to Arthur's and to supper at Mrs George Pitt's'.

A man of fashion would begin his day at eleven, assisted by his valet and his barber and attended by minor relatives and friends (who had surfaced at a less elegant hour). 'We rise by nine' said John Macky in his *Journey through England*,

> and those that frequent great men's levées find entertainment at ten till eleven. About twelve, the *beau monde* assembles in several coffee or chocolate houses. We are carried to these places in chairs or sedans. If it is fine weather, we take a turn in the Park till two, when we go to dinner. The general way is to make a party at the coffee house to go and dine at the Tavern, where we sit till six, when we go to the play, unless you are invited to the table of some great man. After the play, the best company generally go to Tom's or Will's Coffee house adjoining, where there is playing picket and the best of conversation until midnight.

The conversation might well be that of Johnson or Burke, and the gambling more than just picket. Indeed so widespread was the craze for gaming that people of all stations indulged in it. They played whist and picket, hazard and pharoah (or faro), ombre, loo, quadrille, pope-joan, bassett, passage, commerce, costly colours, Queen Nazarean, post and pair. 'The boys and girls' complained Lady Hertford to her friend Lady Pomfret, 'sit down as gravely to whist tables as the Fellows of Colleges used to do formerly. It is actually a ridiculous, though I think mortifying sight, that playing should become the business of the nation, from the age of fifteen to four-score.' The high play which characterised Whites from its chocolate house days spread to Almacks and Crockfords in the middle of the 18th century, and betting books were formed in every club and coffee-house and even in University Common Rooms. A Scotsman at Blackheath bet that a friend would drive his feather bale 150 yards once in three times; the wages in the Combination Rooms at Cambridge dealt with the position of the wranglers; whereas the members of Whites were chiefly concerned with the longevity of their male friends and the fertility of their female ones, or such sporting bets as 'Mr Cavendish bets Mr

H. Brownrigg 2/1 that he does not kill the bluebottle fly before he goes to bed' (which apparently he succeeded in doing!).

If the theatres, the pleasure-gardens, the masquerades and the ridottos, the cock-fights and dog-fights and prize-fights offered plenty of diversion for a man in Society, his daily routine always included a visit to the club and the coffee-house for a game of cards. And as the century wore on and the middle classes grew more prosperous, so they too began to get showy. 'When I see young shopkeepers keep horses, ride hunting, learn dog-language and keep the sportsman's brogue upon their tongues I am always afraid for them', grumbled Defoe, as he noticed that such people were beginning to wear swords and long perukes, and to be seen increasingly at balls and masquerades, as well as on the race-course and at gaming houses. Under the circumstances it was hardly surprising that profligate habits should find their way even into the solid precincts of Lloyd's which until 1769 remained a coffee-house to which all the world had access – and would write any risk on any voyage for any amount. The fat underwriting profits during the Seven Year War were a magnet for speculators hoping to make a quick fortune who were inevitably disillusioned when peace brought a collapse of the high wartime premiums and a levelling-off of underwriting profits.

The result was an outbreak of gambling that had nothing to do with regular marine insurance. Money was free and opportunities for investment limited. To gamble on insurance risks was an obvious temptation. And so people went in for a 'flutter'. Horace Walpole, himself a gambler, considered that insurance was 'nothing more than a particular game, a more solemn species of hazard . . .'.

Gambling policies on ships had been prohibited by an Act in 1746, but wager policies on the lives of prominent people became so popular that Thomas Mortimer was moved to publish a scathing attack on the jobbers of Jonathan's and the merchants at Lloyd's who made bets '. . . insuring on the lives of such unfortunate gentlemen as may stand accountable to their country for misconduct'. There was even less justification for making a book on the lives of well known personalities who happened to be ill. It hardly improved an invalid's morale to read in the paper that 90 percent odds were being offered against his recovery.

Henry Gray notes that the life of Sir Robert Walpole was for a long time a standing dish, the premium varying according to the circumstances of the day. Charles Edward, the Young Pretender of 1745, was another popular risk. Large stakes were placed on the Duke of Newcastle when he was prime minister, on Admiral Byng, and on Lord Nithsdale when imprisoned in the Tower.

Nithsdale's escape by disguising himself as his wife was little to the taste of the underwriters who had made their book on the basis that he already had one foot on the scaffold. When George II fought with his troops at Dettingen, 25 guineas percent was paid against his return.

The fact that news travelled slowly offered plenty of opportunities for exploiting inside knowledge. 'It is a well known fact' said the *London Chronicle*, 'that a certain ambassador insured £30,000 on Minorca in the war of 1755 with advices at the same time in his pocket that it was taken.'

According to Mortimer, the merchants of Lloyd's had put up a notice in the coffee-house banning such wager-policies. But in 1768 the *London Chronicle* carried a leader criticising: 'The introduction and amazing progress of illicit gambling at Lloyd's Coffee House . . .' and going on to say:

> Though gaming in any degree . . . is perverting the original and useful design of that Coffee House, it may in some measure be excusable to speculate on the following subjects:
>
> Mr Wilkes being elected member for London, which was done from five to 50 guineas percent,
>
> Ditto for Middlesex, from 20 to 70 guineas percent
>
> Alderman B--d's life for one year, now doing at 7 percent.
>
> On John Wilkes' life for one year, now doing 5 percent (warranted to remain in prison during that period),
>
> On a declaration of war with France or Spain: 8 guineas percent . . . But when policies came to be opened on two of the first Peers in Britain losing their heads at 10/6d percent and on the dissolution of the present Parliament within one year at 5 guineas percent . . . it is surely time for Authority to interfere, and . . . put a stop to it.

Such a betting-shop atmosphere brought discredit on the place and upset some of the more reputable merchants and underwriters who did their business at Lloyd's. Insofar as this group can be identified at all, the evidence from Braund's papers would indicate that it was the younger (and perhaps more earnest) broking element, such as Angerstein and Brook Watson, who took the matter most to heart. So seriously did they object to the way things were going that a number of them felt that the time for a radical change had come. And so they decided to break adrift from the old coffee-house and set up a rival Lloyd's of their own.

RAYMOND FLOWER AND MICHAEL WYNN JONES
Lloyd's of London, An Illustrated History
(1981), pp. 50–54

4 *The* Lutine

The preamble to [the Act of Incorporation] recites that, 'in or about the year 1799 a vessel of War of the Royal Navy, named the *Lutine*, was wrecked on the Coast of Holland with a considerable amount of specie on board'. It goes on to relate that long subsequent to the wreck, and at a period when the names of the underwriters could not be ascertained, a sum of twenty-five thousand pounds from salvage out of the wreck had come into the possession of Lloyd's. Clause thirty-five of the Act provides with customary solemnity that the said £25,000 and any further salvage 'shall be applied for purposes connected with shipping or marine insurance according to a Scheme to be prepared by the Society and confirmed by an Order in Council on the recommendation of the Board of Trade'. Lloyd's naturally and properly thought that the interests of marine insurance would be best served by the Corporation taking the cash and anything else it could get out of the wreck; so thought the Board of Trade, and so confirmed Her Majesty in Council. It is perhaps the fact that Lloyd's as a body benefited by this salvage which has caused the incident to figure in the annals of Lloyd's and has turned it into a somewhat romantic legend. The Chairman of Lloyd's is privileged to occupy a chair of great magnificence and considerable discomfort made from the rudder, which was recovered in 1859 after the lapse of sixty years. . . . The Corporation possesses also a table made of material from the same source, whilst the ship's bell, always an object of interest to the landsman, is erected in the Room by the caller's rostrum and, diverted from its purpose of disturbing the rest of seamen, is used to obtain silence for any announcement of special interest, especially if relating to overdues.

The *Lutine* has a certain international interest. Built for the French Navy, captured and lost by the British, she was wrecked on the Dutch Coast at a time when this country was at war with Holland, a condition which the citizens of both countries would now regard as happily impossible. After some negotiation the King of Holland ceded his rights in the wreck to His Britannic Majesty, and it was the King of Holland's share which eventually passed to the Corporation of Lloyd's and was dealt with by the Act of 1871.

CHARLES WRIGHT AND C. ERNEST FAYLE
A History of Lloyd's
(1878), pp. 387–389

5 *The* Lutine*'s Treasure*

[According to calculations made in the 1860s, the total value of the treasure on the wreck of the *Lutine* had been £1,175,000.] If this were so, over a million pounds remained – rather more than five times that figure in our devalued currency. At 10.18 on the morning of 29 July 1938, two strokes sounded on the *Lutine* bell itself in the Room at Lloyd's and a red-robed 'waiter' announced from the rostrum that a gold bar marked FFB 57, weighing about 7 lbs had been brought up by the dredger *Karimata* owned by the Billiton Company which, under licence from Lloyd's, had been systematically dredging around the area of the *Lutine*. But this gold bar, along with a cannon ball and a few coins, was the only booty brought up after 1861, and Warren Dawson may have written the epitaph of the *Lutine* when he said:

Although the wreck lies fairly near the shore, the actions of currents and the constant shifting of sand have rendered salvage operations difficult and costly almost to the pitch of impossibility. A change in the current in a single night will undo the work of months, and it is very doubtful if the greater part of the golden treasure will ever more see the light of day.

All the same, it is there for anyone who cares to have a try.

RAYMOND FLOWER AND MICHAEL WYNN JONES
Lloyd's of London, An Illustrated History
(1981), p. 115

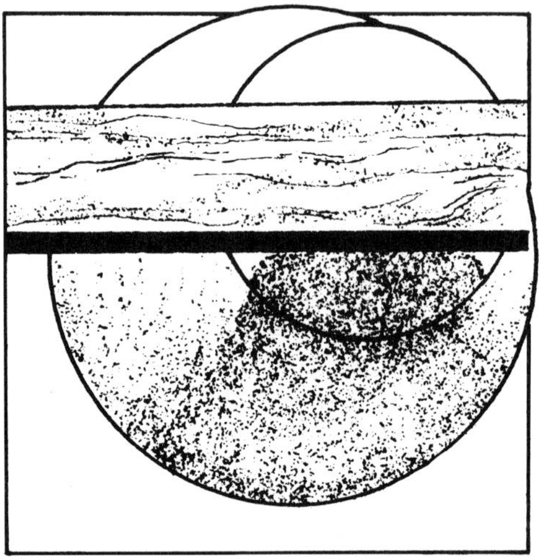

II
Of Ships and Perils of the Sea

1 *Frank Ledwith's World*

How fortunate I was to have my life cast among ships! Most of my time may have been spent in St. Mary Axe, nose to grindstone, but ships and the sea were in everything I did there, and I took every chance I could to go down to see them for myself. I can remember the first time I went on board a cargo ship, accompanying a surveyor instructed to get particulars of some damage to grain. It was in the Surrey Commerical Docks, a longish bumpy ride in a battered car, through the gates, over the cobbles, and then an uneasy climb up the gangway slung alongside. She was a smallish tramp ship, but seemed big and high close to. On deck, I at once went to the open hatch where they were discharging sling loads of sawn lumber, and looked down. The next thing I knew was a smack across the side of the head from a wire rope. Luckily, the brim of my bowler hat took the shock, so all I got was a broad line of black grease down my face, but I never again leant over a hatchway without a good look round first. I might easily have been flicked over the hatch coaming into the ship's hold, a twenty foot drop.

Although I'd seen sketches and photographs I found it more impressive to see for myself the ship's equipment, the heavy cleats and eye-bolts for the wedges and lashings, the derricks swinging round, the speeding and slowing of the winches, with puffs of steam, and drippings of oil. Below, in the hold, were the last few layers of planks stowed, as so often in the trade from Vancouver to Britain, over a bottom layer of bulk grain. I had learnt by then that heavy grain and light lumber together made a good way of utilising the full capacity of the ship, both in space and weight-carrying. Plain to the eye, however, was one of the dangers of this practice. Moisture from the timber had condensed on the ship's side plating, and run down onto the wheat at the edges, where the separating tarpaulins did not reach. The 'grass', which was actually young wheat, showed green and a foot high right along the hold. . . .

In an industrial and workaday age, a launching is always a moment of pure emotion. The words end, '. . . and God bless all who sail in her', the great structure stirs, moves, and begins to slide, and everyone catches his breath. Is it an association of ideas? Or is it that ships have personalities, and this is the point at which the personality is born?

Certainly ships mysteriously acquire characteristics which can well be regarded as personality. Any naval architect or shipbuilder will tell you that it is possible to build two ships which are intended to be exact duplicates, and they will behave quite differently when they are in service. One might be a whole knot faster than the other, a big margin in terms of a twenty years' life. One might ride easily in bad weather while her sister, similarly laden in the same conditions, digs her nose into every wave. Some are always in trouble, some never.

Occasionally, one comes across the freakiest characteristics. For example, most merchant ships have a single propeller with a right-handed 'screw'. It is so set (I hope I understand it correctly) that it drives the ship straight forward, but it is axiomatic that when such a propeller is put into reverse, to stop or send the ship astern, it tends to swing the ship's bows to starboard. It is something to do with torque, and the rule is (mechanically) inevitable. But one ship I dealt with, when the engines were put astern, would sometimes pay off to starboard and sometimes to port. Coming into berth at Colombo, the pilot ordered engines full astern. Away to port went the ship's bows. There was a dredger moored on the port side, and the dredger went to the bottom. There was also a heated discussion as to whether the master had warned the pilot of his ship's playful ways. In the end, the discussion was repeated before a judge, who decided that no warning had been given to the pilot.

Another British ship in the same ownership as that wayward beauty was also in trouble at Colombo. Her trouble was a fire. It was so fierce that in two or three minutes the engine-room was evacuated, and in twenty minutes more the crew abandoned ship. There was 150 tons of dynamite among the cargo stowed in the tweendecks. Fortunately, every one was safely clear by the time the ship blew up and sank. Since cargo owners in the United States were threatening a legal action against the shipowners, we had to investigate the cause of the fire. I got the detailed plans of the ship from her owners. She was a 'Doxford Motorship', one of the simple all-purpose cargo ships with a simple diesel engine, of which many examples were built in the forties and fifties as part of the first replacements of the ships lost in the war. Even so, the engine-room was the equivalent of a three-storey factory, containing 24 major items of machinery, and many minor ones.

I also set out to interview all the ship's eight engineers. Four months after the accident, six of them had left the sea. The second engineer was a boiler surveyor for an insurance company. Two others had formed a partnership and started a garage. And so on. The chief engineer was still at sea. So was the eighth or junior engineer, or at least he was supposed to be. I had to wait a while for him to come out of jail at Antwerp, where he had been put after a fight with his new chief engineer ashore somewhere. This junior, although he denied it, was plainly the man who started the fire. One of the items of equipment in the engine-room was a large oil-fired boiler which provided steam for various services when the ship was in port, and the main engines were not in use. One purpose was to power the windlass which lifted the anchors when preparing to sail. The junior engineer had been detailed to light the furnace under the boiler for this purpose. He turned a drainage tap on a fuel oil tank to make some tests, and obviously allowed oil to flow out onto the deck plating, for when he tried to light the furnace there was a flash-back which ignited oil on the deck. What was worse, he must have left the tap running for there was no other way in which enough oil could have been reached by the fire so quickly as to send a sheet of flame right across the engine-room. He was a large fleshy young man, with a face covered with pimples, and I could not help hoping that he was not a fair sample of the engineer officer of the future.

At least, we were able to prove there was nothing wrong with the ship, and on the basis of this we won the case. . . .

The oddest things happen to ships, and in connection with ships. One broke adrift in the River Tees, and was making briskly for the sea, stern first. The chief officer rushed forward and dropped an anchor. Unfortunately, the ship was at that moment very close to the end of a pier and, due to the overhang of the bow, the anchor (a seven ton chunk of steel) fell squarely onto a small building on the pier, reducing it to a heap of bricks. An Israeli captain was fined in London once for allowing the ship's dog shore leave without its having passed quarantine. A British captain was fined in Venezuela for blowing his whistle for a pilot at eight o'clock on Sunday morning, and waking everyone up. Another ship was accused of emitting smoke from her funnel in London, and damaging the food displayed on a coffee stall in the Rotherhithe Dock Road.

Then, there was the ship which got magnetised. Cargoes of scrap iron and scrap steel are often loaded and discharged with large magnets. The magnet is lowered onto the cargo, switched on, lifted up bristling with pieces of steel, swung over the ship's side, and lowered, and switched off. It is routine for a ship's magnetic compasses to be adjusted by an expert after this process is completed, as the normal magnetic field of the mass of steel which constitutes a ship is affected. The process involves putting pieces of soft iron of appropriate size into the supports of the compass, to compensate. In this case, the stevedores were very careless and kept hitting the ship's bridge with the magnets. When the compass adjuster came on board, he could never get any of the magnetic compasses to work, whatever he did. Whichever way the ship was pointing, the compasses unhesitatingly said that the front of the bridge was north. After a week's delay, the shipowners had to buy a gyro-compass before the ship could sail, and it was a year before the condition wore off. I tried very hard to get the stevedores to pay for the consequential losses, but only recovered a small amount. . . .

[One] case which filled the headlines for a time . . . began with a fire of mysterious origin in the cargo liner *Seistan*, owned by the Strick Line, last of the many shipowning companies of the P & O group to be merged into the great single fleet of today. The company's main trade was the carriage of every conceivable form of general cargo to the countries round the Persian (or as some say, Arabian) Gulf. The fire began deep in the cargo, and could not be reached. Captain and chief officer had quite an argument as to whether it was better to smother the fire with steam, or flood the hold with water. The captain won, and steam was used, unluckily as it turned out, although the captain could not be blamed for something he did not know. The fire spread, there was a violent explosion (one story said the funnel landed five miles away) and the ship became in practical terms a total loss. Nineteen people were killed on the ship and on a tug alongside.

The cargo was a valuable one, and a Pakistani salvage company was given a contract to salve what they could of it. It was known that the cargo had included a large amount of jelly explosives consigned to the oil companies, and the shippers, Imperial Chemical Industries, sent out an expert to supervise its discharge. When he saw its condition, he insisted that the ship (or wreck, as she really was) be evacuated immediately. The stuff was not in the hold where the fire began, but the steam which had been turned into the cargo spaces had part-melted the explosives, putting them into a highly unstable and dangerous condition. After a careful investigation, the explosives were very cautiously discharged into a barge, which was towed some miles out to sea. The expert lit a long slow fuse, and everyone retired hastily. When the echoes died away, the owners of the barge said, 'By the way, who pays for our barge?' – but that is another story.

The death roll appalled both the Strick Line, and ourselves. What caused the fire? There was no direct evidence at all. Indirect evidence appeared a few months later. A sister ship with a similar cargo had a similar fire, only this time the crew managed to put the fire out. When the cargo was discharged, the fire seemed to have originated in some cases of 'toe-puff', a substance rather like celluloid, used for stiffening shoes. Research showed that a shipment of toe-puff was in the *Seistan*, and in the hold where the fire started. The Strick Line asked the Ministry concerned if there would be a government enquiry into the accident. There seemed at first to be a reluctance, even though it was a British ship with British lives lost from unascertained causes. The shipowners and we began to talk of holding an enquiry ourselves, and publishing the results, but luckily the Ministry decided to go ahead. They wrote to the manufacturers of the toe-puff (a company no longer in existence, I believe), and asked them to make a batch of the substance the next Thursday, for their experts to test on the following day. They agreed. On the Tuesday night there was a fire at the factory, and the whole batch was destroyed. At the enquiry, it was established that the stuff was prone to spontaneous combustion. Yet it was not regarded as a hazardous cargo. It was one of the borderline substances, which could or could not fall into a category requiring special precautions when carried overseas. When it was first produced years before, the company got a certificate from the Ministry that it was non-hazardous. Since then, specifications had been changed, but shipments had continued on the basis of the original certificate. After a very long hearing, the official enquiry attached no blame to anyone for this situation.

No comment seems appropriate, but not many years afterwards better regulations for hazardous cargoes were introduced under the auspices of the United Nations.

Ships are big, dirty, troublesome things, but I cannot help regarding them with affection. I remember bucketing along the Dutch coast in the *Tangistan*, when it was so rough that the pilot refused to come out. The captain told us that these were the waters in which Sir Francis Drake learnt his seamanship in raids on the Spanish-occupied Netherlands. What with fogs and the steep short seas in those shallow waters, it must have been a stern school in the fifteen hundreds. I think, too, of the *Apollon*, newly built at Readheads on the Tyne, bowling across the Atlantic with 13,000 tons of coal. With the wind at force 7 to 8 and the swell on the starboard quarter, it was great to sit on the forecastle head looking aft. Dark clouds made a back-drop, but sun sparkled on the spray flung up above the bulwarks, and sometimes green water flooded across the forward hatches just below our feet. I think, too, of the little *Sela*, 1,039 tons, which took us up to her own country of Iceland. Her engine-room was so clean that the chief engineer did not give us the usual handful of cotton waste on which to wipe our hands, and the drums and other cargo on deck were stowed in so seamanlike a manner that when we arrived, I kicked the lashings and found the ropes still bar-tight. We came back from India by the old *Cilicia* of the Anchor Line. Their passenger service now abandoned, she is pensioned off as a school for stevedores in Rotterdam. Then she was still a very friendly ship, and we enjoyed her atmosphere in spite of our prejudice in favour of the cargo vessel pure and simple.

We under-estimate our ships. They are an essential factor in civilisation, and we must never forget that life as we know it is impossible without them.

FRANK LEDWITH
Ships that go Bump in the Night
(1974), pp. 182–190

2 A Prediction

One day someone may write a depressing little monograph on the losses of ships at sea in the last few years of the 19th century. If such a one exists he might well study the first few months of 1897, when the violence of the weather, particularly in the North Atlantic, provoked the following remarks in *Syren and Shipping* (17 March 1897):

> One gale follows another with such heart-sickening rapidity that before underwriters have had time to learn the extent to which they are hit by one there is another whistling round their ears. Already the year is said to be so far the worst known for 25 years, and if this weather continues much longer it will be necessary to requisition the services of the usual 'oldest inhabitant' to supply us with a parallel. Up to March 10th, 208 sailing ships and 168 steamers were entered on the loss books at Lloyd's, as against 166 sailing ships and 137 steamers during the corresponding period of 1896. This tells its own tale, and last week's gale has still further increased the disproportion.

DAVID KEIR
The Bowring Story
(1962), p. 269

3 The Ballad of the 'Bolivar'

Seven men from all the world back to Docks again,
Rolling down the Ratcliffe Road drunk and raising Cain.
Give the girls another drink 'fore we sign away –
We that took the Bolivar *out across the Bay!*

We put out from Sunderland loaded down with rails;
  We put back to Sunderland 'cause our cargo shifted;
We put out from Sunderland – met the winter gales –
  Seven days and seven nights to The Start we drifted.

    Racketing her rivets loose, smoke-stack white as snow,
    All the coals adrift adeck, half the rails below,
    Leaking like a lobster-pot, steering like a dray –
    Out we took the *Bolivar*, out across the Bay!

One by one the Lights came up, winked and let us by;
  Mile by mile we waddled on, coal and fo'c'sle short;
Met a blow that laid us down, heard a bulkhead fly;
  Left The Wolf behind us with a two-foot list to port.

    Trailing like a wounded duck, working out her soul;
    Clanging like a smithy-shop after every roll;
    Just a funnel and a mast lurching through the spray –
    So we threshed the *Bolivar* out across the Bay!

Felt her hog and felt her sag, betted when she'd break;
  Wondered every time she raced if she'd stand the shock;
Heard the seas like drunken men pounding at her strake;
  Hoped the Lord 'ud keep His thumb on the plummer-block!

    Banged against the iron decks, bilges choked with coal;
    Flayed and frozen foot and hand, sick of heart and soul;
    'Last we prayed she'd buck herself into Judgment Day –
    Hi! we cursed the *Bolivar* knocking round the Bay!

O her nose flung up to sky, groaning to be still –
  Up and down and back we went, never time for breath;
Then the money paid at Lloyds' caught her by the keel,
  And the stars ran round and round dancin' at our death!

    Aching for an hour's sleep, dozing off between:
    'Heard the rotten rivets draw when she took it green;
    'Watched the compass chase its tail like a cat at play –
    That was on the *Bolivar*, south across the Bay!

Once we saw between the squalls, lyin' head to swell –
  Mad with work and weariness, wishin' they was we –
Some damned Liner's lights go by like a grand hotel;
  'Cheered her from the *Bolivar* swampin' in the sea.

Then a greybeard cleared us out, then the skipper laughed;
'Boys, the wheel has gone to Hell – rig the winches aft!'
'Yoke the kicking rudder-head – get her under way!'
So we steered her, pully-haul, out across the Bay!

Just a pack o' rotten plates puttied up with tar,
In we came, an' time enough, 'cross Bilbao Bar.
Overloaded, undermanned, meant to founder, we
Euchred God Almighty's storm, bluffed the Eternal Sea!

Seven men from all the world back to town again,
Rollin' down the Ratcliffe Road drunk and raising Cain:
Seven men from out of Hell. Ain't the owners gay,
Cause we took the "Bolivar" *safe across the Bay?*

RUDYARD KIPLING (1890)

4 *The Custom of the Sea*

Her body then they did dissect
Most dreadful for to view
And serv'd it out in pieces,
Amongst the whole ship's crew

–"Ballad of the Brig *George*"

The story of the *Mignonette* [the murder and cannibalism case] was essentially a tale of maritime disaster and of the ensuing fall from grace, through extreme temptation, of the victims. The nineteenth century was a great era for disasters. The Victorians, like ourselves, were always delighted to hear of the latest ones, and ample material lay at hand. Thus the index to the *Times* for 1884 lists, with a slight air of frivolity, the following remarkable examples of sudden death:

Captain Berry, at Nyasa, from a huge Alligator seizing him in the Middle while Bathing.

Thomas Farmer, at Chatham, from taking Liquid Ammonia instead of his usual Cough Mixture.

Mr. A. W. Jesson, who Fell Down and Expired while Running at the Oxford Boat Race.

Mary Jane Butterfield, by having her scalp torn away by a Lion during a panic in Wombwell's Menagerie at Bolton.

Mr. Richards, Thrown into a Millpond as a Joke by Getting Entangled with the Weeds.

The Revd. J. Selby-Watson, by Falling out of his Hammock in Parkhurst Prison.

Josephy Jacklett, who Died from Holding some Dynamite over a Gas Flame, at Aldershot.

Samuel Halliday Smith, Shot Dead by the Explosion of An Explosive Walking Stick.

These improbable events involved individual deaths only; major disasters killing large numbers of people at once usually involved mines, railways, and ships. Shipwrecks provided the most dramatic of all catastrophes, for like air crashes today, they killed large numbers of people at the same time. But aircraft are more efficient and leave less scope for the tales of heroism and precarious survival that grace the stories of the sea; storm and tempest also lent an air of grandeur that is lacking in most air accidents. There were indeed plenty of shipwrecks, and their monotonous frequency was reflected in the grim entry in the index to the *Times:* 'Disasters at Sea, see each day's paper.'. . .

The tale of the *Francis Spaight* is perhaps the most striking of all the nineteenth-century cases, and it belongs to a period in which such incidents appear to have been particularly common in the North Atlantic timber trade. It was, however, by no means the last such case. In addition to the case of the *Mignonette* in 1884, there was the *Euxine* (1874), where lots were drawn and a boy eaten, and, in the same year, the suspicious case of the *Cospatrick*, where cannibalism certainly occurred and possibly death was hastened by bleeding. In 1878 the American press reported the grim case of the schooner *Sallie M. Steelman* (or *Stedman*), which suffered severe damage on January 20 in a gale off Cape Hatteras on a voyage from Charleston, South Carolina, to Baltimore, and became a drifting derelict on which Captain S. G. Higby and his crew of six began to starve to death, their only provisions being coffee. On January 30, when they had been out 43 days, a black sailor, George Seaman, lost his reason and threatened to shoot the captain. On deck he called out to another black sailor, Walter Sampson, to come on deck: Sampson did so and, fearing Seaman was going to shoot him, pulled a pistol borrowed from the steward, Sylvester R. Herbert, and shot Seaman dead. After the body had lain on deck four hours, Sampson cut off the head, which Herbert and another sailor, David Barrett, wrapped in canvas and threw overboard. Barrett then butchered the corpse and salted some flesh; this was boiled and fried, Barrett claiming it tasted 'as good as any beefsteak he ever ate'. They were rescued on January 31 by the schooner *Speedwell*, on passage from Cadiz, and eventually reached New York. Press reports suggested that the men might be brought to trial, and when interviewed, 'the seamen, while they answered inquiries put to them, seemed to do so unwillingingly, and continually enquired if any punishment was likely to be inflicted on them for the act of cannibalism'. But no proceedings were ever apparently brought, presumably because Sampson's story was accepted. The internationalism of the seafaring community is brought out by the fact that this American tragedy generated a Danish street ballad, set to the music of the song 'Amanda Was Sitting with a Garland of Roses', which added a sad but romantic detail – George Seaman was to have married Susan Illit on the ship's return; she stood waiting for him on the shore, not knowing of his death.

In the nature of things, some of these stories of the sea may be inaccurate in detail; no doubt in the aftermath of shipwrecks there was a fair amount of lying and romantic embroidery, designed to place the informant in a better light or to emphasize the horrors from which he had escaped. We shall never know for certain whether the lots on the *Francis Spaight* were really fairly drawn or whether the elaborate ritual actually took place. But our concern is that of establishing the historical context for the case of the *Mignonette*, and for that purpose what really happened hardly matters; what was really important was belief and myth, not reality. Viewed in this way, it is quite clear that the situation confronting the survivors of the yacht *Mignonette* was one for which they were well prepared and that in a general sense Dudley and his companions knew the proper thing to do; someone must be killed that the others might live. They also knew that to obtain blood to drink, a living victim was preferable; to wait until death occurred was unwise. They knew too the appropriate preliminary course of action, which was to draw lots, a practice viewed as legitimating killing and cannibalism, particularly if agreed upon by a council of sailors. Nor was the tradition of the sea as it applied to such critical situations confined to seamen, as a sort of professional secret (no doubt mariners would know of other more private stories, which circulated orally on shipboard or in seaports). The incidents I have described were all public knowledge. There was nothing whatever secret about the matter. What sailors did when they ran out of food was to draw lots and eat someone.

A. W. BRIAN SIMPSON
Cannibalism and the Common Law
(1984), pp. 96, 139–140

5 *The Hope of Gain*

Commercial documents cover a vast range. As the Bench has often pointed out, many a policy of marine insurance is 'a very strange instrument'.[1]

It is wonderful, considering how much property is at stake upon instruments of this description, that they should be drawn up and with so much laxity as they are, and that those who are interested should not apply to some man whose habits of life and professional skill will enble him to adapt the words of the policy to the intention professed by the parties. In construing these instruments we must always look for what was the intention of the parties, without confining ourselves to a strict grammatical construction; for it is impossible in many instances so to construe them without departing widely from the object intended.[2]

In one such case, neither a fine verbal distinction nor the citation of certain decisions on the Workmen's Compensation Acts received an enthusiastic welcome from Lord Sumner. 'Of course perils of the sea are not the same as perils on the sea, but in law epigrams only dazzle, and as for decisions on the Workmen's Compensation Act, they shed even on that Act an illumination

1. *Le Cheminant* v. *Pearson* (1812) 4 Taunt 367 at 380, *per* Mansfield CJ.
2. *Marsden* v. *Reid* (1803) 3 East 572 at 578, *per* Lawrence J.

which is sometimes dim. In marine insurance we shall do better with the light of reason.'[3]

In one case the issue was whether the shipowners were entitled to recover on a policy of marine insurance in respect of their ship *Arnus*, or whether it had been scuttled with their privity. Bailhache J found for the owners, but the Court of Appeal reversed this decision, and the owners appealed to the House of Lords. There, the Earl of Birkenhead regarded the case as 'a particularly clear one.' He referred to the judgment at first instance, and said 'The second officer of the vessel was one Felipi Ybarra, of whom the learned Judge observes: "He gave his evidence on commission, and repeated it here, and I was impressed with his demeanour and his frankness." This impression was somewhat surprising, having regard to the fact that Felipi Ybarra gave no evidence before the learned Judge at all, and enjoyed therefore small opportunity of exhibiting either his demeanour or his frankness.'[4]

After referring to certain of the facts, Lord Birkenhead observed that the plaintiff company which owned the ship

carried on its affairs in a pleasant family atmosphere. Its managing director was Juan de Longaray. He, his two brothers, and his ten step-children held the bulk of the 4,800 shares of 500 pesetas each issued by the company. On the night when the Arnus commenced her last voyage of all the only assets of the company were the ship and the sum of about £400. And there were outstanding liabilities in respect of loans amounting to 936,986 pesetas. The company was insolvent; there was not the slightest prospect of paying its creditors; if such indeed was its purpose. The intimate family atmosphere which was so striking a feature of the company is not altogether lost when we pass to consider the vessel. She was commanded by Thomas Enciendo. The captain was in a position somewhat singular in that he had no shares in the company. The first mate was Jose Ybarra. The second was Felipe Ybarra. Both these men were nephews and also step-sons of Longaray, the managing director. The chief engineer was one Gomeza, who held 80 shares in the company. Each of the Ybarras was the owner of 72. The enterprise had all the elements of co-adventureship.

The voyage, and the loss of the ship which followed, presented remarkable incidents. The course from Vivero to Rotterdam would, in normal circumstances, be laid by a competent navigator so as to pass clear of the dangers of Ushant. A course, in fact, was set which, if prolonged, would have taken the vessel ashore inside Armen Rock; a course altogether unexplained; out of the track of ships passing from Finisterre to Ushant; but presenting the advantage to anyone who had by good fortune foreseen the casualty, that it would bring the vessel nearer the fishing fleet south of Penmarch. This fleet, in fact, by a happy coincidence, picked up the crew when in their boats.

On the night of April 27, in fine weather; with a smooth sea; little or no wind blowing; the vessel sank in deep water. The vessel did not actually founder for five hours after the crew had prudently taken to their boats. No attempt was made to attract attention or secure assistance by wireless or by rockets. To complete a singular chapter of maritime misfortune, we are assured that all the ship's logs and papers perished in an attempt which failed to launch the first boat. No evidence whatever was offered at the hearing of any casualty to which the sinking of the ship could be attributed except the influx of sea water. The second mate indeed says that he saw some wreckage. But his evidence is valueless because he evidently had not formed the view

3. *P. Samuel and Co Ltd* v. *Dumas* [1924] AC 431 at 464.
4. *Compania Martiartu* v. *Royal Exchange Assurance Corporation* (1924) 40 TLR 669 at 670.

that the Arnus was struck by it. Other evidence there was none. I find myself, as I have already indicated, in complete agreement with all the Judges who have reached the conclusion that the vessel was scuttled. Mr Justice Bailhache alone has taken a different view.

The irresistible inference, he said, was that the owners were accomplices in the fraudulent destruction of the vessel.[5]

Lord Sumner pointed out that

Ships are not cast away out of lightness of heart or sheer animal spirits. There must be some strong motive at work and this is usually the hope of gain. In the present case there was no operative motive to lead the engineer and captain to sink the ship on their own account. The engineer, it is true, had 80 shares in the appellant company, but he is not shown to have had any knowledge of the state of the company's finances and insurances, such as would be requisite, if he is to be taken to have had an eye to improving the value of his shares. The captain was not a shareholder at all. Both lost their effects and their employment, and both risked their lives while at sea and their liberty, I hope, when they got ashore. It is idle to suppose that they – strangers to one another as they were, and one of them quite recently unemployed – would have cast the ship away except at the instigation of others interested, since they had no motive of their own, and in the company we find a full interest, and an overwhelming motive. In their case and in theirs alone there was a golden prize in the case of complete success and complete insolvency if the ship was not got rid of on this very voyage. There was further full opportunity for arranging the plot with all the advantage given by the relation of employer and employee. Nothing was easier than to pass the necessary word before the ship left Bilbao, and it seems to me a matter of just and inevitable inference from the circumstantial evidence, of which the whole case is full, that the word was, in fact, passed by someone charged with the management of the company's affairs.

We were told that the principal shareholders were rich and respectable men. Don Jesus de la Roca had a jute mill; Don Luis Leguizamon was brother to a Spanish senator; Mr Longarary had been his college friend; and Bilbao thought highly of them all. I do not know if the proposition intended really was that rich and respectable men do not commit crimes, even for money, but that mariners and seafaring men do so and for nothing at all, but, at any rate, my experience does not bear it out. It is not necessary to name particular persons as the culprits, and as for generalities I am sure the loss of the ship, and of the action too, will bite deeper than any censure. I will only say that I think the decision of the Court of Appeal was right.[6]

R. E. MEGARRY
A Second Miscellany-at-Law
(1973), pp. 276–279

5. *Ibid*, at pp. 670, 671.
6. *Ibid*, at p. 672.

6 Shortlandings

At one time, there passed across my desk many of the outturn figures for meat cargoes discharged in London and other British ports. The short deliveries were then running at from £1,800 to £4,000 or more a ship. And hundreds of cargoes came in each year. Much of the missing meat went out as joints under the coats of the dockers.

Some people, however, had more ambitious plans. A handful of notes were slipped to a tallyman by the driver of a meat delivery van, and the load was recorded as 80 sides of beef, instead of 90. At an unscheduled stop on the way to the depot, ten were delivered to the shop of an unscrupulous butcher. Many transactions of this kind were eventually proved in the criminal courts. One butcher, caught in the act of receiving stolen meat, had in his possession a notebook recording many such deals, and the 'expenses' paid. Another time, as a delivery was being made to a shop in Portsmouth, a car pulled up. Out jumped detectives who had followed it 80 miles from the London docks. 'Where did you spring from?' asked an astonished thief.

All kinds of commodities are affected. At one time, three successive ships in a transatlantic service arrived in Britain with general cargo – thousands of packages in each. Each carried one small case of the synthetic 'flints' for cigarette lighters, worth thousands of pounds. All three disappeared without trace.

For years there were mysterious shortages of raw cotton in bales at Liverpool docks. Investigations produced nothing. Then it was found that loads were going out the gates on cleverly forged passes. The police found that the marketing problem for this valuable stuff had been dealt with ingeniously but simply. A cotton broker, very advanced in years and no longer acute in mind, had been approached, allegedly by a cotton mill which (he was told) had more raw material at times than it could handle, and he had sold the stolen goods for the thieves on the Liverpool Cotton Exchange! A tightening of dock procedures put an end to that little game.

Another gang in Liverpool did very well until the discarded mistress of one thief took her resentment to the police and gave them names and addresses. At one house the garage was crammed with radios, perfumes, spirits and such.

In London, too, a gang operated a big scheme based on forged receipts for goods intended to be transhipped, and therefore shifted from one book to another. Surprised by the police, they resisted violently, and one officer was badly injured. After a big manhunt, the leader was trapped in a telephone box in Epping Forest.

For every big thief, however, there are a thousand little ones. If these could be eliminated, the big criminals would find themselves more exposed and vulnerable. Perhaps the major problem is much more the men who stroll out of the dock gate with a length of silk wound round their bodies under their coats, or those who fit themselves out with new shoes from the cargo so that the ship arrives with the discarded old shoes littering the 'tween-deck, or the long-established custom in Glasgow of bumping down a case of whisky on its corner in a way which breaks the corner bottle, and holding a tin cup to catch what drains out. . . .

Sometimes, of course, cargo just cannot be accounted for. Does it disappear? Or was it never shipped? Or was it delivered somewhere else?

The shipowner, through his crew or agents, acknowledges that he received it, but it is not there to be delivered. Failing some explanation, he has to pay and so therefore does his protecting and indemnity club. Many times I faced this kind of situation. Sometimes the mystery was solved. Sometimes (like the police in many kinds of crime) I was sure I knew, but could prove nothing. Sometimes I was completely baffled.

Consider the Scandinavian ship which brought a cargo of telephone poles from Finland to the London docks, and the consignees claimed 176 poles short. Why? It was hardly likely that a young seaman or stevedore would slip one under his coat as a present for his girl friend. And in this case, there was a complete discrepancy between the counts made by the timber merchants' tally-men on the quay, and a countercheck by members of the crew made as the poles were swayed up by the cranes over the ship's rail. The shore tally showed a shortage: the ship tally showed that all the cargo called for was delivered.

I had the ship's tally-books sent up to the office, and did a hurried check of them. They looked all right to me, small note books, with the tally made in the old well-known 'gate' system, of four vertical strokes with a fifth diagonally across them to indicate five units, totals at the end of each line, and a running total at the foot of each page. So we agreed to put the papers to an arbitrator to decide whether or not the claim for the missing poles should be paid.

He decided against us. Disappointing, indeed. A day or two later, he called in to see me, and returned the papers. 'I thought', he said, 'you would like to have another look at these tally books. First of all, on one of the later pages, the totals do not correspond with the number of gates. But there is something else. They are not suspiciously clean. In fact, they are as dirty as you would expect after hours of handling on the deck of a ship covered with dust and traces of oil and rust. But look at this.' He opened one of the books and put it face down on my desk. Spreading the fingers of one hand over the two covers, he twisted it back and around on the desk top. There were five round smudges on the cover, corresponding to the tips of his thumb and fingers. The book clearly had been artificially dirtied, rubbed in dirt, after it was written up.

The Scandinavians, reluctant to pay for cargo which doubtless had not been shipped (and carelessly counted at the loading port), had prepared books specially to show the wrong figures. All those 'gates' drawn for nothing.

It may seem hard that the shipowners (and thus we) paid for cargo which was never shipped, but they had given receipts for it, and the timber importers had paid on those receipts.

Another far larger discrepancy arose in a different way. After the Second World War, large quantities of army stores had to be brought back from Egypt to the United Kingdom. One ship arrived, to deliver a long list of all sorts of things, all except one item on the list – 250 army trucks! But the explanation was simple. The Strick Line had an arrangement that their ships returning from the Persian Gulf should pick up anything they could find space for when they reached Port Said. The army people produced a bill of lading listing all they had ready for shipment. There was no room for the trucks, and someone just forgot to strike them off the list.

Then a ship was chartered to carry a full cargo of guano (bird droppings) from the Seychelles to Durban for Fisons, the fertilizer people. The outturn showed a shortage of no less than 1,200 tons against the bill of lading figures. The usual enquiries turned up nothing at first. In the case of a cargo measured by weight, a fairly close check can be made by comparing the ship's draught before and after loading. Most people have seen the six-inch high figures, six inches apart, marking each foot of submersion, painted on both sides of the stem, and again on both sides of the ship aft. For a ship of this size, every fifty tons or so of cargo put her another inch deeper in the water. The captain, however, said that he had loaded off shore from barges, and the sea was too rough to measure the draught. He thought the bill of lading figure too high, but could only guess.

More detailed enquiries showed that the barges brought the cargo in bags, which some labourers emptied into the holds. The first hundred or two were each weighed on deck, and the average weight had been multiplied by the thousands of bags emptied each day. It was fairly obvious that as the men got more tired (and perhaps more nauseated) they filled the bags less and less full. Certainly, the total in the bill of lading was a wholly unreliable figure; and this was one claim we did not pay.

For several generations a story has been told against the famous P & O Company. It could even be true. In the old days a stream of P & O ships carried general cargo of all kinds out to India and the East. On one of them a new chief officer was appointed, a conscientious man. One of his duties, of course, was (under the captain) the care of the cargo; and he took an early opportunity to inspect all the ship's holds, accompanied by the ship's boatswain and carpenter. If you have never been down the hold of a cargo ship, I can assure you that physically they had quite an arduous task. Access is by vertical steel-runged ladders, and even in a small cargo liner this means down and up thirty odd feet of ladder five or six times, and walking considerable distances in the holds and 'tween-decks. And every ship has a variety of equipment, pipes, drainage systems, and so on, everywhere.

In the corner of one hold these was a smallish wooden erection, painted grey like everything else, and the officer asked casually, 'What's that?' The carpenter replied, even more casually, 'Oh, just a casing to protect some valves on the pumping system.' They turned away, but the officer found himself thinking, 'Why there?' He turned back, and told the carpenter to prise off one of the planks, and check. With a shrug, he did so. Inside was a grand piano. It was much decayed. Years before, it had doubtless been overlooked in its distant corner, and recorded as short-delivered. There it had been ever since, and each time the hold had been painted, the packing case got painted as well.

Another story was told me by a P & O man. If there is a discrepancy in the loading tallies, as there was in the discharging tallies in the case of the telegraph poles discussed earlier, the usual practice is to issue a bill of lading for the smaller number, adding words such as '47 pieces more in dispute, if on board to be delivered'. My P & O friend told me with a straight face that they had in the office an old bill of lading acknowledging the loading of three live elephants, one more in dispute.

A Norwegian ship carried in wartime a cargo of miscellaneous stores for British troops in the Middle East, including canteen stores. The short deliveries, when she discharged at Basrah, included 557 cases of canned beer, each containing 48 cans. I felt this was rather beyond a joke, and insisted that the ship's managers obtained a special report from the captain. Eventually, there arrived from somewhere on the other side of the world a long report, which must have provided a pleasant occupation for a dull day at sea. It may be summarized as follows: 'I have made exhaustive enquiries as to the missing cases of beer. I find that, by a remarkable coincidence, all my officers on that voyage were total abstainers, so that there is no question of any of them being responsible. The lower-deck ratings were all Arabs, who are enjoined by their religion to abstain from alcohol. When the ship arrived at Basrah, the military authorities, on account of the nature of the cargo, put an armed guard on board to prevent pilferage by the local labour. These guards were assisted in their duties by volunteers from among their comrades. The climate in Iraq being so hot, it does occur to me that some of these guards may have had an occasional drink from the cargo, but I do not think this could have exceeded in all 100 cases, or 4,800 cans. As regards the balance, I cannot suggest any possible clue. It remains a mystery.'

FRANK LEDWITH
Ships Afloat in the City
(1977), pp. 49, 51, 53–56

7 *Grave Losses*

There is in the [Bowring] company's archives a graphic eye-witness account of the impact made upon it by [the sinking of the great new ship *Titanic* on her maiden voyage]:

For those working at Lloyd's, that grim day in February 1912 was a memorable one, during which many rumours prevailed, but the general feeling was that this magnificent vessel of over 40,000 tons – which had started only a day or so before, with all due pomp and ceremony, on her maiden voyage – could not be in such grave danger as to entail total loss. In this connection an incident occurred after market hours which illustrates the faith and goodwill which exists between brokers and underwriters at Lloyd's. A cable was received in our office at 5.30 pm requesting us to place what was, in those days, a large line of reinsurance on the *Titanic* against total loss at 'best possible'. A young broker was despatched to Lloyd's to see whether anything could be done. After searching the 'Room', the Captain's Room and elsewhere with no result, he met on the stairway of the old Lloyd's in the Royal Exchange Mr John Povah, a well respected leader in the overdue market. On being offered the risk he remarked, 'the rate at the moment is 25 guineas per cent but if you want me to write so large an amount as that, I must have 30 guineas.' Having an order at 'best possible' this offer was accepted and Mr Povah said, 'Bring the slip round to me tomorrow and I will put it down – I am in a hurry now.' By next morning there was no doubt about the total loss of the *Titanic*; there was likewise no doubt in anyone's mind that the verbal acceptance was binding.

Here we might look ahead to the next comparable shock in the market – the sinking of *Lusitania* by a German U-boat in May 1915.

'There was no special announcement in the Room,' writes a Bowring underwriter who was there, but a waiter from the information room walked up to the noticeboard and pinned up the usual yellow 'casualty' sheet. The message was short and to the point. It read: 'The Admiralty have telephoned to say that the *Lusitania* has been sunk.' The news went quickly round the Room and although for a short period there was a kind of stunned silence, there was no panic and underwriters resumed their normal activities with perhaps a new and grim resolve to see the thing through.

DAVID KEIR
The Bowring Story
(1962), pp. 274–275

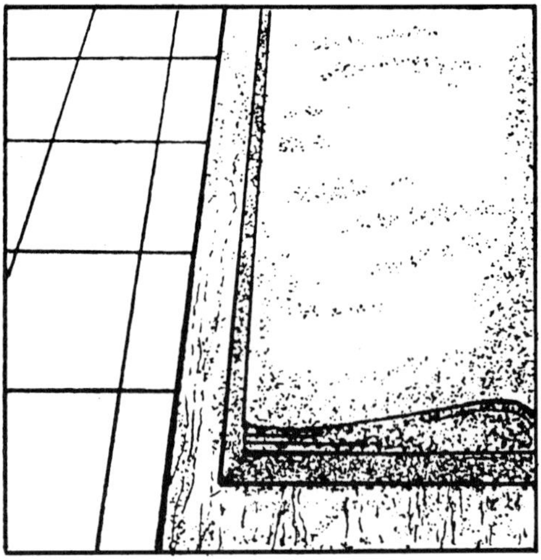

III

Other Accidents of Transport

1 *A misunderstanding at Thorpe station*

At Thorpe station, Norwich, on September 10th, 1874, . . . [a] mundane railway platform became, for sixteen critical minutes, a stage for high tragedy in which no dramatic ingredient was lacking. Unknown to the actors, we, their audience, can watch error upon trivial error leading in remorseless sequence to their terrible conclusion. And only when it is too late, when disaster becomes inevitable, does there come the sudden overwhelming realisation of guilt and error.

Before beginning the action the stage must be set. The single line of the Great Eastern Railway between Norwich and Yarmouth was one of the first in the country to be controlled by electric telegraph. The installation of five-needle Cooke and Wheatstone instruments on the Norfolk Railway (as it then was) in 1848 was considered at the time to be a model of its kind. For twenty-six years it had controlled the traffic over the line without a single mishap. Now, the Great Eastern Company proposed to double the line and by the irony of fate a second set of metals had already been laid between Thorpe and the East Norfolk Junction at Whittingham, the very section upon which the collision occurred, and was only awaiting inspection and approval by the Board of Trade. The movement of trains through this section was controlled by the telegraph instruments at Thorpe and at Brundall, the next station east of Norwich. At Brundall the stationmaster worked the telegraph himself. At Thorpe the instruments were worked by a telegraph clerk acting under the instruction of the station inspector. If late running made it necessary to alter the normal crossing arrangements, the procedure at Thorpe was as follows. The telegraph office had a window with a sliding wicket, like a booking office, which faced the platform. At this window was kept a message pad for the use of the station inspector. The inspector would write his instruction on the pad, sign it, and hand it to the telegraph clerk who would then transmit it to Brundall exactly as written with the signature as proof of its authority. Brundall would then acknowledge it in the same form and both the message sent and the reply received would be entered by the clerk in a record book. At the same time the station inspector would hand a signed instruction to the driver of the train concerned.

The 5 p.m. express from Liverpool Street to Yarmouth was normally booked to cross the 8.40 p.m. up Mail train at Brundall but on this occasion the express was running late. The drama began at 9.16 when Cooper, the night inspector, who had just come on duty, went to the stationmaster's office as usual to receive his orders for the night.

'What about having the Mail up, sir?' Cooper asked. Sproule, the stationmaster, consulted his watch and inquired what time the Mail was due to arrive at Brundall. 'Nine-twenty-five', Cooper told him. 'We will not have the Mail up', Sproule replied, 'certainly not.' 'You know, sir', Cooper reminded him, 'there is an order allowing us to detain the 9.10 down as late as 9.35.' To this the stationmaster made an ambiguous reply. 'All right', he said, 'we will soon get her off.' Now it seems clear that Sproule's 'All right' was delivered in a tone of impatient dismissal and that by 'her' he was referring to the express and not to the Mail. But evidently Cooper thought that Sproule had conceded his point. He left the office, walked straight to the telegraph office, tapped on the wicket and said to the young clerk, Robson, 'Tell Brundall to send the Mail on to Norwich'. Robson wrote the message down on the pad but Cooper had hurried away without stopping to sign it. The time was then 9.22.

One minute later the express drew in to the down platform drawn by the four-coupled mixed traffic engine No. 218. She was met by the day inspector, Parker, who, thinking the train might arrive punctually, had already made out an order authorising her driver to proceed. He was standing by the engine when Cooper came up and he asked him whether he had arranged for the Mail to come on. Inexplicably, Cooper answered, 'No, certainly not; let us get the train away as soon as possible'. Parker then handed the order to the driver and told him to proceed to Brundall. Events now moved swiftly. Parker gave the express the 'right away' at 9.30 and from his office window the stationmaster watched it pull away. It had scarcely cleared the platform when Edward Trew, an inspector of railway police, wishing to speak to the telegraph clerk upon some other business, knocked on the office wicket. Robson immediately opened it and asked where the express was.

'She has just left', Trew replied. 'What, left the yard?' asked Robson. He seemed about to make some exclamation when Cooper hurried up. 'You haven't ordered the Mail up, have you?' he asked. 'You told me to order her up,' Robson retorted. The clerk at once went to his instrument and signalled 'Stop Mail' to Brundall. Immediately the deadly reply came back: 'Mail left.' He returned to the wicket, put the pad with its fatal message in front of Cooper and asked him to sign it. 'No', cried the wretched man, 'No. I never gave you that message. I did not, I did not.' Robson's reply was unanswerable. 'Why, if you did not, have you now come back to cancel it?' At this moment Hayden, the ticket collector came up. 'What's the matter?' he asked, and Cooper answered, 'The Mail is coming up'. 'Good God', said Hayden, 'this is a frightful thing.' The stationmaster, overhearing the raised voices and the word 'Mail', guessed that something was wrong and rushed out of his office. He described the scene at the inquiry. 'What about the Mail?' he asked. Cooper was standing against the window with his back to him as he said this. When he turned towards him his face was as white as chalk; 'he had the appearance', said the stationmaster, 'of a man paralysed.' 'I have ordered the Mail up,' he answered. Both men knew very well what these words meant. They meant that on this dark and rainy autumn night with visibility down to 300 yards Cooper had sent two trains to certain destruction. No power on earth could save them now. Sproule was so unstrung that he said he scarcely knew what happened after this. He felt so deeply for Cooper that he could hardly speak, but he remembered suspending him and telling Hayden to take his place.

While this little stricken group of men stood helplessly upon the platform at Norwich in the overwhelming knowledge of what they had done, the tragedy was being played out in the blackness beyond the station lights where the express and the Mail were speeding towards each other. They met between the Yare Bridge and the East Norfolk Junction, and the noise of their collision, said those who heard it, was like a great clap of thunder. Of the last few terrible moments of that drama there was no witness for both engine crews perished. But on the engine of the up Mail, the 7-foot single No 54, they found the regulator shut and the tender brake screwed hard down. In all, twenty-five lives were lost in the Thorpe disaster and seventy-three were injured.

The unfortunate inspector, Cooper, was not alone to blame. The telegraph clerk Robson was even more culpable and the Board of Trade inspector, Captain Tyler, commented adversely upon the fact that this youth of eighteen had no less than four young men in the telegraph office with him to distract his attention from his work. He knew perfectly well that the working rules stated clearly that no message should be transmitted unless it bore the station inspector's signature. Yet when he had taken down Cooper's verbal instruction he had almost immediately transmitted it to Brundall as 'signed A. Cooper', whereas, in fact, Cooper had never signed it. Asked why he did this he replied: 'I see my error. I did it to oblige Cooper; I never did such a thing before in my life.' He added that Cooper had promised that he would return immediately to sign his order but that he had failed to do so. At this Captain Tyler pointed out that he was provided with a bell with which to summon the inspector if required and that he should have rung it when Cooper failed to return. Robson replied that he did not use the bell because it made the inspectors angry. Cooper, on the other hand, declared that he had no sooner given his order than he heard the express approaching and cancelled it, Robson replying: 'All right, Captain'. Robson denied this.

L. T. C. ROLT
Red for Danger
(1955), pp. 119–123

2 *Early Motor Claims*

Within living memory non-marine risks were regarded as a slightly improper intrusion upon Lloyd's true function, the insurance of risks germane to perils of the sea. But history shows that with all its feeling for the past Lloyd's has always marched with the times. Non-maritime premiums flow into the Room from every quarter of the globe at the rate of millions sterling annually. Such a vast turnover compels the use of modern business mechanisation. . . . I look back to the circumstances of my introduction to this great and august concern in 1907 and still find them, like so many of my later adventures, improbable.

Carefree and twenty-one I was riding a tram along the Thames Embankment in the noon sunshine. The river boats were busy. But it was the road traffic that held my especial interest, for the years I had already spent in my father's law practice had gone largely in handling claims arising from street accidents. So it was with a professional eye that I saw a horse drawing a hansom cab shy at the tram's gong and swerve into an automobile. At the time, 1907, motor cars and those in charge of them were held at worst in hatred or at best in contempt. I knew that none of the bystanders would speak up for the blameless chauffeur. With this in mind I alighted, gave him my card and said he might refer his master to me for the truth about the smash. This gesture wasted most of my ticket (a half-penny one). But I was content to walk the rest of the way happy in having struck a blow for justice.

Some weeks later a shy little man, A. J. Whitcombe of Lloyd's, called upon me at the office. He insured the car which the hansom had damaged. Did I agree the cabby was solely to blame? I certainly did. 'Well,' said he, 'the cabby through his insurance company denies all liability. Can I force him to foot the repair bill?'

I spoke of the heavy pro-horse bias in any Motor *v*. Horse contest; advised him to steer clear of litigation in so small a case as this (there was only £14 10s at stake) and to aim rather at a fifty-fifty compromise. 'See if you can do it for me,' he said, gave me his file and hurried off. Was it conceivable that this modest little chap had it in his power to employ a youngster like me to act for such a world-famous insurance body as I vaguely knew Lloyd's to be? But who was I to question his authority?

Now the cabby's insurers boasted as claims manager one Grant, a dour Scot. He and I had met before. There was no tougher nut to be found in the insurance circles of those days.

I called upon him and played the only card I felt would offer any hope of success. I told him of the tram ride and its sequel. I reminded him that we should, no doubt, be against one another many times in the future. I swore that if on this new claim he would bear half the car's repair bill he might regard his outlay not only as settling a claim but as buying my goodwill for life.

Our talk developed on the lines of a Barrie play. Grant made a show of turning me down flat, appeared to weaken a little, mumbled something about 'liking to see a young man trying to get on', finally yielded ('agen ma better judgment') and no doubt laughed quietly as I left with his cheque (including fee, 10*s* 6*d*.) in my pocket. He never had cause to regret the bargain.

To be able to send A. J. Whitcombe a 50 per cent recovery within twenty-four hours of his visit was a minor triumph. Soon I was handling his claims by the score. And, best of all, I had made my Lloyd's début. Never was a ha'penny better invested. . . .

My Lloyd's work, while heavy, did not grow fast enough to swamp me. This respite – a blessing in disguise, since it left me a few hours for study – was due to the low rating which underwriters put upon the acumen of my sponsor, A. J. Whitcombe. He was a lovable eccentric from a family of parsons and doctors. What freak of fate dumped this modest, kindly and unbusinesslike little gentleman upon the insurance world I never learned. Anyone less like a pioneer it would have been difficult to imagine. And yet, to him must go the credit for producing (in December 1901) the 'A.J.W.' policy under which motor insurance was for the first time subscribed at Lloyd's. No specimen of it is now to be found. It had been drafted with the help of Whitcombe's friend, Franklin Adams, a marine underwriter, and is said to have smacked of the sea, treating the insured vehicle as a ship navigating on dry land. A flat £4 was charged for the accidental-damage section and another £4 covered third-party risks up to £500. At least those were the prices paid by cautious motorists. Folk (known in 1902 as 'road hogs') who tore wildly about the country at breakneck speed (twenty-five miles per hour was not impossible) had to pay through the nose. The happy-go-lucky affairs of the A.J.W. Syndicate were conducted over a baker's shop in Pancras Lane in an atmosphere redolent of new bread. If a claim arose in unforeseen circumstances which left any doubt whether underwriters should pay or not, they paid. Before my advent A.J.W., with little or no experience to guide him, had enjoyed handling his claims unaided on a basis of trial and error. He was especially proud of one 'total loss' where neither he nor the assured had the least idea whether or not it came within the policy wording. A.J.W.'s solution was to toss the assured double or quits and win. It was known that the surveyor who went all over the British Isles for him assessing damage done in motor accidents was a Newbury blacksmith. This was judged an odd choice. It happened to be a very good one. The blacksmith had been in motoring from the start and had opened in his native town one of those motor-repair shops which attracted to them the French name 'garage'. The fact that he was brawny, bearded, cloth-capped and countryfied did not detract from his competence. Most underwriters thought that I, a young unknown, noticed only because I had witnessed a street accident, was another odd choice and to be avoided. I bear them no grudge; they long since made ample amends.

WILLIAM CHARLES CROCKER
Far From Humdrum
(1967), pp. 51–56

3 *Utmost Good Faith*

A memorable collection of motorists' statements made on insurance claims was published by the *Police Review* in their 'Spare A Copper' anthology compiled by Superintendent George Harris. Rarely has the requirement of candour in relationship between insurer and insured been demonstrated so graphically as in these brief extracts:

- Coming home I drove into the wrong house and collided with a tree I don't have.
- I collided with a stationary truck coming the other way.
- A pedestrian hit me and went under the car.

– The guy was all over the road, I had to swerve a number of times before I hit him.

– I pulled away from the side of the road, glanced at my mother-in-law and headed over the embankment.

– In an attempt to kill a fly, I drove into a telephone pole.

– I had been driving for 40 years when I fell asleep at the wheel and had an accident.

– I was on my way to the doctor with rear end trouble when my universal joint gave way causing me to have an accident.

– An invisible car came out of nowhere, struck my car and vanished.

– I was sure that the old fellow would never make it to the other side of the road when I struck him.

– The pedestrian had no idea in which direction to run, so I ran over him.

– I saw a slow moving, sad faced old gentleman as he bounced off the roof of the car.

– The indirect cause of the accident was a little guy in a small car with a big mouth.

Insurance claims statements
from 'Spare A Copper'
Police Review (1982)

4 *The Beult Viaduct Disaster and Charles Dickens*

The Beult viaduct on the South Eastern Railway main line near Staplehurst was a very modest structure. It carried the line a mere ten feet above a muddy stream and consisted of a series of cast iron trough girders resting on brick piers. The work in hand was the replacement of the longitudinal timber baulks which lay in the girders and upon which the rails were laid. It was being carried out between trains and no mention of it appeared in the monthly service timetables. The work had proceeded smoothly and by the afternoon of June 9th only one of the thirty-two baulks on the viaduct had still to be changed. John Benge planned to do this between the passing of an up train at 2.51 and a down train at 4.15. John Wiles, a platelayer's labourer, was protecting the up line. According to the rule it was his duty to place one fog signal on the rail every 250 yards from the viaduct up to an extreme distance of 1,000 yards where he was to place two 10 yards apart and station himself with a red flag. But Benge had posted him at the tenth telegraph pole from the bridge which was only 554 yards away. Wiles was supplied with only two detonators and was told not to use them unless it was foggy. It was a bright and sunny afternoon.

It is obvious that John Benge and his leading carpenter were so sure of their ability to carry out their work between trains that they had come to look upon the business of protection as a mere formality. Beult was not the first bridge they had dealt with in similar fashion and the whole job had gone like clockwork until now when it was practically completed. But on this last afternoon John Benge made a fatal mistake. There was one train in the Company's timetable which did not run to a fixed schedule. This was the Folkestone Boat Express which was known as the 'tidal' because its timing varied with the tides which governed the arrival of the Folkestone Packets. These daily times were shown in Benge's working timetable but he misread it. He believed that the boat train was not due at Headcorn until 5.20 whereas in fact it was due at 3.15. The leading carpenter had also been issued with a copy of the timetable but he had dropped his on the rail where it had been destroyed by a passing train so he could not correct his foreman's error. Disaster was in these circumstances a foregone conclusion.

The new timber baulks had been set in position but two 21-foot lengths of rail had still to be replaced when the express approached running at fifty miles an hour. Her driver acted promptly as soon as he saw Wiles' red flag, but in so short a distance he could not hope to bring his train of thirteen vehicles to a stand. The leading van and the first two coaches were fitted with Cremar's patent brakes, but unfortunately the guard in charge did not himself see Wiles's frantic signal and in response to the brake whistle he first put on his ordinary screw brake. Not until half the critical distance had been covered did he realise the urgency and apply the patent brakes. By that time the engine was practically upon the bridge, and before the eyes of the horrified gang a scene of frightful destruction ensued. Extraordinary to relate, the locomotive, its tender and the leading brake van actually succeeded in crossing the rail-less gap on the timber baulks, but the following train was less fortunate. The strain was too much for the cast iron girders beneath. The offside girder collapsed as the tender and van passed over. The first coach came to rest hanging at a perilous angle supported by the van coupling, but the next five fell through the gap into the muddy bed of the stream where they lay in a confusion of splintered wreckage, one standing on its end and another on its roof. Ten passengers in these coaches perished and forty-nine were injured.

The travellers in the leading coach – so commonly shunned by nervous passengers – were in this case more fortunate than their fellows in the rear. Amongst them was Charles Dickens. He was reading through the manuscript of *Our Mutual Friend* when the accident occurred, and he alluded to his experience in a Postscript which he added to that book.

> On Friday, the ninth of June in the present year [he wrote] Mr and Mrs Boffin (in their manuscript dress of receiving Mr and Mrs Lammle at breakfast) were on the South Eastern Railway with me, in a terribly destructive accident. When I had done what I could to help others, I climbed back into my carriage – nearly turned over a viaduct, and caught aslant upon the turn – to extricate the worthy couple. They were much soiled, but otherwise unhurt. . . . I remember with devout thankfulness that I can never be much nearer parting company with my readers for ever than I was then, until there shall be written against my life the two words with which I have this day closed the book – The End.

That end, unfortunately, was not far off. Although Dickens escaped physical injury his terrifying experience seriously affected his nervous system with results which became apparent later. 'I am curiously weak', he wrote, 'weak as if I were recovering from a long illness. I begin to feel it more in my head. I sleep well and eat well; but I write half a dozen words and turn faint and sick.' It was some time before he could bring himself to travel by rail again and when he did so he preferred slow trains.

> A perfect conviction against the senses, that the carriage is down on one side (and generally that is the left, and *not* the side on which the carriage in the accident really went over) comes upon me with anything like speed, and is inexpressibly distressing.

It is true to say that Dickens never fully recovered from the after effects of Staplehurst, and on June 9th, 1870 – the fifth anniversary of the disaster – the great man died in his fifty-eighth year. We cannot estimate the loss which English literature sustained as a result of John Benge's tragic mistake. Certainly he deprived us of the solution to *The Mystery of Edwin Drood*.

L. T. C. ROLT
Red for Danger
(1955), pp. 106–108

5 *Bird Strikes*

Three fatal airliner accidents have been caused by bird strikes. Damage by a single bird is rarely hazardous: windscreens and airframe engine leading-edge structures are designed and tested to meet the strictest bird-impact airworthiness standards. There was the case of a Viscount which in November 1962 collided with a swan at 6,000 ft near Ellicott City, Maryland. The aircraft was destroyed with the loss of all 17 occupants. The accident investigators found the remains of the bird embedded in the tailplane, which had broken off. There have been sightings of geese and other species at over 15,000 ft, but collisions are extremely rare. In July 1962 the commander of an Indian DC-3 on a domestic flight was fatally injured by a vulture which came through the windscreen. The copilot landed the aircraft safely.

Complete power failure following the ingestion of flocks of birds into the engine air intakes can be disastrous, as in the case of the Electra which flew into a flock of starlings soon after take-off from Boston in October 1960, with the loss of 62 lives. A similar accident occurred to a Qantas 747 taking off from Sydney in April 1973, without loss of life. In December 1969, also at Sydney, a Pan American 707 was severely damaged when the take-off was abandoned following bird ingestion, although none of the 136 people on board was injured.

Particularly vulnerable to bird strikes are military aircraft which spend much of their lives flying at high speeds and low levels where the bird population is highest. Bird strikes are regarded by most air forces, especially those operating single-engined jets, as one of the routine major safety hazards. The Royal Netherlands Air Force has found that up to a third of its accidents are caused by bird strikes. The United States Air Force reports as many as 700 a year.

About 90 per cent of bird strikes take place below 1,500 ft, where nearly 90 per cent of birds fly. Except during migration, more than half the bird population flies below 500 ft. More than a fifth flies between that level and 1,000 ft. Only 14 per cent is found between 1,000 ft and 1,500 ft. From there up to 5,000 ft is found 9 per cent, and above that level the remaining 4 per cent. All these figures change during migration, when the highest density in many areas is between 1,500 ft and 2,500 ft.

The force with which a bird strikes an aircraft is proportional to its weight and to the speed of the aircraft. Doubling the weight of the bird increases the impact force by only half; doubling the speed of the aircraft increases the impact force by more than four times. The speed of the aircraft is more critical than the size of the bird.

Airworthiness-certification standards of bird-proofing design and impact-testing are such that strikes are nowadays more of a nuisance than a danger, except in the rare case of power failure caused by a multiple strike. Typical of the windscreen requirements, which vary with aircraft type, is the ability of the A300 to withstand the impact of a 4 lb bird at 470 m.p.h.

The airlines expect the airport authorities to control the bird population. They expect also that the air-traffic control authorities, in co-operation with the airport management, will give regular warnings of bird-strike hazards.

Temporary advantages have been gained by broadcasting amplified recordings of distress calls. For a time this is found to disperse the birds; but familiarity gradually makes it less effective. The sudden unsettling of a flock can in any case be dangerous. Recorded distress calls are almost ineffective at big civil airports where the runways are too busy and continually noisy. The British Airports Authority has tried the technique at Stanstead but without conclusive results, other than an indication of the cost of the operation.

Some military airfields have employed hawks and other birds of prey to keep down bird life. Falcons operated at RAF Lossiemouth reduced bird strikes by nearly half.

The mediaeval contribution to jet safety requires trained falconers and birds, and is expensive. It has not yet been found possible to colonise airfields naturally with hawks.

The siting near airports of bird-feeding grounds, such as the major sewage lagoons at Heathrow under the western (prevailing) take-off path, is not good safety practice. Ten aircraft in one day were damaged by seagull strikes, according to the Civil Aviation Authority *Civil Aviation Information Circular* of January 28, 1974, at an airport which is assumed to be Heathrow. There have also been numerous warnings about waste food left lying about outside airport restaurants. The dangers should not be exaggerated. Bird strikes have not been a serious danger at Heathrow. This is Europe's busiest airport and it has been bordered by reservoirs and sewage farms for many years. But everything possible must be done to avoid siting bird-attracting amenities near airports, and certainly airports should not be built on sites heavily populated with birds.

The bigger the aircraft the more vulnerable it is to bird strikes. It appears that the number of such incidents is proportional to the size of the air intake. The number of bird strikes for the Boeing 747 is just over 10 per 10,000 hr compared with 1.5 for the Boeing 707.

Investigation of an accident in which a DC-10 was totally destroyed, fortunately without loss of life, at New York Kennedy in 1975 revealed that at least two heavy birds and possibly as many as seven in the 2 kg class (duck, geese) had struck the No 3 engine fan, causing the fan casing to disintegrate.

Fatal bird strikes

Date	*Aircraft*	*Carrier*	*Location*	*Type of Flight*	*Fatalities* Crew	*Fatalities* Passengers	*Remarks*
Oct 4, 1960	Electra (N5533)	Eastern	Boston	SP	3	59	Multiple strike on take-off
July 15, 1962	DC-3 (VT-AVS)	Indian Airlines	Lahore	NSF	1	—	Captain killed by vulture through screen
Nov 23, 1962	Viscount (N7430)	United	Ellicott City, Md	SP	4	13	Hit swan at 6,000 ft. Left tailplane detached

Subsequent debate between the US National Transportation Safety Board and the Federal Aviation Administration disclosed some areas of doubt about bird-strike airworthiness requirements.

An FAA Circular had prescribed that a test engine should ingest flocks of starling-sized birds in volleys of up to 16; gulls, pigeons or small duck in groups of up to 10; and large birds such as duck, geese and buzzards weighing around 2 kg fired singly at the test engine fan.

Doubts exist about the effectiveness of firing volleys of birds at different fan radii compared with single shots fired at critical areas such as the blade tips. The 'worst case' – hitting a flock of Canada Geese weighing about 3 kg each – is being considered by the airworthiness authorities.

J. M. RAMSDEN
The Safe Airline
(1979), pp. 87–89

IV
Fire

1 The Great Fire and Old St Paul's

To an onlooker from Southwark or Westminster it must have appeared as though Old St Paul's was going to survive. At sunset it was completely ringed by fire, yet it remained unburnt, its great single tower rising above the swirling smoke. The fire had come creeping towards the cathedral out of the little alleys and lanes that opened on to the churchyard, but it was only at the north-west corner that the houses came within a matter of a few feet of Inigo Jones's portico with its wooden ceiling.

Just as the goldsmiths had used the Tower as a place of safe keeping for their wares, so the booksellers of Paternoster Row used the churchyard as an open-air store for their stock. First they and the mercers carried their goods into the cathedral precincts, and then as the fire approached they decided that was not safe enough, and the booksellers took their volumes down into St Faith's, the parish church in the crypt. Since St Faith's was the guild church of the Stationers they were in fact using their own place of worship. Before they had finished and sealed up all the openings they had, according to Pepys, deposited no less than £150,000 worth of highly combustible books there. As St Faith's was only half below ground, it was lit by a series of small windows on either side of the choir which had their sills only a foot or two above the level of the churchyard. Against these the traders now piled more books, together with the bales of cloth brought over from their shops by the mercers.

Dusk would have fallen at about 7 p.m., almost unnoticed in the flickering glare reflected off the clouds of smoke rolling away towards the west. The flames of blazing Ludgate must have lit up the main front and strongly buttressed central tower with the power of flood-lights, though with the shadows changing shape and size every instant.

But if anyone found time to rejoice that the cathedral had withstood the fire, it was premature. During the summer of 1666 restoration work had been going on at Old St Paul's, and the central tower was surrounded by scaffolding, also there were builder's materials lying on the roof itself.

Two eyewitnesses saw the beginning of the end for the cathedral. One was Martin, a bookseller who was in the churchyard at the time. Pepys quoted what he was told: 'And he tells me that it took fire first upon the end of a board that, among others, was laid upon the roof instead of lead, the lead being broke off, and thence down lower and lower.' At about the same instant the scaffolding round the tower caught fire, either from the flames on the roof or else from blazing cinders carried across from the surrounding houses. Also, the timber roof of the portico was fired from the house nearest to it. There was nothing anyone could do, except stand and watch.

William Taswell takes up the story:

> . . . just after sunset at Night, I went to the royal bridge in New Palace Yard at Westminster to take a fuller view of the fire. As I stood upon the bridge (landing stage) among others, I could not but observe the gradual approach of fire towards that venerable fabric. About eight o'clock it broke out on the top of St Paul's Church, already scorched by the violent heat of the air, and lightning too, and before nine blazed so conspicuous as to enable me to read very clearly a sixteen mo edition of Terence which I carried in my pocket.

Once before, in 1561, the roofs of the cathedral had been destroyed by fire, but with almost negligible damage to the interior. This time it was a very different story. The timbers which supported the roof, brought from Yorkshire by sea just over a century before, blazed up like tinder, melting the lead covering the roofs. 'Now the lead melts and runs, as if it had been snow before the sun, and with a great noise fall on the pavement, and break through into Faith Church underneath, and great flakes of stone scale, and peel off strangely from the side of the walls' (Vincent). It must have been the molten lead, cascading over the walls, that caused the phenomenon, which was also mentioned by Evelyn. 'The stones of Paul's flew like grenados, the melting lead running down the streets in a stream, and the very pavements glowing with fiery redness, so as no horse, nor man, was able to tread on them, and the demolition had stopped all passages, so that no help could be applied.'

The sight of the molten lead, creeping out of the cathedral by the doorways, and running down Ludgate Hill must have been one of the most terrifying sights during the whole Great Fire. It was as though Old St Paul's had ceased to be an inanimate object, and had come alive at the moment of its death. The lead also poured off the outer walls, spattering cornices, pilasters and buttresses, thrusting down into cracks in the stonework and so causing it to explode and fly in all directions with killing force. All over the vast building, nearly six hundred feet long, the masonry was exploding in the intense heat. Lumps of Caen stone, some weighing as much as a hundred pounds hurled through the air like cannon balls. First the timbers of the roofs smashed through the vaulting of the nave and choir, and in the latter the masonry falling from a height of over ninety feet broke through the pavement and pierced the vaulting of St Faith's. Already the heat from above must have made all the books stored down there tinder dry: now, as the air rushed in, they ignited with the force of an explosion.

According to Pepys the fire also entered the crypt via the goods piled against the outside of the windows: 'they first took fire from the Draper's side, by some timber of the houses that were burned, falling into the church.'

Now the cathedral was an inferno from end to end, the flames bursting out of all the windows and enveloping the tower. As the doors at the west end and on the north side of the nave, and at the ends of the transepts, burnt or warped and burst open, so a terrific draught was caused inside: the high and comparatively narrow walls of the nave and choir acting like a chimney, making a furnace of the interior. A furnace destroying the pomp and grandeur of Medieval London. If Old St Paul's had been the Valhalla of so many of England's noble – though not necessarily royal – ones, this was their Twilight. John of Gaunt, Sir Simon Burley, Sir Philip Sidney, Sir Christopher Hatton, Sir Nicholas Bacon, Sir Francis Walsingham, Dr John Donne, Dr Colet, Sir Anthony van Dyck; and from more remote times SS Sebba and Erkenwald and King Ethelred the Unready. From death they were passing to physical oblivion, and so were their tombs. The exquisite tabernacle-work raised by Henry Yevele over the tomb of John of Gaunt and Blanche, his first wife, must have been crushed in an instant.

Though mutilated and profaned during the Commonwealth, much must have remained (as it did at two other shamefully treated cathedrals, Durham and Exeter). Such effigies as do survive prove that at least those in the choir, which was walled off from the nave and used as a preaching house, were not all destroyed by the narrow-minded bigotry of Puritan iconoclasts.

One monument did survive intact, and it was the last that was set up in the old cathedral before the Civil War. It was to John Donne, died 1631, and was the work of Nicholas Stone. Placed immediately behind the south-east pier of the central tower, it showed Donne as though rising from an urn, in his shroud. Sometime after the pavement was broken open the effigy, which is tall and narrow, slithered from its place and fell right down into the small vault below, where it remained unharmed while the fire still raged through the cathedral itself. Years later it was set up between two windows of the south choir aisle of Wren's building: the only intact relic from Old St Paul's that has survived.

Martin also told Pepys: '. . . one warehouse of books was saved under Paul's; and there were several dogs found burned among the goods in the churchyard, and but one man, which was an old man, that said he would go and save a blanket which he had in the church, and, being weak, the fire overcame him.' This old man, anonymous to history, was not only the last person to see that magnificent interior, but also he was probably only the second casualty in the Great Fire, which had now been raging since Sunday.

By dawn on Wednesday, 5th September, Old St Paul's was quite gutted though the walls still stood, and also the central tower. It went on burning for several hours, while the books in St Faith's continued to smoulder for a week. Among the works destroyed were three hundred copies of Sir William Dugdale's invaluable history of the cathedral (1657), which had plates by Hollar.

It was not until Thursday that anyone could get near the Cathedral, and among the first to do so were Pepys, Evelyn and Taswell. Pepys approached it from Paul's Wharf: 'A miserable sight of Paul's church, with all the roofs fallen, and the body of the choir fallen into St Faiths.' Evelyn walked right through the City from west to east, and back again.

> I was infinitely concern'd to find that goodly church St Paul's now a sad ruin, and that beautiful Portico (for structure comparable to any in Europe, as not long before repaired by the late king) now rent in pieces, flakes of vast stone split in sunder, and nothing remaining entire but the inscription in the architrave which showing by whom it was built, had not one letter defac'd: which I could not but take notice of. It was astonishing to see what immense stones the heat had in a manner calcin'd, so as all the

ornaments, columns, friezes, capitals and projectures of massey Portland stone flew off, even to the very roof. It is also observable, that the lead over the altar at the east end was untouch'd, and among the divers monuments, the body of one Bishop, remained entire (Robert Braybrooke).

But the most touching account of Old St Paul's immediately after its destruction is that by the schoolboy William Taswell.

On Thursday soon after sunrising, I endeavoured to reach St Paul's. The ground so hot as almost to scorch my shoes, and the air so intensely warm that unless I had stopped some time upon Fleet Bridge to rest myself, I must have fainted under the extreme languor of my spirits. After giving myself time to breathe, I made the best of my way to St Paul's. And now let any person judge of the violent emotion I was in when I perceived the metal belonging to the bells melting; the ruinous condition of its walls; whole heaps of stone of a large circumference tumbling down with a great noise just upon my feet, ready to crush me to death. I prepared myself for returning back again, having first loaded my pockets with several pieces of bell metal.

I forgot to mention that near the east wall of St Paul's a human body presented itself to me, parched up as it were with the flames; whole as to skin, meagre as to flesh, yellow as to colour. This was an old decrepid woman who had fled here for safety, imagining the flames would not have reached her there. Her clothes were burnt, and every limb reduced to coal.

In my way home I saw several engines which were bringing up to its assistance all on fire, and those concerned with them escaping with great eagerness from the flames, which spread instantaneous almost like a wild-fire; and at last accoutered with my sword and helmet, which I picked up among many others in the ruins, I traversed this torrid zone back again.

JOHN E. N. HEARSEY
London and the Great Fire
(1965), pp. 153–159

2 *Investigating Arson*

Exclusion of accidental causes

The first step in recognizing arson is the exclusion of all accidental causes. Possibly the best method is to cast out the obviously impossible causes and thus narrow the field of probability. The investigator should be familiar with the generally accepted causes of accidental fire and should inquire into the following:

The Electric System. Fuses, bridged with wire or foil or in which pennies have been inserted; broken or rotted insulation; overloading of circuits; defective switches or fixtures; wiring not installed in accordance with the local code or the National Electric Code.

Electric Equipment. Not of approved type; defective; fire originated close to equipment such as iron or other heating element; fire traceable to paper shades on electric bulbs.

Gas. Leaks in pipes or defective stoves or heating unit.

Pets. Presence of dog or cat and its possible contribution to cause of fire.

Painting Equipment. Carelessness with paint, paint rags, linseed oil, turpentine, and so on.

Heating Units. Overheated stoves; clothing dried too close to fireplaces or open flames; overheated steam pipes; faulty chimneys or flues; explosions resulting from kerosene stoves; stoves overturned in dark by pets, during flight, and so on.

Sun. Concentration of sun's rays on bubbles in glass window panes, convex shaving mirrors, odd-shaped bottles, and so on.

Lightning. Check on duration of storm.

Children. Accidentally, while at play.

Smoking. Careless disposal of cigars, cigarettes, or pipe ashes; falling asleep while smoking in chair, auto, bed, and so on.

Storage of Hay. Date stored and condition.

Other causes are less common, but any possibility should be thoroughly explored. Some of the less common causes are sparks from electric motors or friction caused by running machinery; rubbish and brush fires spreading to a nearby building; ignition of hot grease, tar, oil, or like substance; explosion of natural or artificial gases; fireworks; sparks from an outdoor fire or a passing locomotive; or improperly combining chemical solutions.

A good rule for an adjuster to remember is that no listing of possible accidental causes can be considered all-inclusive. Some fires are the result of odd and unusual accidental ignition, but in order for a fire to start, it is necessary to combine combustible material with a source of ignition. These ignition sources are fairly well established and include open flames, electric arcs, heating and cooking devices, moving machinery, chemical processes, and spontaneous ignition. If any of these sources can be located in a specific section of the building, it should be determined whether it was possible for the source to combine with a combustible material and result in a fire.

Firefighters can help in the discovery of suspicious fires. Seek their active cooperation, talk to them, and listen to their stories. After all, fire and fire prevention is their business. Every day they risk their lives to fight fire, and aiding the arson investigation is just another means of doing so.

One of the explanations for the great activity of the professional torches during the Depression of the 1930s was the commonly held belief that a fire could be set and in burning obliterate all evidence of incendiarism. The smart criminal today realizes that this is far from true. The development of laboratory facilities and techniques such as the spectograph, the gas chromatograph, the ultraviolent light, the infrared ray, and the vacuum distillation process; the high level of training among arson investigators; and the alertness of firefighters are all increasing the likelihood of detection.

Set fires leave telltale signs. These signs may be so obvious that the first firefighter on the scene will suspect arson, or they may be so well concealed that months of patient investigation will be required to show that the fire was set. However, the sign is always present. It may not scream out 'This is arson!' but it may whisper 'This is a suspicious fire'.

The superior officer on the first fire truck to near the scene, on coming into view of the fire, will 'size up' the fire and the building. If two or more separate fires are noted, this officer will immediately be aware of the probability of arson. So will the first firefighters to enter the building if they detect a strong odor of kerosene or other petroleum products – unless their presence is accounted for by the occupancy of the building. An unaccountably rapid spread or intensity of a fire is also suspicious.

There are many of these signs which are encountered again and again at fire scenes; some point directly to arson, while others serve to alert the firefighters and officers at the scene. From a study of the burned building to a search of the debris, the telltale signs most encountered are listed in the following paragraphs:

The Burned Building. The type of building in which the fire occurs may indicate a set fire under some circumstances. A fire of considerable size at the time the first apparatus arrives on the scene is suspicious if it is in a modern fireproof building. Modern loft and warehouse construction has also eliminated many of the accidental causes of fire as well as provided means for preventing fire travel.

Separate Fires. Perhaps the most conclusive sign of fire setting is a number of separate fires. When two or three separate fires break out within a building or group of buildings or even in one room or store, it is almost certain that accident or misfortune can be ruled out and arson definitely suspected.

Color of Smoke and Flames. Some fires burn with little or no smoke, but they are the exception rather than the rule. Combustion of materials is usually incomplete and there is some smoke. The characteristics of smoke very often assist in identifying the substances which started or boosted the fire.

As H. Rethoret notes in his fine book *Fire Investigations*, the observation of smoke must be made at the start of a fire. Once a fire has assumed major proportions, the value of an observation of smoke is lost, for the fire is then consuming the building itself and the smoke will not indicate the materials used by the arsonist. It is therefore extremely important to locate and question the first person who saw the fire and the first firefighters at the scene.

When white smoke appears before the water from the fire hoses comes into contact with the fire, it indicates humid materials burning. Burning hay and vegetable matter in stable and barn fires give off a heavy white smoke but with a distinct garlic odor and a noxious effect on those inhaling quantities of it. (Phosphorus is used in the preparation of wartime chemical agents.)

Biting smoke, irritating the nose and throat and causing lachrymation and coughing, indicates the presence of chlorine – another wartime chemical agent. The inhalation of smoke containing chlorine gas is also dangerous.

Black smoke indicates lack of air; but if accompanied by large flames, it generally indicates the burning of a material with a petroleum base. Unless petroleum, tar, coal, rubber, or like compounds are stored within the burning building, it is possible that some fire setter used a petroleum product to accelerate the blaze.

Reddish brown, thick yellow, or brownish yellow smoke is an indication that films, or substances containing nitrocellulose fiber, sulfur, or sulfuric, nitric, or hydrochloric acid are burning. If later investigation fails to reveal that any quantities of such substances are normally stored in the building, then incendiarism can be suspected.

To a great extent, the appearance of smoke is also governed by the supply of oxygen available to the fire. This also governs the flames. No flames or comparatively small flames indicate lack of air. More flames than smoke indicates the burning of dry substances. Large flames indicate a good supply of oxygen, while erratic flames shooting at odd and unusual intervals indicate the presence of an accumulation of some gases. When the flames swirl around in a sort of pattern and are accompanied by a cloud of dust and fine ash, it indicates better-than-average ventilation at the fire. Sparks in large quantities indicate powdery substances are burning in a well-ventilated fire.

The color of the flames is a good indication of the intensity of the fire, an important factor in determining incendiarism. A reddish glow indicates a heat of about 500°C, a real light red, about 1000°C. Red flames also indicate the presence of petroleum as does the appearance of tongues of flame on the water running off from the fire. A fire temperature of close to 1100°C is indicated by a yellow glow, and a blinding white fire usually reaches a temperature of 1500°C.

Though large quantities of alcohol will burn with an orange flame, a blue flame reveals the use of alcohol as a fire accelerant, and although not used frequently because the color of the flames readily identifies it, there is a possibility an investigator many encounter its use.

Size of Fire. This is important when correlated with the type of alarm, the time received, and the time of arrival of the first apparatus. Fires make what might be termed "normal progress." Such progress can be estimated after an examination of the materials burned, the building, and the normal ventilation offered to the fire. Thus, the time element and the degree of headway made by the flames become important factors to anyone probing into possible incendiarism.

Direction of Travel. While it is acknowledged that no two fires in buildings burn in identical fashion, it is also necessary to point out that fires can be expected to make normal progress through various types of buildings. Experienced firefighters can usually determine whether a fire has spread abnormally fast when they take into consideration the type of construction, the channels of ventilation, the combustibility of the contents of the building, and the circumstances surrounding the sending of the alarm.

It is known that hot gases rise and fire tends to sweep upwards until blocked by some obstacle. It then seeks holes, cracks, or outlets through which to escape. If none is present, the flames mushroom out horizontally until the fire can bend around the obstruction or find some break through which to continue its progress. Dumbwaiter shafts in tenement houses and elevator shafts in hotels and apartment houses have furnished tragic examples of the speedy progress of a fire and then the mushrooming of the smoke and flames horizontally into hallways when the fire meets the dead end at the top of the shaft.

A fire does not spread nearly so rapidly in a horizontal direction unless favorable ventilation is present, or possibly the wall surfaces have been treated with a flammable substance. When a fire has spread in a direction which normally would not be expected, it might be suspected to have been incendiary.

Another point to be borne in mind when seeking to determine the direction of the burning is the depth of the charring at various points on the studding or beams in a building and the pattern of burning as indicated by the charring, scorching, blistering, and soot deposits in a room or about a building.

Sometimes a fire setter will seek to better ventilate a building by cutting holes between rooms or floors, opening windows, tying back doors, or blocking up fire doors. Sprinkler systems have also been made inoperative to permit a fire to spread. In most cases, the means used to ventilate a building or damage a sprinkler system are readily visible if the fire is quickly extinguished. Unless the structure is burned to the ground, a close inspection may reveal the arsonist's techniques; and even when it is burned to the ground, the unusual speed of travel may cast suspicion on the fire.

Intensity. The degree of heat given off by a fire and the color of its flames often indicate that some accelerant has been added to the materials normally present in a building and alert the firefighters or investigators to look for further evidence of the use of flammable liquids or compounds. Possibly some difficulty in extinguishing the fire will lead firefighters to suspect the presence of such fluids as gasoline and kerosene. Fires react to a stream of water in various fashions. If a flame burns brighter when hit with a hose stream or if the flames change color when the water strikes them, any experienced firefighter is alerted to the probability of arson.

Odors. There is little question that the odor of such flammable substances as gasoline, kerosene, and alcohol has trapped more arsonists than any other tell-tale sign. Because arsonists seek a substance which will make the blaze certain and which will burn up any evidence of arson, kerosene, alcohol, and gasoline spring to their minds. All three will burn, but in burning up the evidence of arson, a readily identifiable odor is given off and this points to a fire setter.

An investigator can easily learn to recognize the odors of various flammable liquids. By placing small amounts in wide-mouthed glass jars, shutting the eyes, opening a jar, and guessing its contents, the investigator will soon be able to promptly identify the various odors.

Condition of Contents. Persons intending to touch off a fire frequently remove objects of value or items to which they are sentimentally attached. Clothing; personal papers – particularly bankbooks and insurance policies; and such articles as typewriters, television sets, and objects associated with the arsonist's hobby are likely to be removed before household fires are set. Pets are frequently left with relatives before the fire. Stores and other business establishments sometimes remove the major portion of their inventory or replace valuable merchandise with 'distress' out-of-style articles.

Doors and Windows. Locked doors and obstructed entrances and passageways sometimes point to an effort to impede firefighters in their attempts to fight the fire. Doors or windows showing marks of forced entry may point to arson preceded by burglary or possibly arson by someone without a key to the premises.

Windows which are obstructed frequently point directly to a touch-off. The arsonist does not want the fire detected by a chance passerby and therefore will pin down shades and cover windows with drapes, blankets, and even papers. In one case on the West Coast, an investigator found the inside of the glass in the hallway door of a recently burned tenement painted black. Not satisfied with the owner's attempt to blame it on children in the neighbourhood, the investigator cited it as an attempt to obstruct the view of the hallway from the street. Since the fire originated in the rear of the hallway, it was promptly classified as suspicious. Children would have splashed the paint carelessly on the door, but examination of glass fragments revealed two coats of paint had been skillfully applied with all the brush marks running neatly in one direction, apparently the work of an expert painter.

Familiar Faces. Pyromaniacs – psychopathic fire setters – are marked by their tendency to remain at a fire scene 'to watch the fun', as one of them remarked when questioned by a fire marshall. Numerous good arrests have been made because of an alert firefighter or police officer noting a familiar face in a crowd at a fire. Such recognition usually occurs when several fires take place within a few days or hours of each other.

Interested Bystanders. Persons in the crowd about a fire who strive to help when no help is needed or who seem unduly interested in the fire are prime suspects. This is particularly true in 'vanity' fires because the fire setter's object is to appear as a hero. Other arsonists cannot refrain from questioning firefighters and police about the origin of the fire and whether there is anything to mark it as suspicious.

Other Suspicious Circumstances. What may alert a firefighter or an adjuster at a fire scene may be difficult to define. Many times there is just 'something' about the fire that is not quite normal. It may be that a search of the debris revealed a trace of candle grease or some object which might be part of a mechanical fire-setting device. It may be something about the time of the alarm – shortly after the storeowner left for the night – or it may be failure to fully explain an attempt to fight the fire with inadequate equipment without sending an alarm. Or possibly the point of origin or the weather does not tie in with a householder's explanation of the cause of the fire. Whatever the sign that alerted those first on the scene, the investigator must exploit the first telltale sign, the sign that labels a fire 'suspicious – worthy of further investigation'.

Set fires

When a fire is classified as suspicious, it is then the task of the arson investigator to determine if it is in fact a 'touch-off' – a set fire. At this point, all plausible accidental causes have been excluded and observation at the fire scene has pointed to either the possible use of some fire accelerant or the setting of a fire without the use of a recognizable accelerant. It is now up to the arson investigator to determine the modus operandi of the fire setter.

Point of Origin. Initially, the important point to be established at any fire is at what point in the building it originated. This point of origin frequently may be established by an examination of witnesses, by an inspection of the debris at the fire scene, or both.

The first person to be questioned is the discoverer of the fire; the second is the person who turned in the alarm; and, last, any other witnesses who can be found. All should be interrogated about their identities, their business in the area of the fire, what attracted their attention to it, the time of observation, and their positions in relation to the fire at that time. When it has been ascertained that a witness was in a position to view the fire (time and place of observation), then the investigator seeks to learn the exact location of the blaze, its size, its intensity, and the speed of its spread. Witnesses will also be questioned about other persons in the vicinity. Did they observe one of the other witnesses? Did they observe anyone in or about the premises just before or immediately following the fire?

In many cases, there is only a single witness; one person discovered the fire and turned in the alarm, and diligent inquiry fails to uncover any other witnesses.

The person who turned in the alarm will also be questioned about whether a fire box, telephone, or other means was used. It is also important to try to learn the length of time that elapsed between the discovery of the fire and the time the alarm was dispatched.

All experienced arson investigators know that the identity of these witnesses, their business in the area at the time of the fire, and what attracted their attention to it are three vital questions in any investigation of fire setting. It is astonishing the number of times, year after year, that investigators have come across the fire setter among the small number of persons who 'discovered' the fire, who turned in the alarm, or who were on hand before the fire apparatus and helped direct the firemen to the scene. Individuals who have come to the attention of police and fire departments as chronic 'false-alarm ringers' have, in many instances, later blossomed out as thrill-seeking fire setters.

An inspection of the debris must always be made, first to determine the point of origin and, second, to uncover the arsonists's technique.

Charring of wood occurs as a fire burns, the 'alligatoring' of the surface varying as the wood is consumed. When a fire is extinguished quickly, the charring is only slightly below the surface and the alligatoring shows large segments or squares. As the fire continues, the charring goes deeper into the wood and the segments of the alligatoring become smaller. The search for 'alligatoring' will not only help locate the point of origin but may also reveal the existence of two or more separate fires.

Tracing liquid accelerants to the place of spillage aids in definitely locating the point of origin of any fire in which such fluids were used. Any fluid will flow downward to a lower level and in such movement will flow around any fixed object in its path. Therefore a fluid fire accelerant such as gasoline, kerosene, turpentine, or alcohol may be traceable from the point of spillage to its lowest point. Quite frequently, unburned quantities of such liquids are found in rooms below the fire, in cellars, or in portions of a foundation, as a considerable quantity of such fluid sometimes runs down to a low point out of range of the fire. These fluid accelerants will sometimes pool on a large, level floor and burn from the outside of the pool toward the center, leaving a distinctive mark on the floor. These accelerants also cause deep charring, which sometimes neatly charts the flow of the flammable fluid used by the fire setter. Cases have been encountered in which charring traced the path of the accelerant into cracks of the floor to the underside of the floorboards. In addition, these fluids will mar furniture and painted surfaces upon which they may have been splashed and which may be found untouched by the fire.

The point of origin itself points to many suspicious fires. Arsonists place their fire-setting devices where the flames will take hold, while many accidental fires occur in locations where they burn out instead of gaining headway. Thus the location of the point of origin may be of great help in excluding accidental causes.

Fire-setting Mechanisms. It is the duty of an arson investigator to search the debris of a suspicious fire, particularly around the point of origin, to gather evidence pointing to the mechanism used by the fire setter.

Any arsonist may use the simplest of methods – a match and some paper – or elaborate mechanical or chemical means to start and accelerate a fire.

An incendiary mechanism may be mechanical or chemical. It consists of an ignition device, possibly a timing mechanism, one or more 'plants' to feed or accelerate the initial flame, and frequently 'trailers' to spread the fire about the building, sometimes from plant to plant.

Ignition and Timing Mechanisms. An ignition device may be simple (a match, for instance) or it may be a complex mechanical or chemical device which can be timed to go off hours or even days after it is set. This latter type provides a time lag between the time of setting and the outbreak of the fire and gives the fire setter an opportunity to leave the scene and possible establish an alibi for the time of the actual fire.

Matches. Frequently a match is struck by the arsonist, but only juvenile arsonists and pyromaniacs seem to favor this method. Other fire setters want some delay, so they adapt the ordinary match to some timing mechanism.

Several matches may be affixed to a lighted cigarette with a rubber hand or scotch tape, with the heads of the matches about halfway down the cigarette from its glowing end. In some cases, the matches are just laid alongside the cigarette. Books of paper matches have also enjoyed popularity. Since cigarettes will continue to burn when laid on their sides, they are effective ignition devices; the slow-burning cigarette allows the fire setter a few minutes to get away from the scene before the fire makes any headway.

Matches are also used in conjunction with numerous mechanical devices. One misguided arsonist hooked them up with his telephone, strapping them to the ringing mechanism in a wall box and inserting a piece of abrasive board in place of the bell. This 'brain' thought he could set a fire from miles away by calling his home. However, his estranged wife had a change of heart and came home unexpectedly. She settled down to await the amateur fire setter's return. It was not long before she noticed a wisp of smoke from a pile of old clothing on the floor of the living room. Frightened, she called the fire department. The ignition device had been activated but had fizzled out. The firefighters carefully preserved the rags (wet down with lighter fluid), the matches, and the abrasive board, and arranged a warm reception for the husband who had planned 'the perfect crime.'

Unburned or partially burned matches about the point of origin should be carefully preserved for examination and comparison. A suspect may be carrying similar matches or the book from which paper matches have been torn.

Candles. As a timed ignition device, candles have been in use by arsonists for over a century. A candle will burn at various times, depending on its composition and size. Thick candles burn slowly, and long candles naturally burn for a longer period than short candles.

Some years ago, Dr. Richard Steinmetz established a table of the burning time of candles of various compositions and sizes in his fine text *Arson Investigator's Manual*. This table can be summed up as follows:

Composition	*Diameter*	*Time to Burn 1 in.*
Tallow	3/4"	61 minutes
Wax	7/8"	57 minutes
Paraffin	13/16"	63 minutes

Arson investigators sometimes work on a rule of thumb of an hour's burning time for each inch of candle of above diameters. Of course, this is only guesswork, and the investigator must arrive at a more definite time when a little more information is secured about the candle used in the fire. The fire setter makes experiments before a fire so that the burning time will fit into the arson plans. Once the average burning time of the candle is known, the arsonist can adjust to a desired time lag merely by cutting the candle to the proper length. The candle is therefore not only an ignition unit, but also a device which can be adjusted within certain limits to set a fire hours after the arsonist has departed from the scene of the crime.

Candles are mostly used in conjunction with containers of easily combustible materials, which are sometimes set within or close to other containers of flammable liquids or in an area sprinkled with such accelerants. However, candles leave a deposit of wax as their telltale sign. It may have soaked into the wood of a floor or it may be found in a pool at the low point of a floor or table top. Another sign is the protection afforded the floor or table by such wax – the spot upon which the candle rested will show less charring than the surrounding area. In many cases, a part of the candle and possibly the container in which the candle was placed may be found in a search of the fire scene.

Chemicals. Various chemical combinations have been used to set fires. Saboteurs have used such means for years. Units which provide for an acid to be released upon some combination of chemicals is a favorite device, with the acid releasing itself by eating its way through the cork or even the metal of its container. The time lag from setting to ignition can be estimated with some certainty by an arsonist with a little knowledge of chemistry.

Various rubber receptacles, such as hot water and ice bags or contraceptives, have been used for a phosphorus and water ignition device. A pinhole is made in the rubber container, allowing the water to seep out. Once it drains below the level of the phosphorus, ignition takes place. As this chemical ignites on contact with air, a time lag is secured by controlling the amount of water and the size of the hole in the container.

Even the ordinary fire setter sometimes utilizes a chemical which ignites on contact with water, setting up a device actuated by the next rainstorm. Holes in the roof or some connection to the gutter system have been used to trigger this device. Another device is the diversion of the sewage line in a building, set up at night but planned to trigger off the next morning when the toilet is flushed for the first time.

Most chemical ignition units leave some residue or have a distinctive odor, or both. Naturally, the debris must be analyzed at a laboratory when it is suspected that chemicals have been employed for ignition.

Fortunately, most arsonists are not equipped with the knowledge required for the use of chemical ignition or timing devices, nor are the machinery and tools necessary for the construction of some of these devices readily available. Unless prepared for a saboteur, the device will probably be fairly simple. The more complex units are encountered as a rule only in time of war, and usually in the possession of a frustrated enemy agent who has not had the opportunity to use them.

Gas. Although not commonly encountered, the combination of gas and the pilot light on the kitchen stoves of many residents is always a possibility. Illuminating gas rises to the ceiling, being lighter than air, and then slowly moves down to floor level as it continues to escape. When it reaches a combustion build-up, it is close to the pilot-light level and an explosion, usually followed by fire, takes place. A candle placed in a room adjoining the kitchen has also been utilized as a means of ignition. Therefore arson investigators must remember that while such explosions normally follow suicide attempts or stem from accidental causes, it is possible that an incendiary may use an ordinary gas range as an arson tool. In such cases, the investigator should get help from an engineer of the local public utility. The time lag between the initial release of the gas and the explosion can be estimated from the size of the room involved, number of openings, type of gas, and related data. For example, a normal kitchen of about 10 by 15 feet with a 9-foot ceiling equals a total volume of 1350 cubic feet. When 71 cubic feet of gas is introduced into the room, the lowest limit of explosive range will have been reached. In a well-ventilated room it is almost impossible to build up to this limit, but an arsonist will seal off the room or rooms concerned so that the gas volume will build up. In a fairly well-sealed room, a single burner left open on a kitchen gas stove will deliver sufficient gas to reach the explosive range in about 5 hours. The oven jets will build up the same volume of gas in 2 hours, and if the stove has an oven and four burners and all of them are left open, the lower explosive limit of gas volume can be reached in from 30 minutes to 1 hour.

What has prevented the widespread use of gas as an arson tool and thwarted some attempts to use it is its smell. Neighbors detect the gas odor and call police or firefighters, or break in themselves and thus ruin a carefully planned arson attempt.

Electrical Systems. Any wiring system, including doorbell and telephone circuits, can be used in fire setting. Ignition devices hooked to the wiring systems of buildings have been used throughout the country as arson tools. The time lag can be established by a study of the habits of the persons using the premises in which the fire is to be set. Possibly a security guard may switch on the light every hour while inspecting the various portions of the building on rounds of inspection; employees turn on the lights at the time of opening; and so on.

While a doorbell system can be used in the same manner to trigger an ignition device, the possibility of flaws in the timing precludes any widespread use. The bell may be rung by some chance visitor and upset the carefully laid plans of the fire setter.

Telephone timing devices have the same fault; a 'wrong number' or an unexpected call and the fire is under way, possibly days ahead of schedule.

Electrical appliances have also been used to set off fires. An open heater is placed close to a flimsy set of curtains, and an apparently accidental fire results. An iron can be set in its usual position; overheating serves to ignite the ironing board cover; and, again, an apparently accidental fire results. Or perhaps an electrical circuit is deliberately overloaded with several appliances until some portion of it heats up. Sometimes an accelerant or 'booster' such as kerosene is dropped into a switch box; and there have been a few cases in which a length of normal wiring was removed and a lighter wire substituted so that it would overheat and, without blowing the fuses, serve as an ignition device.

Investigators will generally find that some physical trace of an electrical ignition device can be discovered after a fire. Some portion will not be completely destroyed.

Mechanical. Alarm clocks were once a favored weapon of arsonists. A simple alarm clock, some wire, and a small battery – and a fire setter was 'in business'. But after a search of the fire debris disclosed the remains of an alarm clock, the arsonist was in trouble and usually on the way to prison. The aronist utilized the lead hammer which normally hammers away at the alarm bell as a tool – to break a glass tube which will then feed flammable matter to a fixed flame; to push over a container of chemicals into a container of other chemicals; to close an open electrical circuit; or, by attaching matches to the hammer so that they will be pressed back and forth against an abrasive surface, to ignite a previously prepared 'set' of flammable material. The clock is actuated by simply setting the alarm for a certain time, at which point the alarm 'goes off' and the lead hammer starts to swing. The weights in a grandfather's clock have also been utilized in a similar manner.

Mechanical devices which the minds of fire setters have dreamed up beggar description. Some are childish, some are worthy of master craftsmen, and others are truly fiendish. Unfortunately for many of these ingenious incendiaries, their infernal machines will not burn and can later be hung like millstones around their necks.

Plants. Any preparation for the unlawful setting of fires is termed a 'plant'. It is the material placed about the ignition device to feed the initial flame. Newspapers, wood shavings, excelsior, rags, clothing, curtains, blankets, and cotton waste are some of the materials used in plants. Newspapers and excelsior seem to be the most frequently used material, with cotton waste being used extensively in factory or industrial fires.

Accelerants or 'boosters' to speed the progress of the fire are also part of the plant. Kerosene and gasoline are favored boosters, with alcohol, lighter fluid, paint thinners and other solvents enjoying some popularity. However, any flammable fluid or compound may be used to accelerate the blaze.

Trailers. Trailers are used to spread the fire. A trailer is ignited as a result of the blaze kindled in the primary plant by the ignition device, and it carries the fire to other parts of a room or building. Sometimes the trailer will simply carry the fire to these other locations, the arsonist depending on the flames from the trailer to spread the fire; but usually a trailer will end in a secondary plant, that is, another pile of papers or excelsior sprinkled with gasoline, kerosene, or some other booster.

From the primary plant, a fire setter may lay four trailers to an equal number of secondary plants, thus securing four separate fires from the one ignition device.

Rope or toilet paper soaked in alcohol or like fluid, motion picture film, dynamite fuses, gunpowder, and other such substances have been used as trailers. Sometimes rags or newspapers are soaked in some fire accelerant and twisted into a rope. On other occasions, an arsonist will use a fluid fire accelerant such as kerosene as a trailer by pouring a liberal quantity on the floor in a desired path.

Incendiary Fires. When any fire-setting device, any components of the various ignition and timing units, or any of the materials used in plants or trailers as previously described are found in premises in which a suspicious fire has occurred, then the classification of the fire can be made. Unless the presence of materials used by fire setters bears some relation to the occupancy of the premises, the blaze should be classified as incendiary.

When kerosene, gasoline, excelsior, candles, and like substances are discovered about the point of origin of a suspicious fire, it is evidence of arson, and if the investigator can prove this material had no right to be in the premises, then the corpus delicti has been established; that is, the presumption of accident has been overcome as established by law and the body of the crime has been proved – that the fire occurred from some criminal agency.

Property Claim Services:
American Insurance Association,
'Arson Insurance Investigation'

3 *Fire at the Grammar, Bedford*

It is now necessary to attempt to cover the most unpalatable aspect of the fire – how it came to be started.

In charge of the police investigation was Superintendent (then Detective Inspector) Roy Rogers. He has said that the major problem in trying to discover the cause of a fire is that, by its very nature, any evidence there may be is likely to be destroyed. However, the make-up of the human mind is such that, should the cause be arson, the person who lit the match feels a compulsion to be present and to watch his handiwork. For this reason Superintendent Rogers likes to be present at a fire in case he can pick up clues from the behaviour of one or more of the people watching it. On this occasion he was certainly aware of a discordant element amongst the large number of spectators, but was nevertheless unable to feel positive that this fire was due to arson. In spite of that, on the Sunday morning he called in Dr Michael Fereday, a forensic scientist from the Home Office Forensic Science Laboratory at Aldermaston, to search the remains of the building and make a report of his findings. These were negative: there was no evidence of arson. Superintendent Rogers therefore briefed the Press that arson was not suspected.

In his deepest mind, though, the Superintendent may not have been totally convinced by the lack of evidence. For one thing, for a period of two months starting shortly after Christmas there had been an unexplained increase in the number of fires in Bedford, and these fires seemed to be concentrated in an area north of the river. Moreover, he worked in close collaboration with Assistant Divisional Officer Holloway of the Fire Service in whom the conviction was growing that there was an arsonist at work. Assistant D/O Holloway personally undertook a searching and comprehensive investigation into every aspect of the Bedford School fire, interviewing, with police assistance in some cases, every available person known to have had any connection with the building in the hours preceding the fire. But these investigations yielded nothing beyond the obvious possibilities, namely: failure properly to extinguish smoking materials; electrical faults; malicious ignition by person or persons unknown. And of these possibilities, no single one had a stronger claim than the others.

In the event, the true cause of the fire was discovered by chance. A member of the Fire Service overheard a conversation in a pub which made it quite clear that the speaker was boasting of his exploit in setting Bedford School on fire. The fireman reported to Asst D/O Holloway who in turn notified Superintendent Rogers.

Thus the name of Ian Ludman came to the ears of the police who, of course, knew of his previous criminal record. But at this time there was no actual evidence to connect him with the fire.

The precise date of this information is not altogether clear, but it was, significantly, after the next incendiary incident, the setting on fire of the Chicken Bar-B-Q in Harpur Street. Also important, it transpired, was the fact that the premises had just been burgled and a quantity of frozen foods removed before the fire was started.

Superintendent Rogers therefore instigated and personally took part in a search of the back areas, dustbins included, of the addresses which he knew were frequented by Ludman, in particular that of his parents in Goldington and that of Flat 6, 8 St Andrew's Road, where Ludman was known recently to have been. In the very early hours of 22 March, in the dustbins of Flat 6, he found the evidence he needed: the wrappers of catering packs of frozen foods normally purchased only by retailers. On the basis of this evidence he obtained a magistrate's warrant and at 8.40 a.m. entered the flat, roused the occupants and conducted his search. He had not far to look. The refrigerator was crammed full of catering packs of frozen food, and a refuse bin held the cardboard remains of more frozen food. Superintendent Rogers therefore arrested the three occupants. Ludman was not present but the evidence suggested that he had been staying there, and newspaper cuttings referring to the fire at Bedford School were discovered, as well as other property later discovered to have been stolen from the School.

At first these men were unwilling to give any useful information. They could not, however, deny the connection between the frozen food in their possession and the fire at the Chicken Bar-B-Q, nor their association with Ludman. Eventually, with the realisation of the weight of the penalty for those involved in or associated with arson, they did talk. It emerged that Ludman had spent the evening drinking with others at the George and Dragon which he left at 11.20 p.m. before proceeding through the School grounds from the Howard's entrance in St Peter's Street. Ludman then, having separated from his associates, went his own way. One of them said he heard the sound of breaking glass behind him as he himself went on to the St Andrew's Road flat. Some time later – it would have been close on midnight – Ludman entered the flat and invited them to come out on to the fire-escape to see the sight. They saw the early flames leaping out of the School roof. Later they went down on the field and watched from close quarters.

After this there was no doubt in Superintendent Rogers's mind. The thing was to get hold of Ludman quickly. He knew his haunts. At 11.20 a.m. Ludman was found in the King's Arms and arrested. At 11.55 he was taken by the Superintendent to a house in Goldington where a number of items of stolen property and some cannabis were found. And after this it was Greyfriars Police Station and fuller questioning.

Superintendent Rogers took Ludman to Bedford School the next day, 23 March, to confront him with what he had done. He showed no remorse. He said, 'It's something to look at'.

On Monday, 23 July 1979, Ian Ludman was brought before His Honour Judge Robert Lymbury QC, accused on eleven counts of arson, burglary, obtaining by deception, and possession of cannabis. What follows is a summary of the proceedings at the Crown Court, Bedford.

The Prosecution stated that Ludman was interviewed twice. At the first interview he admitted the burglary and other counts since the evidence was undeniable; but the fire charge (count 8) he denied, saying, 'There is a little bit of history there, I would not like to see that go up'. When he was interviewed the second time he admitted responsibility for the fire, saying that he did it to destroy his fingerprints.

Giving evidence on Ludman's background, Superintendent Rogers showed that he had never been able to hold down a steady job. Moreover, there was a record of ten previous convictions, one of them for the arson of an army jeep.

In his judgment Judge Lymbury said:

> You pleaded guilty to count 8 on 3rd March, the fire at the Great Hall of Bedford School, which destroyed a building of architectural interest and the contents, portraits, books, records, 780 chairs, many of these donated by Old Boys and irreplaceable. This struck at the very heart of that school, but no doubt it will survive because it is made of sterner stuff than you can appreciate. The damage caused was approximately £2.5m and you watched the burning with glee.
>
> You are void of social conscience and feelings for other people. The charge in count 2, the arson of 3rd February at 122 Howbury Street, causing £7,600 damage, was small by comparison, but more serious because you destroyed this woman's home. The charge in count 10 is arson of the Chicken Bar-B-Q in Bedford where the damage was £1,800. Each of the three offences of arson were committed in buildings in the town, where the fires might have spread and caused further damage and injured persons. But for the timely intervention of the Fire Brigade, people might have been injured and untold grief caused.
>
> These are crimes of the utmost gravity and you have a previous conviction for arson. You are a social menace and there is a strong probability that you will remain a serious risk for many years. I am clear as to where my duty lies.
>
> On counts 2, 8 and 10 (the arson charges) – imprisonment for life;
> The burglary charges (counts 1, 3, 4, 5, 7 and 9) – 30 months' imprisonment;
> Obtaining by deception (count 6) – 12 months' imprisonment;
> Possession of cannabis (count 11) – 6 months' imprisonment.
> All concurrent.

The work of the police, Superintendent Rogers and his team, in tracking Ludman and bringing him to face the consequences of his crimes was commended in court, and the then Chief Constable of Bedfordshire, Mr Anthony Armstrong QPM, paid his own tribute to the tenacity and professional ability, including skilful and determined interrogation, which had led to Ludman's conviction.

As a postscript to this side of the story it is interesting to note that from the time of Ludman's arrest there was a significant reduction in the number of fires in Bedford.

M. E. BARLEN, M. P. STAMBACH AND D. P. C. STILEMAN
Bedford School and the Great Fire
(1984), pp. 58–61

4 *The Least Successful Attempt to Light a Coal Fire*

In 1972 Derek Langborne, a scientist from Upton, near Didcot, built a fire in his grate and lit it. He then popped outside to fill the coal scuttle.

When he returned, he observed that, in its enthusiasm to heat the room, one log had rolled out of the grate and set fire to the log box. He picked it up and carried it out into the garden. On the way out he brushed against a curtain covering the front door. By the time he returned the curtain and the door were both in flames.

While telephoning Didcot Fire Brigade, he noticed that the log box, which he had deposited in the garden, had now set fire to his car.

He then put on his overcoat and approached the car with a bucket of water. In the process he tripped over a partly-filled petrol can.

Seeing that Mr Langborne was in good form, his neighbour called the fire brigade. By the time the fire brigade arrived, Mr Langborne himself was on fire with flames now leaping freely from his overcoat.

STEPHEN PILE
The Book of Heroic Failures
(1979), p. 32

V
Other Acts of God

1 Lighting Strikes in the Danube Delta

When I had bought the villa in Galatz and the ink on the conveyance was hardly dry, the 'Olympia's' insurance agents came running to my door: had I given much thought to insurance?

For a long time my resistance was total but in the end it did not prevail; I insured my aunt against accidents, my villa against hail, and my furniture against fire. I must, however, state that my experiences with the Olympia have hardly been pleasant.

What I can say – on 13th June, a Friday, lightning struck – it killed my aunt, destroyed an umbrella and the piano caught fire.

All right, I said to myself – seeing that auntie's dead – I am myself totally unmusical – let it burn! In the interim I read through the policy, past the printed rules, and came across a certain paragraph 19: claims were to be notified without delay.

I could only notify damage when I was in a position to know how far the piano business had gone. In the event, the fire extinguished itself after the right-hand half of the piano was consumed up to around F-sharp.

At the speed of the wind came Dominul Ghizu, Director General of the Olympia-Provincial.

'Now then', he said 'What seems to be the trouble?'

It was plain from this rough interrrogative that there was little point in looking on the brighter side of things. I led him to the piano and pointed to it in silence. He inspected the piano and spoke only to disapprove.

'Hardly the latest model, is it? Anything else?'

'Yes', I answered, 'This article which you might have mistaken for a metal broomstick or an oversized whisk was in fact my umbrella until this afternoon.'

'The entire matter is very suspicious', he answered' 'Not to say odd. How is this supposed to have happened?'

'Oh, it all happened so fast, around three. We were sitting quite comfortably . . .'

'Around an open window?'

'Yes.'

'A-n o-p-e-n w-i-n-d-o-w', he repeated, noting it down in his little book.

'We were sitting in this way. My aunt was playing the piano – I was sitting on the chair – the weather was a little stormy outside. My aunt was giving us a gentle rendition of the "Eroica" and asked at some point in the proceedings over her shoulder "Do you like goose crackling?". Those were her last words. Suddenly there was a terrible peal of thunder – everything went blue before my eyes – when I looked up, the piano was burning.'

'More than odd', the Director rumbled, shaking his head, his eyes glowing, 'This is something the courts will have to rule upon.'

'My dear Sir', I replied, 'Whatever can you mean? Do you suppose I set my aunt on fire?' Without answering he walked over to the piano and he pressed one key after the other.

'The low keys still work', he said. I answered, but by now I was angry.

'You don't seem to have the slightest understanding of music. The low keys of themselves mean nothing. They are the accompaniment. How do you suppose we will experience the exaltation and joy pulsing through our veins at the sound of song if the entire right-hand side of the piano, the joyful half, is broken?'

'My dear Mr Roda, I may know but little of conducting and composing – but one thing I do know: really serious and sustained music is always made here on the left by means of the low keys. The lightning struck to the right – your aunt appears to have been playing, how shall we say, a popular piece of a lusty nature at an open window. During a storm. Did you open the window?'

'No.'

'Well who else did? That much ought to be capable of ascertainment. The thing which really puzzles me, Mr Roda, is the umbrella. From whence came this umbrella? Umbrellas do not fall out of the heavens. Show me the invoice if you claim to have bought the umbrella. One hears so much in the coffee houses these days of stolen umbrellas. By the way, was your aunt playing under the umbrella? – Holding a window open, my dear Sir, is calculated to attract lightning. Just imagine how many lightning strikes are experienced in Romania in a typical summer. If our company had to pay for an umbrella each time – where would we be then? – What is the value you place on your aunt?'

'The policy is valued at ten thousand gold francs.'

'Ha, ha, ha! The old lady – ten thousand francs. Don't make me laugh so, dear Sir. Your aunt had no income, she was only a burden on the family. You should be paying us something! And the lady – how sad at her age she should feel no shame at seeking attention by playing indecent songs during thunder storms – and to make things worse beneath an open umbrella. – No, no, no, my dear Sir, you must read our rules, Paragraph 31a: "the company may make restitution for losses *in natura*, by supplying objects of equal value to those which have been lost." It so happens as a consequence of a fire in Bucharest we have a spare lady of this age – you may have her. We shall have your piano repainted and restrung at our expense and then *basta*, that will be all. In no way can it be the duty of a Public Company to steal an umbrella from a cafe, you had better do that yourself.'

Such then have been my experiences with the Olympia AG.

ALEXANDER RODA RODA
Die Versicherung
(1905)
Translation by the Editor

2 *The Broad Definition*

DAHLIA, LTD *v.* YVONNE

An interesting point was argued yesterday in the House of Lords. The House, by a majority (Lords Sheep and Bottle dissenting), allowed the appeal of Dahlia, Ltd, against a decision of the Court of Appeal, reversing a judgment of Mr Justice Tooth. The Lord Chancellor had read a learned judgment to this effect, awarding damages of five thousand pounds with costs against the respondent, Madame Yvonne; and the House was in the act of rising when Mr David, for the respondent, a young barrister making his first appearance before the House, asked that costs in the appeal should be borne by the Crown on the ground that the judgment was in the nature of an Act of God.

The Lord Chancellor (*resuming a sitting position*): I beg your pardon?

Mr David: An Act of God, milord.

Lord Flake: What is an Act of God?

Mr David: The decision of this House, milord. Milord, in the case of *Rumble* v. *Spatt* (1893) 2 HL, at page 147——

The Lord Chancellor: Mr David, the authority of this House is without doubt very great, and I do not like to discourage junior counsel from making proper expressions of their respect, but it is never wise to exaggerate. Would you kindly explain yourself?

Mr David: May it please your Lordships, it is well settled that, in the absence of any express provision to the contrary, a defendant cannot be held liable to make good any damage caused not by his own default but by the Act of God. An earthquake, milord, which destroys a theatre will relieve the manager from his promise to produce an author's play in that theatre before a given date; an insurance company will not be held liable to replace furniture destroyed by a sudden and unprecedented flood in London unless the risks specified in the policy include damage arising out of the Act of God; a conflagration, milord, which swept——

Lord Mew: Earthquakes, floods, conflagrations? What has all this to do with us?

Mr David: Milords, in *Rump* v. *The Stepney Guardians*——

Lord Flake: There is no question of a conflagration here. The jury found that the bun was in fact composed of salicyclic acid, and we have found for the appellants on the point of law.

Mr David: Milord, with great respect, in *Rump* v. *The Stepney Guardians* – milord, in all these cases the principle is that a man can only be held responsible for damage which he might reasonably be expected to anticipate and so to avert or control. Milord, in the case of a volcanic eruption——

Lord Mew (*sharply*): Yes, but there is no volcanic eruption here.

Mr David: Milord, with great respect, milord, the point is a little delicate——

Lord Flake: So delicate, Mr David, as to be, so far, invisible.

Mr David: If your Lordships will bear with me for a very few moments, I hope to show—— Milord, the definition of an Act of God laid down by Lord Mildew in *Turbot* v. *The Mayor of Swindon*——

Lord Bottle: Was that the Violin case?

Mr David: No, milord, the Bicycle case. Milord, in that case an Act of God was defined as '*something which no reasonable man could have expected*'.

Lord Sheep: But the respondent had a *duty* not to supply buns which were composed, or mainly composed, of salicyclic acid.

Mr David: Milord, I was not referring to the bun.

The Lord Chancellor: Then what in the world are you talking about?

Mr David (*who appeared to be suffering some embarrassment*)*:* Milord, in my submission – milord, if your Lordships will forgive me – milord, with great respect, milord, the contention is that a decision of your Lordships' House is something which no reasonable man could have expected——

Lord Flake: What did you say?

Mr David: Something which no reasonable man could have expected, milord – a decision of your Lordships' House, milord – an Act of God, milord. And therefore, milord, no man can be made responsible in costs or damages as a result of it.

(For a few moments, our correspondent informs us, there was complete silence in the House of Lords.)

The Lord Chancellor: Are you quite well, Mr David?

Mr David: Yes, milord.

The Lord Chancellor: I should be reluctant to send your name to the Bar Council, Mr David. Perhaps we did not hear you correctly.

Mr David: Milord, it must be evident *a priori* that no reasonable man can foresee a decision of the House of Lords, for otherwise no reasonable man would appeal to the House of Lords, only to lose his case. In the present appeal, milords, three of your Lordships have found for the appellants and two for the respondent; and by the definition already cited, milords, the working of your Lordships' minds——

Lord Bottle: We accept the definition, Mr David, but must not the event, to fall within the rule, be some large and cataclysmic operation of nature – an earthquake, flood, hurricane, or conflagration?

Mr David: In my submission, not necessarily, milord. I can conceive that a widespread epidemic of plague or infectious fever might be held to be an Act of God, though caused by a single minute and invisible bacillus——

The Lord Chancellor: Are you now comparing their Lordships' minds with an infectious fever?

Mr David: Not exactly, milord. Milord, to take another example, it might be held that the going off the Gold Standard——

Lord Mew: That was due to the King's enemies, not the Act of God.

Mr David: I am obliged to your Lordship for the interruption, which greatly assists my argument. The principle is the same in both cases, milords, that is, the incalculable nature of the event. No man can foresee an Act of God or the conduct of the King's enemies, and therefore no man is mulcted in money by the Courts for anything that follows from these proceedings, since it would be inequitable to hold a man responsibile in law for that for which he cannot *ex hypothesi* be responsible in fact. A decision of your Lordships' House on a difficult point of law, with great respect, milord, is as incalculable as the onset of a flood, fever, or fire, and by the same reasoning it would be inequitable for either side to be compelled to pay for it.

Lord Bottle: But would not your reasoning apply with equal force to the costs of the hearing in the High Court or the Court of Appeal?

Mr David: In the Court of Appeal, perhaps, milord, but not in the High Court, for there the proceedings consist mainly in a finding of fact by the jury, and a reasonable man may be expected to foresee that a British jury will discover the true facts. But the appellate Courts are concerned with discovering the state of the law, and here the element of uncertainty is so great as to make the event incalculable. Moreover, in this tribunal there are five judges, not one judge, so that the chances to be calculated are much more various and numerous. Where there is one judge he is either dyspeptic or he is not; but where there are five, three may be dyspeptic and two not; one may be irritable, one deaf, and three dyspeptic; or there may be one dyspeptic, two——

The Lord Chanceller: I do not think you need work out all the permutations, Mr David. We see what you mean.

Mr David: I am much obliged to your Lordship. It follows, therefore, that he whose fortunes depend upon a decision of your Lordships' House is involved, as it were, in a speculation or gamble; and where, as in the case of my client, he is dragged into the speculation by the act of another, it is against equity and the rule of law that he should be called upon to pay for the result. In the case of *Rump* v. *The Stepney Guardians*, milords——

The Lord Chancellor: Mr David, you will have an opportunity to conclude or withdraw your argument to-morrow. And we advise you in the meantime to consult a doctor.

The House then rose. In legal circles the decision of the House is awaited with much interest. It was observed by legal spectators that Lords Bottle and Sheep appeared to be considerably impressed by counsel's argument.

NOTE – In the event, the costs were paid by Madame Yvonne, Mr David's client. A little later Mr David was offered a legal appointment in the Home Office, and he has not been heard of again. EDITOR

A. P. HERBERT
Uncommon Law
(1935)

3 *The San Francisco Earthquake*

It is strange how behind the great urban fires of the English-speaking world there lurks a meaty legend. The Fire of London, it was said, began in Pudding Lane and ended in Pie Corner, a celestial judgement upon the gluttony of the citizenry. In Chicago the conflagration was attributed to Mother O'Leary's cow and in San Francisco the blaze which destroyed the plush but gimcrack town built from the fortunes of pioneers and golddiggers was blamed on a great earthquake, a fallen chimney and one family's attempt, notwithstanding the excitements of the morning, to enjoy a breakfast of ham and eggs.

It all began on Wednesday, 18 April 1906, at twelve minutes past five in the early morning. What San Franciscans long inured to such things first mistook for yet another tremor emerged over several very long minutes as an earthquake of legendary intensity. One widely-quoted account of the actual earthquake was by James Hopper who worked for one of the city's newspapers:

My head on the pillow watched my stretched and stiffened body dance. It was springing up and down and from side to side. The bureau at the back of the room came toward me. It danced, approached not directly, but in a zig-zag course, with sudden bold advances and as sudden shy retreats – with little bows and becks and nods, with little mincing steps: it was almost funny.

Hopper's sense of fun no doubt wore a little thinner as the full severity of the earthquake dawned upon him:

Br-r-r went the quake, raising the plane of violence another notch. Up to that time I had only felt and seen. Now I seemed to turn on my sense of hearing as one turns on an electric light. I heard the crash of falling buildings, the rumble of avalanches of bricks, the groans of tortured bridges.

Among the first reports of the disaster to reach the outside world was this laconic but accurate account sent by a post office telegraph clerk:

There was an earthquake hit us at five fifteen this morning, wrecking several buildings and wrecking our offices. They are carting dead from the fallen buildings. Fire all over town. There is no water and we lost our power. I'm going to get out of the office as we have had a little shake every few minutes, and it's me for the simple life.

As people emerged from their houses into the streets to survey the damage, many at first believed they had got off lightly. The older, low-lying parts of the city suffered the most initial damage. People made excursions to see the worst afflicted areas for themselves, walking down streets littered with fallen, live electric cables and smelling gas escaping from the fractured mains. Chinatown, for instance, at that time a quarter of disreputable shanties perched on insubstantial footings, collapsed almost entirely. The worst damage was hidden from sight. All three conduits bringing water to the city were cut. The power supply to the city continued unabated for some fifteen minutes after the initial shock until the engineer's assistant used his initiative and shut the supply off. Fires began to break out all over the city.

On the far side of Van Ness Avenue in Hayes Street, an area where timber-built houses formed the majority, a housewife decided to cook her family breakfast. Unaware that the earthquake had brought her chimney down, she lit the "ham and eggs fire" which rapidly consumed the roof, the house and, fanned by a gentle Pacific breeze, the whole neighbourhood before going on to consume the rest of the city.

The fire brigade, deprived of its highly regarded Chief Sullivan who was mortally injured during the earthquake and lacking a reliable supply of water, watched helplessly. The leaderless condition of the fire-fighters was doubly aggravating because Sullivan was also knowledgeable on the use of explosives and the efforts to create fire-breaks undertaken by the brigade were not notably successful.

The spread of fire was inexorable but slow enough to allow the evacuation of the population. By Saturday, 21 April, when the rains came, four square miles containing 500 city blocks – some four-fifths of the city known as the Pride of the West – were reduced to isolated blackened walls standing in fields of ashes. The property damage was colossal, the death-rate, in the circumstances, surprisingly low, only one in a thousand in a city of half a million souls. Most of the loss of life had occurred during the initial shock of the earthquake itself.

* * *

The insurance implications of the fire were daunting. Six years into the American century, no sane underwriter could be blind to the opportunities presented by the rapidly expanding economy of the United States. Nevertheless, the claims arising out of the earthquake amounted to some £45 million. The annual premium derived from insuring the city against fire amounted to a mere £200,000. Underwriters clearly faced massive losses.

To tempt the insurance companies of lesser fortitude or substance, it emerged that some of the insurances covered only fire or only earthquake, others covered fire if caused by an earthquake and some even excluded loss caused by earthquake. A whole city backed by press and politicians clamoured for the settlement of its claims.

Of the 120-odd companies financially concerned in the fire, five went bankrupt instanter. Eighteen of the companies were British: they incurred losses of £15 million but none defaulted. Fifteen of the 90 American companies defaulted. Only four of the 15 continental European companies concerned defaulted, but these unfortunately were companies with large liabilities. It was not the insurance industry's finest hour by any means, but the British companies and Lloyd's at least emerged with their reputations enhanced. The Heath Syndicate, leaders on Lloyd's earthquake policies, paid in full irrespective of the policy wordings. C. E. Heath's commercial farsightedness was, in the gloomy circumstances, exemplary. The underwriting loss suffered in the earthquake exceeded the underwriting profit made on all United States fire insurance business for the 35 years previous to 1906.

Yet since the purchasers of insurance part with their premiums in exchange for nothing more substantial than a promise, underwriters must await the day of the mega-claim in a positive frame of mind if only to demonstrate to society at large that insurance is worth its price and its providers are worthy of trust.

JONATHAN S. IGNARSKI

4 *Balm of Gilead*

Back in January, about the middle of the first week, Ned Jones received a letter from the fire insurance agent's office in Bangor. The letter said that the company, effective January 1st, last, had discontinued allowing a discount on premiums covering farm houses and barns which were equipped with lightning rods. Therefore, the letter said, the cost for protection on his buildings would be raised to twenty-two-fifty from twenty-fifty.

However, the letter went on, if the rods were already installed on the buildings, a lightning rod expert would call and inspect the terminals, ground wires, brads, and so forth, and if the expert found them in first-class condition, the discount would be reinstated. The charge for all of this, the letter concluded, would be three dollars for the inspector's time.

'Thunderation', Ned said when he had finished reading the letter the third time. 'Hell and thunderation!'

It did not take him long to figure out that he would save a dollar by not having the lightning rods inspected, but even so he could see that it was going to cost him two dollars a year more to keep his buildings covered by insurance.

'That's thunderation', he said.

His wife, Betty, was silent about the whole matter. She always froze up inside whenever something came up like that and threatened to cost an extra penny.

The insurance premium was not due and payable until February 1st, but a week before that time, Ned got ready to make a trip to Bangor and pay a call at the insurance agent's office.

He and his wife started out to Bangor after breakfast, driving the old car slowly along the black-top road, taking care to stay as far on the right-hand side of the road as possible. The law was that a car owner would not have to carry liability and property damage insurance as long as he did not have a mishap. Ned was set on not having that first accident on the highways that would force him to pay insurance premiums for the right to drive his car. It was an old car anyway, about twelve years old, and he did not intend buying another one when it was worn out.

They got to Bangor just before ten o'clock in the forenoon, and, after finding a safe place to park and leave the automobile, Ned and his wife went straight to the agent's office.

They sat down on a bench in the hall and waited for several minutes, and then a girl took them to see Mr Harmsworth.

'Now, about that insurance on my stand of buildings out at Gaylord', Ned said, shaking his head and his finger at the agent. 'I take it you're upset about the new lightning rod clause, effective January 1st, last', Mr Harmsworth said, smiling at Ned and his wife. 'You see, Mr Jones, and Mrs Jones, the company at the home office in New Hampshire rewrites the contracts, and we agents have nothing whatever to do with the terms the company dictates.'

'What do people in New Hampshire know about lightning rods anyway?'

Ned said. 'Now let me tell you, I once knew a man in New Hampshire who——'

'Let's not get off the subject, Mr Jones, and Mrs Jones', Mr Harmsworth said. 'After all, both my parents were born and raised in New Hampshire, and I'm sure there is a New Hampshire connection somewhere in your family, too.'

He smiled at Mrs Jones, beaming upon her all the force of what he knew was a sunny smile. Betty refused to be disarmed. She was frozen up inside, and she intended to remain unthawed as long as the insurance company refused to make an adjustment that would not cost them an extra penny.

'Now, I've lived down here in the State of Maine for all my life', Ned said, 'and I'm sixty and more right now, and lightning rods are the only things in the world that'll keep lightning from striking and setting fire to a house or barn. All my life I've seen lightning strike a spire and run down the cable into the ground without even so much as smoking up the roof and clapboards. If it wasn't for lightning rods——'

'Are you sure lightning runs down lightning rods, Mr Jones, and Mrs Jones?' Mr Harmsworth said. 'I was under the impression it ran up the rods, or rather made contact on the point of the spire. However——'

'Lightning is lightning, whether it runs up or down, or slantwise, if it has a mind to', Ned said, rising up.

'I see you know a lot more about such things than I do', Mr Harmsworth laughed, beaming upon Mrs Jones, 'I was raised here in the city, and I never had a chance to observe how lightning behaves when it comes in contact with a rod-equipped building. But, just the same, there's nothing either you or I can do about this here clause, because the home office rewrote the contract and sent us the printed forms, and I'm merely their representative. I carry out their orders, but I have no authority to alter a clause in a contract.'

Ned looked at his wife, and she shook her head. That was all he wanted to know. No insurance company, with a home office in New Hampshire, run by New Hampshire people, was going to tell him whether they thought lightning rods were protection or not. He looked at his wife again, and shook his head. Betty tightened her mouth, freezing tighter inside, and nodded at Ned.

Mr Harmsworth shuffled some papers on his desk, and, bringing one out with much crinkling and creasing, laid it before Ned. 'This is your bill for fire protection coverage, due February 1st', he said, glancing quickly at Ned, but not looking at Mrs Jones.

Ned pushed it back at him.

'Now, about this Balm of Gilead', Ned said, edging forward in his chair.

'What Balm of Gilead?' Mr Harmsworth asked, startled. 'What's that?'

Ned looked at his wife, and Betty nodded. That was what he wanted to know from her. He pulled his chair closer to the desk.

'My Balm of Gilead', he said. 'I've got one in my dooryard, fourteen feet from the west wall of my dwelling house, and twenty-two feet from the east wall of my barn.'

'What's a Balm of Gilead?' Mr Harmsworth asked, still startled. 'Wasn't that something in the Bible? How'd you get something that was in the Bible?'

Ned and Betty looked at each other, but neither of them made any motion of the head.

'Balm of Gilead is a tree', Ned said. 'My Balm of Gilead was set out by my father, seventy-seven years ago, and it stands in my dooryard.'

'What about it?' Mr Harmsworth asked, wild-eyed.

'It's a lightning rod', Ned said. 'It's the finest lightning rod on earth. After a Balm of Gilead——'

'You want us to give you a discount because you have a tree——' Mr Harmsworth began, sitting forward in his chair.

'——passes its fiftieth year, it turns into a lightning rod,' Ned continued doggedly. 'Lightning won't strike any other thing within fifty yards of it. Lightning strikes the Balm of Gilead every time.'

'I don't know what you're driving at exactly', Mr Harmsworth said, 'but I wouldn't suppose you expect to get any discount on your fire insurance for having a tree like that.'

Betty stiffened her backbone.

'I don't know why not', Ned said. 'Why shouldn't I get a discount when I've got a Balm of Gilead located almost half-way between my two buildings, and the farthest is twenty-two feet from it. A tree like that is two or three times more protection than rods on the buildings. Why, it even makes the buildings proof against lightning! I figure I'm due five or six dollars discount for having that tree where it is.'

Mr Harmsworth scratched his head and took a swift look at Mrs Jones. He had time to see that her mouth was drawn in a tight line across her face. He did not look at her again.

'If you insist upon it,' he said, 'I'll take it up with the home office in New Hampshire. I won't be able to do a thing until I hear from them. But I shouldn't think they would allow anybody a discount on fire insurance for having a Balm of Gilead tree.'

'If they wasn't those New Hampshire people', Ned said, 'they'd know how much protection a tree like that is.'

'I'll write you a letter and let you know what the home office has to say just as soon as I get their answer', he said, standing up.

Ned and Betty got up and went out into the hall. Mr Harmsworth followed them trying to shake hands with at least one of them. Betty kept her hands clasped tightly across her waist. Ned outwalked the agent to the street.

'Ignorant young cuss', Ned said. 'Associates with New Hampshire people.'

Betty nodded her head.

They bought a few things in a store, and then got into their car and drove home. Neither of them mentioned the insurance during the rest of the day.

During the remainder of the week, and through the first three days of the following one, both Ned and his wife watched the mail for the letter from the agent in Bangor. On the third day the letter came.

They went into the kitchen and sat down in the chairs by the window before opening it. Ned first took out his glasses and carefully polished the lenses. Betty put her handkerchief to her nose, and then put it away. Ned read the letter aloud.

'Dear Mr Jones: I have taken up the matter of the Balm of Gilead tree in your dooryard with the home office in New Hampshire, and I am herewith advising you of their decision. It seems that the company thought it was all a joke or something because, in their own words, they wished to know if your Balm of Gilead tree would "catch mice, scare cows away, and cure painter's colic". Further along in their letter they state most emphatically that under no circumstances would a discount on fire insurance premiums be allowed for possession of a Balm of Gilead tree.'

The letter did not end there, but Ned read no farther. He handed the letter to his wife, and she laid it aside on the table, drawing her mouth into a thin straight line across her face.

'I never did waste any feelings for the people of New Hampshire', Ned said, putting away his glasses, getting his hat, and standing up.

His wife did not say a word when he left the kitchen and went out into the dooryard.

When she saw him come out of the woodshed with the ax and the crosscut saw, she put on her jacket and went out to help him.

First he cut a notch in the Balm of Gilead on the side in order to fell it in the direction where he wanted it to fall. When that was done, he picked up one end of the crosscut, and Betty picked up the other end. They began sawing silently, their faces bright but drawn in tight lines, and both hoping that an electrical storm would come early in the spring, and each of them praying silently that lightning would strike the house and burn it to a heap of ashes on the ground.

ERSKINE CALDWELL
The Complete Stories of Erskine Caldwell
pp. 23–26

5 *Volcanoes*

Vesuvius, in southern Italy, is today probably one of the best-known volcanoes in the Western world. But in the year AD 79 it was just an attractive conical mountain, thought to be an extinct volcano, overlooking the Bay of Naples. The people who lived in the towns and villages nearby were basking in the prosperity of the Roman Empire at its height. On Vesuvius itself, intensive cultivation reached almost to the summit, reaping the benefits of the rich soils which typically develop on volcanic ash. All that was to change.

Nobody paid much attention to the earthquakes which had rocked the area around Vesuvius for the previous seventeen years – after all, earthquakes were common enough in southern Italy and the volcano was supposed to be extinct. Early on the morning of 24 August, few people were at first concerned by the cloud of ash and steam which rose above the volcanic cone, but their complacency rapidly disappeared as Vesuvius started to shoot ash thousands of feet up into the sky in a massive eruption which continued for two days and nights. Fine ash mixed with larger pebbles (known as lapilli) rained down on the surrounding villages and countryside. There was so much ash in the air that sunlight was completely blotted out, and the unceasing inky darkness added to the confusion. In some places rocks the size of a man's fist or even larger hurtled down from the sky, making it dangerous for people to walk in the open without pillows tied over their heads, and the presence of noxious volcanic gases made breathing difficult. Meanwhile the static electricity in the rising plume of volcanic ash caused violent lightning and local storms, and earthquakes continued to rock the area; tsunamis in the Bay of Naples caused the sea to retreat from the foreshore and pound back relentlessly.

When all this activity had continued for a whole day, the people must have thought that their world was coming to an end, and most had had enough. Thousands of them ran for the open country away from Vesuvius, or set sail in their boats, and over most of the region the rate of accumulation of the ash was slow enough to allow the majority of people to escape. In the town of Pompeii, however, conditions were rather different. Being immediately downwind of the volcano, it was rapidly covered by a thick layer of ash. By the time the terrified inhabitants realised the seriousness of their plight the ash already lay thickly in the streets and continued to rain heavily down – the whole scene in pitch darkness, as no sunlight could penetrate the hanging ash cloud. Eventually most people tried to escape, but many left it too late. The combination of soft ash on the ground, ash raining from above and the air full of sulphurous fumes was too much. They stumbled and fell to their deaths in the streets, their hands clutched to their faces, and were rapidly buried by more ash. Some chose to stay in their homes, protected from the ash – but the fumes were insidious and hundreds died indoors of asphyxiation, while others were killed when the roofs of their houses collapsed under the weight of the ash. At the end of the eruption, Pompeii lay buried beneath 10 feet of ash, and of the original population of 20,000, one in ten lay dead in the ruins of his town.

On the other side of Vesuvius the town of Herculaneum had not been buried by ash, but still it was doomed. High on the slopes of the volcano huge amounts of ash were balanced precariously on slopes, and were then inundated by really heavy rain from the local storms generated by the eruption. Fortunately, by then, most of the population of Herculaneum had been driven away by the terrifying activity of the volcano, and only about fifty people remained in the town when it met its own special fate handed out by Vesuvius. The saturated slopes of loose ash became unstable and started to slide, developing into semi-liquid mudflows which swept down and completely buried Herculaneum – some parts to depths of over 50 feet.

After two days of furious activity the eruption ceased, and the survivors could see that the top of Vesuvius had been replaced by a caldera – an enormous crater two miles across, formed by inward collapse due to the weakening of the underground pressure which had powered the eruption. Part of that caldera wall is still visible as Monte Somma, for the present summit cone of Vesuvius had been built up just south-west of the original one by various periods of rather milder activity which still continue today. Meanwhile the mudflow of Herculaneum set solid, and both it and Pompeii, under its preserving layer of ash, lay forgotten – until their discovery turned yesterday's catastrophe into today's archaeological bonanza. . . . An active volcano can never safely be described as peaceful, but there are certainly degrees of violence to which any eruption may rise. Santorini and Pelée were both extremely violent in their own ways, but perhaps the best known of all the world's violent volcanoes was Krakatoa. Lying in the Sunda Straits between Sumatra and Java, the island of Krakatoa was just part of a massive complex volcano which rose barely above sea level, and on the island were three distinct vents built of andesitic lava and ash. As first recorded by Europeans, Krakatoa had been dormant for two centuries before bursting into activity on 20 May 1883. For three months it variously exploded and produced ash clouds. Nobody lived on the island and the people of nearby Sumatra and Java had almost become used to it, when on 27 August of that year it blew up in four enormous explosions. The third was the greatest and it was heard over 3000 miles away, and ash was blasted so high into the air that it encircled the world. Tsunamis generated by the explosion swept the surrounding shores, and a town called Merak at the head of a tapering bay was annihilated by a wave 130 feet high. Over 36,000 people died in these mammoth tsunamis. Most of the island of Krakatoa just disappeared. The ash which landed nearby was shown to be 95 per cent original material and only 5 per cent broken rock, so much of Krakatoa must have fallen back into a caldera collapse. The power of the explosion may have owed much to its location at sea level. It is probable that the early phase of activity, violent enough in its own right, opened up ground fissures which let the sea into the magma chambers below, there to generate enormous quantities of steam. The combination of this steam and the volcanic gas in the viscous magma was enough to blow up Krakatoa.

TONY WALTHAM
Catastrophe – The Violent Earth
(1978), pp. 30–36

VI

Caveat Assecutor: The Life Business

1 *Lives at risk*

[The Legal & General Assurance Society's] first red-letter day was on the 11th October, 1836, when Mr Thomas Smith, a solicitor of Furnival's Inn, having made a proposal to insure his life in the sum of £1,000, was scrutinised carefully, considered eligible and accepted, his policy being Number 1. This their first policy-holder (so aptly, as I think, called Smith) was not a good 'risk' as events proved. For he died, four years later, on the 30th June, 1840 (the Society having only received £177 16s. 8d. in premiums), from 'a congested state of the brain, accompanied by effusion', though his medical report had evidently been considered good at the time, the Doctor reporting 'Mr Smith has naturally a slow pulse, but I cannot discover any disease of the heart'! The exclamation mark is mine.

Their first Claims Book – a much-thumbed leather-bound volume – drew me at this point into its faded pages with a profound fascination. For it reflected so clearly the customs and conditions of life prevailing at the dawn of the Victorian era.

Tuberculosis was far more prevalent than, happily, it is to-day. But medical science in respect of it was still fumbling towards the nebulous goal of its arrest and cure. A doctor would ask, 'Do you spit blood?' And if you did not, then, obviously, you were not a TB patient.

The first claim on the Society, for £200, was made within a year of the policy being taken out. Poliy No 104, dated 7th August, 1837. The assured died on 8th May, 1838, aged 41, from haemorrhage. The medical referee said he had attended the proposer two years previously for an abscess in the perineum. But this does not seem to have weighed against the acceptance of the risk.

Their second claim was even less profitable. A country gentleman, aged 40, took out a policy for £2,500 on the 5th October, 1837, and died of consumption on the 11th June, 1839, having paid two premiums amounting to £191 9s. 2d. The medical referee at the time 'believed him to be now temperate'; and the Society's doctor's report was good, 'supposing his habits to be temperate'.

Their third claim will make the present-day lawyer raise a questioning eyebrow. A solicitor, aged 38, insured for the sum of £1,000 on the 5th January, 1837, and died on the 14th of August, 1839, of inflammation of the bowels, having paid three premiums amounting to £87. His medical referee reported that he had 'seen him occasionally with slight illness', adding the cryptic remark: 'He lives like most lawyers.'

I gaze with astonishment, but no solution, upon the enigmatic case of one of their earliest policy-holders who, having taken out a policy – on a good medical report – for £1,000 at the age of 32, pays only three premiums amounting to £74 5s., and then dies of *gangrene of the liver*. Again the irresistible italics are mine.

The Society's predominant aversion to accepting a proposal was if the applicant was at all addicted to gout. Many a proposal was declined for that reason. 'Three or four attacks of gout, to which he is predisposed', brought invariably the verdict, 'Resolved that the Proposal be declined'. The sinister record crops up at nearly all their early meetings. For these were the hard-riding, hard-drinking days. Caution, in so far as the enlightenment of medical science allowed them, was the Society's watchword in all things. A private referee reports on a proposer: 'He is an irritable man and wears a false nose.' You feel that there was an immediate outburst of unanimity in 'Resolved that the Proposal be declined': almost a shudder of dissent quivering round the Board Room, although the medical report on the case had been very good.

Yet many proposals were accepted from men who were 'tolerably sober in their habits'. About 75 per cent of the deaths of the country gentlemen of those days, as the book shows, were caused by accidents in the hunting field or while out hacking, or from a seizure during an acute attack of the gout. Such phrases as these are common occurrences in the doctors' reports: 'As sober as young gentlemen of twenty-five usually are' . . . 'Keeps late hours and lives generously' . . . 'As sober as most gentlemen of quality' . . . And of a barrister: 'I cupped him once for deafness. Believe he is reasonably sober; but he lives well and takes his wine nightly.'

But despite all these growing pains of adolescence they moved steadily forward with a suavity, tact and a polished courtesy that is apparent from all their beautifully written, meticulous records.

E. P. LEIGH-BENNETT
On This Evidence
(1936), pp. 53–56

2 *Burial Insurance and Infanticide*

Since the Friendly Societies Act of 1793, the insurance habit among the working classes had grown by leaps and bounds. The Act allowed friendly societies whose rules were approved by the county quarter sessions to register with them, and this gave them important legal advantages over non-registered societies: they acquired quasi-corporate status and could, for example, sue and prosecute as a legal entity. After 1828 local registration was superseded by a centralised national system of registration under an official later to evolve as the Chief Registrar of Friendly Societies.

'Friendly Societies' in their most rounded form offered a range of benefits – sickness, widow's, emigration, and funeral, for example; their subscriptions were relatively high – perhaps sixpence a week – and were designed for the thrifty artisan class. Some, however, offered only funeral benefits, and because their subscriptions were much lower, reached down among the lower strata of the working classes and went for quantity of membership rather than quality.

Side by side with these were the unregistered funeral clubs – 'funeral briefs' or 'death briefs' as they were known in the north of England. They were commonly got up by the local publican in association with the undertaker; their rules were non-approved and their administration was amateurish, lax and often corrupt. Meetings were held on pub premises, and accompanied by much heavy imbibing encouraged by 'mine host'; and rules sometimes even allowed for benefits to be part-paid in drink. The publican acted as banker, and the funeral clubs were conducted with no regard to actuarial or accounting principles; embezzlements and collapses were quite common. Yet they had a wide following because they were cheap (subscriptions were ½ or 1d a week), offered a spurious aura of conviviality, and did not ask too many questions when an insured life was claimed upon.

Some idea of the popularity of working-class insurance may be gauged by the fact that by 1858 there were over 20,000 *registered* societies in England and Wales with over 2,000,000 members; so that, if we include members' beneficial dependants, some 40 per cent or more of the population were covered; to this we must add the unknown membership of unregistered clubs; but multiple memberships, perhaps combining registered and unregistered societies, were common. Although the resulting accumulation of benefits accruable in the case of life policies on members' children was to arouse the worst suspicions, we must also remember that multiple-insurance was a way of spreading the risk at a time when burial societies were so unstable.

Societies sprang up all over the land, in town and country alike, but they were especially thick on the ground in the industrial north-west, and it is from the Lancashire-Cheshire marches that the earliest criminal cases involving the alleged murder of children for the burial money were to emanate from 1840.

Some of the more successful funeral societies expanded beyond their own locality to a regional or even national network, and came to be popularly termed 'collecting societies'; their impersonality precluded informal subscription meetings at the local tavern; instead an army of doorstep agents went round collecting weekly premiums and touting for new members. The largest of these was the Liverpool-based Royal Liver with 550,000 members in 1872. The collectors depended entirely on commissions for an income, and had to be a hard-boiled, pushy and not over-scrupulous breed to hustle successfully for a living. Many of their malpractices were to have a direct bearing on the link alleged between insurance abuses and family murders, particularly infanticides.

To clarify our terminology, we have the 'death briefs' or 'funeral clubs' – these were the local, tavern-based unregistered associations; and the 'Collecting Societies', which offered death benefit only, but were technically and legally 'Friendly Societies' if they were registered as such. The term Friendly Society in *popular* parlance meant those registered societies that offered other benefits besides funeral payments.

From 1854 the commercial insurance company (a joint-stock enterprise whose profits went to the shareholders, not, as with Friendly Societies, to the insuring subscribers) entered the field and was destined to dwarf the other forms of burial insurance. This commercial business was called 'industrial life assurance' because the companies were venturing from their traditional market, the middle classes, into the industrial classes. Their benefits were lower than those offered by the meretricious 'funeral briefs' but they offered actuarial soundness and proven success. The pioneer was the Prudential, which in 1856 was to start recruiting collectors – the 'men from the "Pru"' – to make it viable and, after some hesitation in 1860, extended its portfolio to infant life insurance. It was very conscious of the cloud of suspicion hanging over this area, but found that it really made the market for industrial life assurance; its tables pitched the benefits low, particularly because it was the actuarially sound thing to do in view of the high infant mortality rate among the working classes, and partly to guard itself against any accusation that it was tempting people into infanticide.

Burial clubs would not admit child lives from birth, as the neonatal death rate was so prodigious, but admission ages might vary from a fortnight upwards, and the less sophisticated the society, the less regard it had for the principle of graduating benefits (and this could be fatal to its solvency). The Preston Original Legal Friendly Society, founded in 1831, admitted children after 2 months old, and in 1853 was paying out a flat rate of £2 15 shillings on the death of any child member under 4, provided there had been at least sixteen weekly contributions of ½d. The Prudential would not admit infants before 3 months old, and they had to be in contribution at 1d a week over three months for a benefit of only 10 shillings in its 1860 table. This rose to £1 after a year's contribution, and £2 after two years. The scales were designed to keep the benefits low for the younger infants, and then accelerate them if a child was enrolled after 4 years old; thus a child entered at 4 received 15 shillings after three months, but a child entered at 5 received £2 10 shillings after the same period.

Lodges of 'true' Friendly Societies offered even lower rates; in 1891 the Order of the Sons of Temperance offered only £1 on deaths under 3, for example.

What was the actual cost of a child's burial? Propagandists against infant life insurance played down the sum, to 'prove' that the benefits were a profitable bounty and an incitement to infanticide; the Reverend John Clay in 1854 gave it as 25 shillings and Benjamin Waugh in 1890 put it as low as 15 to 18 shillings. Defenders of insurance emphasised the cost of the extras, considered so important in Victorian funerals, such as bell-tolling, the pall and bearers, and the hire of mourning clothes; and a variety of sources indicates that the real expense was two or three times the figures just cited.

Now any claims to purity by any single society, like the Prudential or a Friendly Society, in respect of the modesty of their benefits, must ring hollow in view of beneficiaries' practice of topping up benefits by multiple insurances; and though laws were to be passed to regulate this, they were to prove ineffectual, as we shall see.

One thing must be emphasised here. The whole field of child-life insurance was non-legal. The law deemed that normally parents and guardians had no legal 'interest' in the continued survival of the child and such insurance contracts were void in the civil courts. The whole industry grew up on good faith alone; societies paid out readily because it attracted further custom, and they frequently made additional *ex gratia* payments – for instance, if the child died before eligibility – to promote goodwill in the neighbourhood. Life insurance was a cut-throat business – rival collectors were known to come to blows on doorsteps – and a society could not afford a reputation for fussiness over pay-outs.

The Prudential, which prided itself on careful management and selectivity over its collectors, became the giant in infant life insurance. Growth was rapid; in 1871 it had about 309,000 children up to 10 on its 'industrial' books, and by 1891 this had risen to 2,400,000 in a working-class child population up to 10 of some 6,500,000. The total numbers of insured children in the population around 1891 were a matter of dispute; estimates ranged from 2,750,000 to 4,000,000, and accurate figures were impossible, as companies and societies counted *policies*; and many – 30 per cent was one estimated – were duplicated among different societies on the same child. But even on the lowest figure, the fact stands out that infant life insurance had grown immensely popular among the working classes and was big business at the end of the nineteenth century. Of the £13,000,000 total value of child life insurance among the commercial companies alone at the end of the 1880s, £9,500,000 were held by the 'Pru'; the Pearl Life Assurance Company came a poor second with £1,400,000.

The two earliest official exposures of infant life insurance in its worst light came in Edwin Chadwick's Report on Interment in Towns in 1843, part of his pioneering public health study, followed by the Reverend John Clay's special report for Preston for the Commission on 'The State of Large Towns and Populous Places' in 1844. Clay was chaplain to Preston jail and an active social reformer, and was associated with Mary Carpenter and Matthew Davenport Hill in the campaign for reformatories for juvenile offenders; he became perhaps the most authoritative single voice against infant life assurance from his base right in the heart of burial-club country in the north-west.

Chadwick's attention had been drawn to the death clubs by a poisoning case – the first of its kind to come into the courts – from Stockport, in the same part of the country, in 1840, and before his report was completed, another case at Chester Assizes in 1843 was brought to his attention.

The 1840 case involved two poor, related couples Robert and Anne Sandys, and George and Honor Sandys, who lived in adjoining cellar rooms in Stockport. Robert and Anne had four children, all enrolled in a local (unregistered) burial club, the 'Philanthropic', which had over 2,000 members, and paid (after administrative deductions) £3 8s. 6d. plus 2 shillings-worth of drink on a child's death. In September 1840 a daughter, Elizabeth, died, and Robert obtained the burial dues from the club the next day, giving 'inflammation' as the cause of her death. The club was very lax, and evidently no doctor's certificate was required. Henry Coppock, Stockport's town clerk, described how the club's officers disposed of claims: 'The officers met at a public house at 12 o'clock at noon; they got the men there at their dinner hour, and the sooner they got quit of the payments the better.' In the Sandys case, typically, they made no check.

On October 12th two of the three surviving children developed severe stomach pains after eating bread and butter, and were taken to two local doctors in succession. Both prescribed emetics, and one of them indeed diagnosed arsenic. (This did not necessarily suggest foul play, as arsenic could be commonly purchased then, for example to kill bed bugs or as a rat poison in the slums, and would be left lying about.) However, both doctors testified later that the mother had failed to give the children the emetics. (This illustrates a suspected crafty ploy that became more widely adverted to later in the century: late in the children's illness parents would make a show of resorting to a busy doctor, to deflect criminal accusations and ensure a subsequent medical certificate of death. For example Dr C. S. Redmond, a Gateshead dispensary doctor, was to comment in 1890: 'Over and over have I been called to cases too late to do any good but where it was only too apparent that the doctor was sent for, not in the hope of rescuing the child from death but of saving the parents from punishment. . . . In many of such cases I find the infants' lives insured.')

One of the two sick Sandys children, Marianne, died. The Sandys accused another woman of poisoning her, but Anne Sandys's odd behaviour at the inquest aroused suspicion. Elizabeth's and Marianne's bodies were exhumed and found to contain arsenic. The police were now alerted to the fact that George and Honor Sandys's daughter Catherine had died in July and the cause of death was registered as 'measles'; she, too, had been insured.

Robert and Anne Sandys were tried for murdering the two girls; Robert was found guilty but Anne was acquitted, as the jury, misunderstanding the law, believed that a wife was presumed to be acting under her husband's influence and could not be guilty. Much suspicion surrounded Honor Sandys and she was charged with Catherine's murder; but the evidence against her was less conclusive than that against Anne, and in view of the unsatisfactory verdict against the latter, Honor's case was dropped.

The prosecution also faced disappointment in the trial of Robert Standring at Chester Assizes in 1843, accused of poisoning his mentally defective daughter for the £8 burial money. The jury acquitted him, against overwhelming evidence, owing, it was suggested, to their qualms over capital punishment.

John Clay's description of the burial clubs in Preston in 1844 was a classic, if statistically defective, study unrepeated anywhere else in the nineteenth century. He followed it up with a long and detailed letter in *The Times* in January 1849, which in turned formed the basis of a noted pamphlet on 'Burial Clubs and Infanticide' in 1853, a copy of which was read by the then Home Secretary, Lord Palmerston, who asked for its circulation in the Cabinet.

Preston was a rapidly growing town; in 1841 its population was 50,000; in 1851 nearly 70,000. The 1849 letter does not mention Preston by name but it must be the anonymous town of 61,000 he is referring to. It had then 52,000 enrolments in its eleven burial clubs (three-quarters of which were children), compared with only an estimated 2,000 in the town's dozen or so sickness clubs which offered sickness as well as burial benefit; the enrolments, remember, must exaggerate the numbers of actual persons, owing to multiple memberships. In 1844 he had estimated that two-thirds of the town's working-class 0–5-year-olds were enrolled in the 'Preston Original Legal Friendly Benefit Society' alone. Clay was struck by the contrasting infant death rates among the town's social classes: among the 'gentry', 'tradesmen' and 'operative' classes in 1844 the death rate of 0–5-year-olds was 17.6, 38.2 and 55.4 per cent respectively. Now he saw that ignorance, poverty and filth were the basic factors, but when he became aware of the near-universality of child life insurance among the working class, the suspicion was kindled that this had something to do with the excessively high infant death rate among that class. He pointed out in 1849 that despite the prevalence of sickness among working-class infants, Preston doctors who practised in the poor districts had told him that only 13 per cent of their patients were below 5. Clay acknowledged that wilful murder was exceptional, but was certain that insurance fostered parental indifference. As he told the 1854 Select Committee of the Friendly Societies Bill: 'I must do the parent justice to say, that the parent herself is not conscious of the influence which is actually taking place in her mind; she might be startled if it were put to her directly, "You are letting this child die for the sake of the burial fees".'

Clay purported to prove that infant deaths in the 'Preston Original Legal' were higher than they ought to be compared with the rate of infant death in the town at large, but his statistical approach was fallacious. He did not compare the proportion of infant members to all members in the Society with the age-structure of the town's population, to draw any sound conclusions. Moreover, since he gives the impression that working-class children were overwhelmingly insured in *some* society, how can he distinguish between 'insured' children and 'town' children?

Before the 1854 Select Committee on the Friendly Societies Bill, Clay presented another statistical case: the death rate among the poor working-class 0–5-year-olds in Preston was 55–60 per cent; yet a sample survey from the burial clubs indicated a death rate of 62 to 64 per cent; the first set of figures included all infants from birth, while the latter excluded the first 2 months of life, the most vulnerable period, so the comparison was even more adverse to the societies, he claimed. Yet again, we know nothing about the sample, and the same objection – how can you distinguish 'society' deaths from 'town' deaths? – still applies.

The year 1846 saw two 'infant burial insurance' trials: Joseph and Mary Pimlett of Runcorn, Cheshire, were tried for murdering two of their infants and poisoning a third. The two dead children were insured with the 'Victoria Legal Burial Society', and their corpses showed traces of arsenic when exhumed. Murder was not proven, however, and the couple were acquitted. However, John Rodda was convicted at York Assizes of murdering his 1-year-old child – insured for £2 10 shillings – by pouring acid down its throat. His three surviving children were all insured.

The Friendly Societies Act of 1846 made the first crude and totally ineffective attack on infant life insurance by banning it altogether on children under 6 in registered societies. The unregistered clubs, where one would imagine that scope for abuse would be greater, were ignored; and the ban only applied to registered societies coming into existence *after* the Act was passed!

In 1848 the connection between murder and burial insurance shifted its focus away from the Mersey region to rural Essex from where news broke in September of a series of suspected poisonings in and around the villages of Thorpe, Kirby, Ramsay, Wix, Mistley, Bradfield and Great Oakley, in those days secluded backwaters.

In July 1848 one Mary May of Wix had been convicted at Chelmsford Assizes of murdering her half-brother with arsenic; unbeknown to him she had insured him in a Harwich burial society for £9 or £10. Some of her children, it transpired, had died quite suddenly, and tongues started wagging. In March 1849 her sister Hannah Southgate was tried for poisoning her first husband, to be free to marry her lover, but was acquitted. Mary May and her sister were rumoured to have been at the centre of a whole web of poisoning conspiracies; for the inquiries conducted by the north Essex coroner into the 'Essex Poisonings' in the aforementioned villages had been instigated by the exposure of Mary; and the suspected perpetrators (nothing more seems to have been proved) all knew Mary and her sister. The newspaper accounts are somewhat obscure, but suggest a burial club connection.

The 'Essex Poisonings' episode shows that the same motivations were at work in the more remote rural areas as were imputed to Merseyside. Infants were not uniquely vulnerable as insurance victims. The pattern of exposed crimes, which almost invariably featured the use of poison, suggests that the perpetrators were psychopaths and unusual types. They usually had a succession of victims, child and adult alike; indeed the financial motive was even greater against adults for there was to be no legal limit set on the amount of their life insurance. The infamous Mary Ann Cotton of County Durham in 1873 and the Liverpool poisoners of 1884, Catherine Flannagan and Margaret Higgins, were murderesses of this type. Margaret's murdered husband, Thomas, for example, had been insured in a number of societies by his wife for a total of £108 19 shillings.

In fact it was not the poisoning cases that worried the critics of infant burial insurance so much as the suspicion that the far more typical and elusive kind of infanticide was murder by neglect, for the defence could so easily raise the plea of 'ignorance' to get their client off the hook. As the Surrey coroner, Athelstan Braxton Hicks, was to observe later in the century it was not possible to convict for manslaughter 'unless a medical man can state positively that the child's life might have been prolonged by medical aid or other necessaries or that its death had been accelerated by the want of such aid or necessaries'; no doctor could do more than state an opinion in court, and this was insufficient for a conviction. John Bransom, the Medical Officer for Rotherham, told in 1890 of a case he had once attended where a child was on the point of death while the two women of the house were 'singing and laughing away' at the washtub. When he upbraided them for plying the child with sops it could not take from a filthy container, and warned them that he would refer the matter to the coroner if it died, they blithely replied, 'Oh master, we are ignorant and young'.

For the most part, then, the evidence was tantalisingly suspicious and laced with hearsay, but legal proof was another matter. Chadwick's report mentions a Manchester family in which six infants had died; one of these was worth £20 from multiple insurances; another, enrolled in ten clubs, yielded £34 3 shillings. A rent collector told him: 'The poor people have often told me that they were unable to pay at that time; but when a certain member of the family – generally a child – died, they would be able to pay. Most of the children at the houses which I visit are in the burial clubs.'

And John Clay told of a lady friend who offered to send medical help to the ailing child of the woman she was employing as a wet-nurse. The woman replied, 'Oh! never ma'am; it's in two burial clubs'.

Against blanket class innuendo of this sort representatives of working men waxed indignant. The Select Committee on the Friendly Societies Bill of 1849 heard protesting evidence from two burial society spokesmen, embarrassed by the recent poisoning cases. William Jenkins, Secretary of the United Legal Friendly Benefit Society of Liverpool, with 47,000 members, said: 'I have made it my business to watch very closely and I have never yet found a case where there was the least suspicion of anything of that kind. I generally find the poor people are very strongly attached to their children.' The same protestation of working-class affection for their children was to be offered cogently before the House of Lords Committee on Child Life Insurance in 1890 by Will Crooks, the dockers' leader and Poplar resident and councillor.

Parliamentarians were only too aware that legal curbs on infant life insurance were politically fraught even long before the working classes got the vote, and so were loath to do anything really effective; apart from the implied class slander, they would be undermining the cherished Victorian totem of 'self-help' – for without private insurance, the working classes would be burying more children at the Poor Law's expense. The new approach tried in the Friendly Societies Act of 1850 was to allow a maximum insurance of £3 in registered societies for children under 10, and make the presentation of a medical certificate compulsory upon a claim. However, it also added the 'undertaker clause' which the working classes found provocative and insulting. As a disincentive to infanticide, the proceeds were to be kept from the claimants' hands. Instead the money was to go directly to the undertaker appointed to make the funeral arrangements.

The hated clause was destined to last five years, and was repealed by the Friendly Societies Act of 1855. Yet despite experience of the reaction it triggered off, Benjamin Waugh, whose political touch was conspicuously maladroit, was to seriously try and revive the idea a generation later, when working-class resistance to class paternalism was even more highly matured.

LIONEL ROSE
The Massacre of the Innocents
(1986), pp. 136–145

3 INA Life Policies

'Consumer buying habits are changing', Zalinski [of the Insurance Company of North America (INA)] said. 'The buyer wants one-stop service. He wants to go to one man for all his insurance.'

To help property-liability agents learn life-insurance selling, INA-Life was ready to send experienced field representatives out to call on selected prospects with the agents. And it was quick to cut red tape that might block a sale.

A San Francisco man wanted a $250,000 policy. Because he traveled a good deal, investigating his medical history was difficult.

'We found that he had had medical treatment in Barcelona', Donald S. Vincent said,

> so we telephoned his physician in Spain. We also needed a statement from a clinic in St Paul, Minnesota, and telephoned them for information. They would not release any information without a signed authorization. Our doctor arranged through one of the press services to have a photo of the authorization sent by wire, and he also made arrangements to have it picked up immediately and delivered to the clinic. The clinic then telephoned us and discussed the case in detail. We were able to issue a standard policy.

Another man was preparing to leave on a trip, and he wanted a $500,000 policy. INA-Life found that the parent company's Bonding Department had a file on him going back to 1935, showing that the company had bonded him for as much as $2,500,000. The policy was approved in two days.

Sometimes applications were rejected for unusual reasons. In June 1966 an application for a $50,000 accident insurance policy on a woman was received. Before issuing the policy, the company looked into the circumstances. Four acquaintances of the woman told INA-Life's investigators that if she were insured for a substantial amount of money, they would not 'give a plug nickel for her life'. The company turned down the application, and four months later her body, with four gunshot wounds, was found in a burning car. The husband was charged with murder.

The INA tradition of liberal treatment of policyholders was implemented in the life company. On January 13, 1967, a man applied for life insurance and paid the initial premium. Four days later, before the policy had been approved by the company, the man had a heart attack which would have made him uninsurable. Examination of the application showed that he had made a mistake to filling it out. Nevertheless, since he had paid the premium in advance and had been insurable on the day of the application (having no prior history of heart trouble), the company issued the policy.

In Apple Valley, California, a restaurateur named Salvatore Testa was murdered by a bandit in a tavern on August 9, 1961. Testa had applied for a $5,000 ordinary life policy on July 6, paying the premium with his application. At the time of the slaying the application had not yet been approved. Nevertheless, INA-Life determined that Testa was insurable on the day he applied, so it honored the policy.

Fraudulent policy applications and strange claims flowed into Philadelphia. INA vice president James W. Ferriman, later head of the Policyholder's Service Division, worked on the life company's claims for a time.

'I swear that in our first couple of years we must have run into every kind of screwball situation', he said.

One chap left the hospital after an exploratory operation for cancer, which was found to be incurable, went right to our agent's offices, and applied for a life insurance policy below the medical limits, so that there would be no examination.

Another case involved an insured who took a raft trip down the Colorado River with thirteen other people. The raft hit a rock, and five of the people went into the water. Three of them were fished out immediately, but two were swept downstream. The body of one of those two was found subsequently; but the last body has not been found to this day. And that was the one we insured for $80,000 or $90,000. It was almost certain that he had lost his life. It was very wild country.

Another disappearance involved a city councilman in the Midwest who was leading a civil reform drive, investigating crime and corruption personally. One day his car was found abandoned; the councilman had vanished. INA-Life's investigators began to dig into the case when a claim was presented on his life insurance policy.

'Ultimately we located him in the South', Ferriman said. 'He had been beaten, transported South, and thrown out of the car. We found him in a hospital.'

Among the most bizarre claims have been several dismemberment injuries that turned out to be intentional.

'It is hard to believe that a man will go out and buy a $250,000 worth of insurance and then cut off a hand or put out an eye', said Alan Waters. 'But it happens. Of course, this is very difficult for us to prove because it's so unbelievable. You really have to dig for information.'

A Florida man was suspected of having deliberately shot his leg off after buying insurance from several companies, including INA-Life. When they began to probe into the case, INA-Life's claims men found that the man had lied about a kidney problem when applying for his policy, so the company simply rescinded the policy on grounds of misrepresentation. The other insurance companies were less fortunate; feeling that it was doubtful they could persuade a judge and jury that anyone would intentionally maim himself, they settled the claims against them. The self-made cripple collected $134,000.

'Some time later we got a claim from another fellow in Florida', Waters remembered.

His leg had been shot off, too. And then we discovered that he was a next-door neighbor of the first man.

At that point, as you can imagine, we really got suspicious. In the course of our investigation we found that the first man had set the whole thing up for his neighbor, even to writing the letters to the insurance companies for him. We were able to break that case because our insured had failed when he tried to blow his leg off by himself, so he had hired another man to do the job for him. But he welshed on paying the fellow, so the guy was ready to talk.

During the investigation, the first crook, the one who had collected and had written the letters for his neighbor, started following his fellow self-made cripple around to see how he was making out. They said it was funny to watch. Here would go our insured (the second crook), and the first fellow would follow him, and our investigator would follow the first man, all of them running around Florida in a line of parade.

And then there was the 'Case of the Man Who Sold His Life'. He lived in North Carolina, but during a visit to Florida, suspecting that something was wrong with him, he went to a doctor. The doctor discovered that the man had an inoperable brain tumor. He probably would not live more than a year.

So the man went back to North Carolina, contacted some gamblers, and offered to sell them his life. If they would give him a large amount of money to enjoy while he was still alive, he would let them buy $1,500,000 accidental death coverage on him, with them as beneficiaries.

They agreed to the deal. He got a fat wad of bills, and they got a fistful of insurance policies. While the money held out, the tumor victim acted like the last of the big spenders. His last weeks were a frenzied search for pleasure.

When he went broke, it was time to fulfill his side of the deal. He killed himself by driving into a bridge abutment at about ninety miles an hour.

There was a sequel. About the time he died, his beneficiaries were found to have been involved in an automobile insurance frauds ring. The state authorities sought a connection between the death of the tumor victim and the operations of the insurance swindlers.

'They are all in jail now', Waters said.

But INA-Life knew that there would be other cheats to take their place.

WILLIAM H. A. CARR
Perils Named and Unnamed
(1967), pp. 352–356

4 *William Palmer*

William Palmer, the notorious poisoner, . . . was convicted of the murder of J. P. Cook, by administering strychnine, and hanged in 1856, after a trial that was the sensation of the times. The main details of his case are too well known to bear repetition, but its insurance aspect is interesting and illuminating enough to merit a little space.

The one murder, that of Cook, was enough to hang the 'sporting surgeon' of Rugeley, but there is no doubt that he killed his wife with antimony, and, although the Grand Jury threw out the Bill in respect of his dipsomaniac brother, Walter, the latter's death probably lay at his doors. Walter Palmer died on the 15th August, 1855. The previous year he had insured his own life with the Prince of Wales Assurance Company for £13,000, being charged the premium for a man of fifty-five, although he was only thirty-three; this in consequence of his intemperate habits. He stated at the time that he intended to assign the policy to his wife, but subsequent enquiries elicited the fact that it was actually assigned to his brother William. The alleged consideration was £400, which in itself was a somewhat odd figure since Walter's total indebtedness to his brother only amounted to £60. Not that this mattered very much since the £400 was given in the form of a bill which nobody would discount!

William also paid the first and only premium on this policy. A little later he offered assurances – again for £13,000 in each case – to the 'Indisputable' and 'Athenaeum' companies, but these were declined. Possibly things were already being said in insurance circles. William's wife Anne had died in somewhat mysterious circumstances in 1854, and the husband had collected £13,000 from the Norwich Union, the 'Sun' Office, and a Scottish office. Very decidedly the number thirteen, reiterated in terms of thousands, seemed to be unhealthy and unlucky.

Then Walter Palmer died, and the insurance claim was duly lodged with the 'Prince of Wales' office. Although that prudent company had only retained £500 of its liability, having reinsured the balance of £12,500, it took advantage of the breathing space allowed by the terms of the policy. While waiting, a letter was received from a Rugeley citizen which convinced the company's actuary that this was a case for investigation. The other companies interested were communicated with, a committee was appointed, and certain details of William Palmer's past activities in insurance were discovered. The £13,000 paid on account of Anne Palmer's decease came to light. So did the fact that William Palmer had recently acted as medical referee to the 'Midland Counties', and had been turned away for undesirable conduct.

The account of the latter transaction as given in the *Post Magazine* of this date is a little confusing in its chronology, but one can gather the main facts. There was a solicitor named Pratt, who appears for a while to have been intimately associated with William Palmer; although in a letter to the *Post Magazine*, published while Palmer was awaiting trial, he was at pains to deny this. At any rate Pratt got himself appointed the Rugeley agent to the 'Midland Counties Assurance', and having, in accordance with the custom of that office, the right to nominate the medical referee for that district, chose William Palmer. Shortly afterwards Pratt submitted a 'proposal' to his company for an insurance of £10,000 on the life of a man called George Bates, who was 'described as a gentleman'. There was apparently some difficulty in locating this 'gentleman', but he was eventually discovered cleaning out William Palmer's stable! He proved to be an ingenuous yokel who regarded his life assurance as a joke on the part of his employer, who was apparently going to pay for it, and to give him 'something for himself' for the privilege of using his name.

Palmer's object can only be surmised, but it is more than likely that if he had succeeded in insuring George Bates and had escaped the consequences of murdering Cook, George Bates would have found the 'joke' a sorry one for himself. As it happened, the office declined the insurance on the grounds that neither Pratt nor Palmer could adduce any 'insurable interest'.

The matter of Palmer's insurances was not fully cleared up till two years afterwards. The 'Prince of Wales' office, as already mentioned, only retained £500 of the Walter Palmer risk. The balance of £12,500 was taken over by the

'Athenaeum', which in turn retained £2,000, and partitioned the remainder among no fewer than twenty-one other companies. More fortunate than the insurers of Anne Palmer, all these escaped on the plea of no valid 'insurable interest' or 'non disclosure of material facts'. But one gathers that the refusal of the criminal's mother, who was the only possible beneficiary, to take any part in the proceedings for recovery had some little influence on the verdict.

F. J. MACLEAN
The Human Side of Insurance
(1931), pp. 93–95

5 *Brides-in-the-Bath Smith*

To the agent who had sold him this annuity (Mr Plaisance), Smith, in October 1913, brought new business, and at the same time made an enigmatic promise to buy another £500 worth of annuity 'out of land transactions in Canada' the following January. For this business he was obliged to return to his real name, and even to forgo all mythology and produce his birth certificate. So the next episode, his marriage with Alice Burnham, is played out in the name of Smith. It was this young woman, a stout merry nurse, in the best of health and spirits, whose life Smith insured with Plaisance. At first Smith wanted the sum to be £1,000, payable at death; but learning that marriage would make the premium on this amount out of his means, he contented himself with one for £500 on a twenty-year endowment.

His confidence in the 'Canadian' deal shows that he had fully made up his mind to continue in the trade for which Bessie Mundy had paid his apprenticeship. To make it pay, he was resolved to turn to the most common and dangerous method of life-insurance, which has hanged innumberable murderers before him. The exploitation of death ranges from the horrible sale of the body itself, as with Burke (but there are even simpler means than that, as we shall see in the case of Haarmann), which solves the problem of disposal of the body and covers its tell-tale witness to the cause of death; through the simple despoliation of the personal possessions of the victim – furniture in the case of Landru, trust funds in the example of Bessie Mundy – to the insurance fraud, which Smith was now premeditating. There is no other method to gain money by the death of a person who has no possessions, and Smith was, for whatever reason, unable to venture on another moneyed spinster. But the essence of mass-murder, to be profitable and safe, is that the victims must stand in a loosened relation to the rest of society. The wolf who knows his business only attacks the isolated members of the herds, the wanderers, the outliers. To strict observance of this principle, Burke owed his immunity. It was in a terrific attempt to snap the chains that bound Kinck to his fellow-men that Troppmann peopled the plain of Pantin with corpses. But the exploitation of life-insurance, while it allows on the one hand of the selection of poor strayers – riches being the most powerful chain to hold society's interest in a man's personal fate – yet the very act of giving a powerful commercial organization a direct interest that the victim should not die wakens an enemy whose determination and acumen is more dangerous to the assassin than all the Dogberrys of all the local inquest courts. Thus, while apparently cunning, it is the stupidest folly for a professional murderer to pick out a friendless victim and then give the victim's life over to the protection of a most powerful and interested corporation. It is a common folly, and tempted that stupid rogue, Smith. Nor indeed was his intended victim, this Alice Burnham, without friends. Her father was a retired coal-merchant, immensely more shrewd than the small shyster that thus pushed into his family circle; there were brothers, sisters, and a mother who loved her. Only over the girl herself, whom he had met in his accustomed manner at Portsmouth, had the murderer any advantage; not one, to be sure, of intellect, but given to him, an eligible male, by nature and the social system. Miss Burnham is a less enigmatic character than her predecessor, though hardly less tragic. She was a strong capable woman, hard-working in her profession, to whom celibacy with all its accompaniments was as irksome as it was despairing to Bessie Mundy. Every atom of Miss Burnham's body and her tastes repelled her from the state to which the customs of her country had condemned her. She was twenty-six years old when she accepted the company of this man, on whom she could have had less illusions even than Bessie. She was eager to risk all the smug-faced monotony of comfort and esteem, even the affection of her family, for the single chance of a natural life; and she was a cheerful gambler.

But first she made a bold attempt to impose her 'young man' (Smith was now 40) on her family. Smith cut a pitiable figure at the family home in Aston Clinton, where he was invited; the bluff father had met many such before, and concealed neither his contempt nor dislike for this stranger whose manner wavered always between brag and servility. The mother, whose ideas of the minimum qualifications of a husband were less exacting than those of Charles Burnham, tried to moderate her husband; but in the end the prospective son-in-law was kicked out, muttering threats, and Alice accompanied him to the station. That was the 31st October 1913. On the 4th November following they were married, without anyone of the family being present.

On retiring from business, Mr Burnham had presented each of his children with £40, the eldest son taking over the succession. To this sum Alice, from her savings, had added £60, and given the whole £100 to her father for safe keeping. He paid her 4 per cent on it. This nest-egg Smith now set himself to collect, with his mixture of greed and legal stupidities. He poured forth a stream of letters to the father in his usual county-court cum lay-reader tone; he accused him of 'taking refuge in obdurateness, contempt, and remorse', and threatened 'to take the matter up without delay'. In the course of the correspondence, a post-card from Smith conveyed the genealogical information at the beginning of this study. Another ran, 'I do not know your next move, but take my advice and be careful'. Another pointed this vague threat (which sounds nastier to us who know the man's past than probably it was intended) with the explanation, 'I am keeping all letters that pass for the purpose of justice'. In the end, Burnham, dreading a long and vexatious law-case with this sinister sea-lawyer, yielded and sent the money.

By this ungainly procedure, Smith had achieved the opposite of what he no doubt intended, and set an estrangement between the daughter and her family. A similar action about a paltry sum owed by her sister completed the effect. But without meaning it, he had blundered into the only possible chance of the success of the deed he was planning – the isolation of the woman. The next act in his fixed repertory which he had composed from the circumstances of his first crime, after the habit of mass-murderers, was to take Alice Burnham on a trip to Blackpool. In the choice of this distant resort, he showed both a knowledge of geography and a nice science of the social usages. Blackpool in winter is out of season, yet the relaxation of censure and curiosity still might be hoped to prevail. The respectable by-roads of Herne Baye suited admirably in his former venture; but both the life and death of the gay little nurse would fit better into the setting of the People's Paradise of the North. And it was as far as possible from her family and any friends her infatuation for him could have left.

When they arrived in the cold grey air, there were no tunes from the merry-go-rounds to greet them; the shooting-galleries were quiet; the promenade empty and windy. They put up for their unseasonal honeymoon with a family named Crossley, in lodgings in Cocker Street. Previously Smith had tried elsewhere, but failed to find the convenience of a bathroom. In the Crossleys' house, for ten shillings a week, they could use the bath when they liked. All they had brought for luggage was a brownish hold-all and a paper parcel. The Crossleys were good Lancashire folk, very anxious to please in this lodgerless month. Mrs Crossley agreed to cook the visitors' meals. They would buy the materials themselves. Smith knows no other method of preparing himself for great acts than to soak his mind in petty meannesses. He grumbles astonishingly at the departure of every penny. Mrs Smith seemed to the Crossleys charming; it is a pity that this Mrs Smith has a train-headache from the journey. But in spite of it and Mr Smith's noticeable stinginess, she insists on going out the same evening to the kinematograph.

Smith is desperately quick this time; he is afraid this lively little Alice will either escape him or ruin him. Nevertheless he does not scamp a detail of his plaster-of-Paris plan. The morning after their arrival, he takes her to the doctor; naturally this time he does not dare to talk of fits (she is a nurse), but insists that the railway-headache alarms him. The doctor is not at a loss: he prescribes a mild purgative.

Two days later, that was a Friday, they went out for a walk, leaving instructions for a bath to be prepared. The bath was to be for Mrs Smith. Smith had already inspected the bathroom. Before this look-round the bolt worked perfectly. It was above the kitchen. At tea-time, the evening meal, the Crossleys, the mother, the son, the grown-up daughter-in-law, were sitting round the kitchen table, when one of them noticed a great stain of water on the ceiling. They all looked at it and saw it enlarge and drip down the wall, behind a picture. Such a thing had never happened before. The elder woman said, 'Oh, Alice, go and tell Mrs Smith not to fill the bath so'. But the girl answered,

'Oh, mother, they will think we are grumbling already, and they not two days in the house'.

Then suddenly the pale Smith came into the kitchen. He lumped a package on to the table and said, 'I have brought these eggs for our breakfast in the morning'. The girl got up to take them, wiping her mouth with her napkin. Smith then went upstairs. They heard him call shrilly, 'Alice, put the light out'. The daughter-in-law, who had this Christian name, thought he was speaking to her, rose and went up to him. He said, 'No, I was speaking to my wife, Alice, to put the light out'. The living Alice went back into the kitchen. Then Smith, who was standing on the mat on the bathroom landing, said suddenly again, 'My wife will not speak to me'. Good Mrs Crossley stood up at this sort of scream, and said, 'Oh, what is it?' 'Fetch Dr Billing in a hurry', he said.

Mrs Crossley: Dr Billing lives quite near. I ran for him and he came to my house for a few minutes. I waited on the stairs and when he came down I asked him what was wrong, and he said, 'Oh, she is drowned. She is dead.' Smith was upstairs on the landing then. I went back to the kitchen and my daughter, called Mrs Haynes, came in. After the doctor had gone, Smith came down into the kitchen. I said to him, 'How dreadful: what an awful thing this is!' He said he would not be surprised at anything that would happen afterwards.

Behind this stiffness that shocked we may catch a glimpse of a soul clinging with all its might to unreality, a wretch, terror-stricken to the heart, striving with all his might to believe that he had simply done a good stroke of business. Under the water-splash on the ceiling, amidst the remnant of an evening meal, the two eyed each other, he helpless to relax his grip, not daring even to pretend to cry, she with an angry uneasiness growing every second. They are both tongue-tied. She breaks it off finally, in a new tone. 'Now, Smith, you cannot stop here to-night.' He can only say, 'Why?' 'Because I'll take good care not to have a callous fellow like you in the house.' He gulps, but does not protest, except, 'When they're dead, they're dead'. He had to write his letters in the next-door house that night. Across the post-card on which he left with her his address, Mrs Crossley wrote, in spite of the inquest, in spite of the verdict, the memento, 'Wife died in bath. We shall see him again.'

This bungler had succeeded again. The mere fact that the woman had died in a bath and that no one as yet had heard of this stealthy form of murder seemed alone to be in this favour. Hang-dog and perpetually busy, he fixed his affairs, collected the money from the company without a murmur, and paid over to Plaisance the promised £500. Acting more near instinct than by free thought he repeated the chain of his acts as he had devised them in the former case, down to their least detail. He had prepared the doctor, prepared her parents, killed on Friday to avoid their presence, made up the same trumpery alibi of a small purchase outside. Now he completed the chain, sold the dead woman's jewels and clothing and cleared out to another sea-town, then sent for the Bristol wife, with another tale of dealings in Canada.

The success of this second murder must have confirmed the man in the complicated unreality he had adjusted round himself. He no longer found it hard to believe that he was a bold business man, successful in a very serious line, who must, after all, look after his health. He became exacting with

Pegler; with those annuities locked in his private drawer, he dared to begin to believe he had done it 'all for her'. The thought of another long sea-voyage to Canada, to find another valuable antique, oppressed him more than it did his companion; he had made symbols like this for everything in his life and used them even in his private thoughts. Every day he seemed more cynical about the hardness of the world. He pitied himself profoundly, because his nature was a handicap. He confided to his wife sometimes parts of what he had suffered in his last journey: how a certain man had tried to humiliate him about his birth, how the miserable suspicions of boarding-house keepers and the like just showed you. So by these symbolisms he managed to relieve himself of the only burden that weighed, the memory of humiliations, the scratches on his pride. Then he would spend hours reading the small print on the backs of his annuities and checking his old house-accounts. At intervals he would be stung with the recollection of what he had lost and he would leave the Bristol house for a week's trip. But never as far as Canada – lesser affairs in the earlier manner. Matters of savings, small deals with servants and the like.

At last those higher powers, who had so whimsically rejoined him and Bessie together, again intervened. At Clifton, near the spot where a man he knew named Henry Williams once met a girl called Mundy, he fell in with Miss Margaret Lofty, a small, wistful shape, who was walking in the cool of the evening to calm certain private anguishes. She was the daughter of a clergyman, dead for years, a lady's companion no longer young. A year before, she had been happy, but the man she was engaged to had turned out to be a married man and now she was alone. She was struck by Smith's eyes, eyes that showed he, too, had suffered, eyes that gave her the sensation of 'having been there before'. She learned that his name was 'Lloyd', a man beneath her station, of course, but a God-fearing, handsome fellow who understood.

She clung to him as if she were drowning. She made a show to him of all her accomplishments, fell in eargerly with all his ideas. When he talked about insurance and how it was a principle of his to make provision for the future, she picked up all its mechanism in an hour or two's quiet chat. He complimented her on her intelligence, regretted he had not had himself the advantage of much education. A shy and retiring man, he was too nervous to meet her family, which suited her, as she felt a tiny grudge against her mother and sister for their uncomprehension in the terrible affair the year before, and how they might not understand. At thirty-eight a woman's affairs are her own concern, and seldom easy to tell. She told them nothing about Lloyd, and made up an innocent story about a new position (which was true after all) when she went away to be married. After she had gone to see the insurance-manager (she struck him as 'having the business at her finger's ends') and taken out a policy for £700, 'Lloyd' had the licence ready. They took train to Bath and the same day were man and wife.

Miss Lofty drew out her life savings, £19, and advanced it to her husband. This money carried them to London, where Smith, who knew the neighbourhood from one of his former existences, had booked lodgings in the superior district of Highgate. Coroner's juries would push complaisance to its limits in such a neighbourhood. But when they arrived at the address, Smith-Lloyd had a great shock. He stumbled across the war.

For during all these years while the man intent in his own cult pursued his private ritual of murder, a mightier killing was being prepared, a world-wide massacre, one of whose immense circuits of force lay through the very house he had selected for his last crime. As absent-minded as a weasel on the blood-scent, possibly until this moment he had never heard of the war. It was the 17th December 1914, the miraculous year. The day before, his own hunting-grounds, Scarborough, Whitby, were shelled by German cruisers. Two months before the London mob in a patriotic ecstasy had sacked the German shops, and every unfortunate German in the country was still trembling. Amongst them the mistress of the very house that he had chosen. On his first visit he had noticed her attitude. Little in a woman's manner ever escaped that professional eye. So automatically he had swelled in *his* manner, played the masterful. When she asked timidly for references, he did not give her an easy lie, but pulled six shillings out of his pocket and tapped them on the desk. She was afraid to refuse them; but more afraid, in such times, when every one of her actions was dangerous, to step even for an inch outside the safety of law. When he returned with the woman, this foreign woman had fortified herself with a supreme reinforcement, a real detective, friend of the family. It was this man (Dennison) who met the couple when they arrived and told Smith-Lloyd, with one of those precognitional glances of which those of his calling have the secret, to be off, and quickly.

The couple went out in silence, at hazard, when Smith had been paid his deposit. In a side-road near by, Bismark Road, they found another place, kept by Miss Blatch. His formula, for a moment checked, begins to run: 'Have you a bath?' They are accepted. Then Mrs Lloyd sits down to send the letter mentioning an illness; then they visit the nearest doctor, then the preparation of the bath, and the full canon of the slaying: with this exception, that there was a splash, a sigh, a strange visit of the man to the harmonium where he played 'something' for a few minutes. Mrs Lloyd is dead. There is again the rushing through the house, the terror of the landlady, the calls, the doctor's dash upstairs, the splashing in the bathroom, the policeman's knock on the door; evidence; a grim man who has a clear story and a bad manner, a word-for-word repetition in the coroner's court. Letters, packings, bargainings with grave-diggers, another £700 safely received.

But this time something more. A coincidence, one of those queer logical figures with which the stream of becoming sometimes playfully diversifies its course, one of life's punning rhymes, which science hates and art abhors, but which fascinate the attention of mankind. Smith, painstaking imitator of nature, who had modelled his ferocity on her accidents, had unthinkingly composed a perfect, a triple coincidence. He had been betrayed by the first law of murder: repetition. Let but one man stumble upon this coincidence of the bath, and Smith, by it alone, like an incurable poison, will die as surely and cruelly as Bessie Mundy.

That man was Charles Burnham. He noticed an account of the Highgate inquest in a Sunday newspaper, the *News of the World*, which is a collection of the happenings of the week, curious, dramatic, horrible and comic, immensely diffused among the English masses. 'Death' and 'Bride' are index-words to the tastes of the readers of this journal; their conjunction in one case gave the news a good place in the paper. Almost with greed, this quiet unhurrying man, lying in not hopeless ambush for the return of the phantom who had destroyed his daughter, caught the devilish assonance, the infernal rhyme with all the circumstances of his own loss. The description of this Highate mystery made Burnham's long-waited revenge as simple then as the pull of a trigger; he cut out the printed account, pinned it to that in his possession of his own daughter's end, and sent them both to the police.

Thereafter there are two feverish activities running side by side, one out of sight and below the other. The figure of a man grown greyish, with an intangible history, working at accounts, very intent on the business of settling his wife's affairs with solicitor, Somerset House, the Insurance Company; and below him, like hounds out of sight in a sunken road, the detectives grappling with his faint and twisted trail back into the past. All that Smith may have noticed in this fortnight is a slight clogging of his affairs, an almost imperceptible increase of the customary delays, the shadow of obscure inhibitions behind the Insurance Company's formal letters. All his senses were sharpened in the darkness in which he worked. At times, deep in his correspondence, he would pause and listen as if through their typed formalities he could hear a far-off noise of running steps. Sometimes for two days in succession he would stop on his way to the solicitor's office and turn back thoughtfully: then for long hours fight with himself to pull back to the *business standpoint*. On the 1st of February 1915, as he left the solicitor's office, he saw with a great start that three soberly-dressed men wanted to speak to him. They came round him so close that he felt their coats, and one said something about Alice Burnham. As in an accident, it was too sudden for him to have any fear. If he had heard 'Miss Mundy' he might have screamed; but the man said, 'Alice Burnham', a name that only recalled a long and nasty business affair, in which he was in the right, quite in the right, and no jury would give a verdict against him. So, without any blink he admitted that he did know her, that he was the George Smith who had married her at the Portsmouth Registry Office: what about it? He was arrested at once on a charge of causing a false entry in the marriage register. He did not need the customary caution not to say more.

England found time to try the man at the Old Bailey; for the nine days between 22nd June 1915 and the 1st July his affairs competed for public interest with the first defeats of the Russians in Galicia and the first victories of the Italians in the Dolomites. A prosy judge, a high-spirited defender (Marshall Hall), let out the regulated driblets of information allowed by English law on the surly, absent-minded mystery fenced in their midst in dock. Under the weight of contrasts, Smith's deeds seemed more terrible than the crash of armies, his tin baths more evil things than bridge-destroying artillery, this minor devil more sinister than all the hell outside.

At times he would take his own part and yell at them. The whole court would stare at him with amazement as if his chop-law was speaking with tongues, and his blind belief in his own innocence – because they could not tell him the precise method he had killed, whether by pulling the feet, or by holding the heads – a thing never heard of in experience. But to this, and other last consolations of the mass-murderer – the inanimation of his victims, all trace of whose living personalities had long been expelled from his brain: the joy in the legal bickerings, so much to his taste: the sense of consideration and elevation that the dock confers – Smith, like Burke, like Troppmann, now felt himself entire. Alone in the court he neglected to look at the iron coincidence, three women identically killed, for identical motives after marriage with the same man, and attached importance to the cunning details which that recurrence contemptuously destroyed. Alone in the court, like a rigid juryman, he refused to believe in his own guilt, because a coincidence was not evidence.

These fundamental errors of thought no doubt sustained him in the condemned cell in which, a safe for precious objects, he was carefully preserved for death by hanging. Irreality has lordly rewards for her devotees, whether solipsists or drug fiends or murderers. In her humblest, more eerie form which had rotted this mass-murderer's imagination, she stood staunch by Smith to his end; if, on the scaffold, with the ropes round his elbows and a bag over his mouth, his legs failed, it was a physical, not a moral, terror that prevailed.

WILLIAM BOLITHO
Murder for Profit
(1953), pp. 108–119

6 Sidney Fox

At morning coffee on October 29th, 1929, Vernon Wood handed to me a thin sheaf of papers which had just come from our clients, the Cornhill Insurance Company. In his rich Lancastrian accent (always richer under any emotional strain) he asked, 'What do we do with this lot, Will?'

The facts recorded in the documents were simple. Less than a week earlier, on October 23rd, a bedroom in the Hotel Metropole at Margate went on fire. An old lady, Mrs Rosaline Fox, when carried from the room was found to be dead. The chief witness at the inquest was the victim's son, Sidney, a well-mannered and handsome man of thirty. His very moving story was this. On the night of the tragedy he had left his mother reading the evening paper by her gas fire and had gone to bed in the adjoining room. Barely an hour later, at about 11.30 p.m., he was aroused by what he thought was the rattling of his window. On rising to deal with this minor nuisance he smelled burning, and opening the communicating door he found his mother's room alight. He tried to reach her, he said, but was beaten back by dense smoke. He rushed downstairs for help, and one of the guests, with a handkerchief over his mouth, crawled through the blinding smoke into the room until he came upon the legs of Mrs Fox hanging over the side of her bed. She was on her back. He succeeded in dragging her to the corridor before he lost consciousness. A doctor, C. C. Austen, was on the scene almost at once. Having examined the woman, he satisfied himself that she was dead 'as the result of suffocation from inhaling fumes and shock'. The news was broken to the son. To help him bear up, and enjoy a night's sleep, he was given a hypodermic injection of a powerful soporific.

The inquest, for the convenience of the key witnesses (commercial travellers who wished to be on their way), was held next morning, within a few hours of the death. The coroner, accepting the medical evidence (he had no cause not to) and dispensing with an autopsy, returned a verdict of 'misadventure'. If the doctor and the coroner before reaching their conclusions had seen the documents which my partner and I were now digesting they would have believed, as I did, that here was either an astounding coincidence or one of the rarest crimes known to British criminal experience – matricide. Sidney Fox, as those documents showed, had effected upon his mother's life a series of short-period insurances with the Cornhill under policies such as are often issued through travel agencies. The sum payable in the event of accidental death was to be £2,000. The first policy covered a period of fourteen days, but this had been extended on eight successive occasions. Subject only to a break of ten days the insurance had been kept in force from August 10th to October 23rd, 1929. In accordance with Cornhill routine, policies of this nature expire at noon on the last day of the cover. The first eight of the Rosaline Fox policies had so expired. The last cover (one for three days only) at Sidney Fox's specific request (and how sinister it now seemed!) had been timed to expire at midnight.

My opinion, which I have never had cause to modify, was that Fox, bent upon his crime, had kept the policies open by extensions, a few days at a time, until he could screw up courage enough to carry it out. It was no doubt in desperation that he ultimately committed the murder, for the final policy had not many minutes to run when his old mother breathed her last. By her will she left him all she had. The Margate solicitor acting for him was asking our clients for the £2,000 payable under the insurance. One does not lightly assume that a mother's sudden death points to matricide. Perhaps I was over-hasty in exclaiming across the coffee table, 'My God, this is murder!' But if the story told by the Cornhill file did not in itself justify that exclamation it did at least cry aloud for speedy investigation.

Where was I to begin? Sidney Fox had said that he and his mother were making for their newly bought home, End View, at Lyndhurst, Hampshire. A telephone call to a Lyndhurst friend told me that there was no such address. Among our staff investigators at that time were Harry Goodrich (ex-CID) and W. J. Emmens, with the innocent blue eyes and the incomparable flair for detection. They set out at once. Soon it transpired that Fox had insured his mother not only with the Cornhill but also with the Ocean Accident Corporation for an extra £1,000. The shrewd and experienced claims inspector of that company, Mr R. E. Hawkins, made a few local inquiries and, concluding that the 'water was muddy', handed his company's interests to me for attention. In cases of murder one looks for a motive. In this particular crime there was motive and to spare. More murderers than have been caught have killed for much less than £3,000 a head; and inquiries revealed that to Sidney Fox, £3,000 meant great wealth. Before the coroner he had described his mother as 'of independent means'. This statement, like most made by this man, was intended to deceive, but it was not wholly false. Mrs Fox had 'independent means' in the shape of a pension of 10s. a week granted to her for the loss of a soldier son killed in France. Although he had never been submitted to the inconvenience of service overseas, Sidney Fox himself drew a 'war' pension of 8s. per week. This joint weekly income had proved inadequate to support mother and son in the style of living to which they aspired. For weeks before the Margate adventure they had lived by bilking hotel after hotel. Inquiries made by Goodrich showed they had been victimising innkeepers six months earlier when the son, pretending to have lost his wallet, had borrowed, with sublime effrontery, from the Coventry police 10s. with which to get home and had omitted to repay it. The publicity given to Mrs Fox's death roused these various creditors to action. The luck which had produced what all murderers must hope to hear, a 'death by misadventure' verdict in the coroner's court, was turning against him. That Sidney and Rosaline Fox were little better than paupers became evident when Emmens questioned a Metropole chambermaid. Neither mother nor son had sleeping attire, neither had a toothbrush, nor any other hygienic equipment. The young man had only the suit he stood up in. The old lady had two stockinette dresses which she wore one over the other. Their luggage, according to the son, 'had all gone on'. It says much for his carefully developed 'Oxford' accent and for his remarkable histrionic talent that while reduced to this miserable state he and his mother were able to pose successfully as an affluent couple and to live comfortably on credit in one of Margate's best hotels without any show of embarrassment. Their method had been to drift, usually by 'bus, from one country town to another. Their luggage, if any, would be carried in a paper parcel. On arrival at an hostelry that attracted them the son would settle his mother comfortably in the hall and then, smiling charmingly, would ask the reception clerk to reserve two rooms. He would add in his cultured voice, 'I must just put my car away – I'll sign the register when I come back'. He would disappear for a short time to deal with his nonexistent car and would then return, his credit thus well established. He 'would not bother to bring in the bags'; their stay was to be 'only a short one'.

Sidney Fox after his mother's death had gone to Norwich. Harry Goodrich's assignment was to run him to earth there and to take from him a signed story with sufficient details to justify his claim against our clients. This written story would have been full of interest and lies. It must, I think, be the common experience (it has certainly been mine) that a crook, whether an old lag or a mere beginner, invariably esteems himself highly as a spinner of a plausible yarn. He not only tells unavoidable lies but also adds many unnecessary ones, apparently for the sheer joy of exercising his craft. As a rule it is easy to disprove the irrelevant falsities – which the crook ignorantly imagines will never be checked – and so to cast doubt upon all his other allegations. This simplicity among villains has helped me in many a difficult case but it was not to avail me with Fox.

The Margate police had, naturally enough, accepted Fox and his mother at their face value. Any doubts they might otherwise have had were lulled by the confident but faulty medical evidence on which the coroner had acted. Once suspicion was aroused, however, they moved swiftly, too swiftly to suit my own plans! In supplying the Chief Constable of Margate, Mr C. J. Haycock, with a photostat copy of our damning Cornhill and Ocean insurance files I told him I meant to get from Fox a full statement in writing. But the police realised that he had a passport and might flee. When Goodrich called at the Royal Hotel, Norwich, during the morning of November 2nd, 1929 (eight days after the inquest), he learned that Mr Fox, although still in residence there, had gone out 'to make some purchases'. He had not returned by 1.45 p.m. and since it was unthinkable that a guest at that high-class establishment should be disturbed during his luncheon hour, an appointment was made for Goodrich to return at 2.45 p.m. Mr Fox, whose apprehensions may have affected his appetite, perhaps lunched lightly, if at all, elsewhere. He went back to the Royal Hotel only to be snatched away by the Norwich police almost from under Goodrich's nose, to face charges of obtaining credit by fraud. We thus lost the chance of securing what would, I feel sure, have been a document of deep dramatic interest and one in which a superb liar would have made a supreme effort to escape the hangman's noose.

Once Fox was in custody his fingerprints were taken and he was found to have a criminal record. This showed that he had turned a strong homosexual urge to financial advantage, among men similarly afflicted, and had also practised forgery, embezzlement, plain theft and various forms of fraud. Although he had been sent to prison on four occasions, he had never been charged with any crime involving violence. The most striking characteristic of the habitual criminal is his inability to change from his regular line of crime to another of a different type. Since for that reason one does not expect an ordinary swindler to threaten life, the police would not have suspected the peaceful Sidney Fox of murder had they not become aware of a nearly successful attempt he had formerly made to gas a wealthy woman whose misguided lust for him had led her to insure her life and make a will in his favour. As soon as Fox was safely in custody Chief Constable Haycock asked for the help of Scotland Yard. Chief Inspector Walter Hambrook was put on to the case. Like most of the really good detectives with whom I have worked there was nothing about him to suggest even remotely any connection with police activities. He was on the small side, mild-mannered, quietly spoken and a lover of good literature. His overcoat pocket invariably held not the paraphernalia of his calling but a volume from the Battersea Public Library with a 'bus ticket as a bookmark. I knew him as a profoundly experienced, astute and indefatigable officer. His appearance on the scene meant that Fox's days were numbered.

The Margate undertaker who buried Mrs Fox (of course on credit; he was never paid) did his work with reverent care. The body was packed tightly in its coffin with sawdust and the lid was sealed with putty. When, therefore, an exhumation was carried out sixteen days after the death the corpse was dry and in an exceptionally favourable condition for examination by that prince of pathologists, the late Sir Bernard Spilsbury.

Sidney Fox had been held in custody on the accusations of fraud from November 4th, 1929, to January 9th, 1930. He was then charged with murder. His trial before Mr Justice Rowlatt and a jury (with only one woman member) began at Lewses Assizes on March 12th, 1930, and lasted nine days. I sat within six feet of the prisoner and watched his handsome face intently. He had, I thought, decided to play the part of a wronged young man whose outward calm should indicate the inward calm of a clear conscience. It was a difficult role and he overacted it. An innocent man facing the possibility of capital punishment naturally shows patent signs of tension and horror as the circumstantial evidence in all its gruesome detail closes upon him. Fox betrayed superficially no more emotion than the court usher. I am convinced that this air, almost of indifference, made a very bad impression on the jury. One had to be close to him, as I was, to detect the throbbing pulse at his temple and to realise that for all his studied detachment the blood was racing through his guilty heart. Once Fox had been arrested my own duties were officially limited to preparing for the police the formal but deadly insurance testimony. But unofficially I was privileged to see stage by lethal stage the case for the prosecution brought to perfection.

Mrs Fox had been easily killed. Under the steady pressure of her son's hands on her throat she died very quickly. There were no signs of external bruising. Corpses do not bruise. And Mrs Fox was a corpse before the pressure was relaxed. One hesitates to record the additional and obvious fact (so often overlooked by criminals) that neither do corpses breathe. Alive and breathing in a room on fire a body draws smoke and soot into the air passages and lungs. A dead body does not. The absence of soot in Rosaline Fox's air passages showed that she was dead before the fire was started. Moreover, a smouldering fire such as that to which she had been subjected produces the poisonous gas, carbon monoxide. The blood of anyone who has inhaled carbon monoxide undergoes a marked change of colour, which, ironically, produces the cherry-red complexion and lips of healthy youth. Spectroscopical analysis of Mrs Fox's blood showed it to be as free from carbon monoxide as her air passages were from soot. These circumstances were embarrassments for Fox, but how could he have avoided them? To collect under the accident policies he had to stage a death that looked sufficiently accidental to deceive the authorities. There had to be a fire and if he gave a thought to the possibility of an autopsy, and what it would reveal, he had to gamble on none being demanded. He would have been justified in regarding his chances in that direction as a bit better that evens for this reason: three days before the murder, with the anxiety to be expected of an affectionate and dutiful son, he had asked a doctor, recommended by the hotel staff, to examine his mother, who, he said, had fainted. The doctor who called on that occasion was cheerfully intoxicated, and on leaving his new patient had crooked a finger on either side of his forehead and said playfully, 'Bogey-bogey', by way of farewell. It was fair to assume that so blithe a practitioner would not be too exigent about the manifestly accidental death which was shortly to take place. Nor was he; for when he came to the hotel on the night of the fire and saw a fireman or a policeman (he did not afterwards recall which) applying artificial respiration he bade them 'stop that damn' nonsense' and said the woman was dead. To that extent only his diagnosis was right. He drew an unscientific conclusion from a casual glance and in waiving a post-mortem examination he came within an ace of giving Sidney Fox success.

Fox's luck, which had produced the 'death from misadventure' verdict, proved fickle. We all have in our throats just above the sound-box a circular bone called the hyoid. In aged people it is so brittle and fragile that with rare exceptions it breaks under the hands of a strangler. Sir Bernard Spilsbury found Rosaline Fox's hyoid bone intact. This was clearly one point in favour of her son and it looked as if his good luck was holding. On the other hand, Sir Bernard, whose trained and powerful eyes saw things which others could see only with the aid of a microscope, spotted a couple of bruises, one inside the old lady's windpipe and the other on her tongue. The former from Sidney Fox's point of view was bad enough: it was a sign of strangulation. But the tongue bruise meant that the victim (whose gums were toothless and smooth) had been throttled while wearing her dentures. This bruise could have been caused in no other way; and since the woman's dentures were found in the washstand basin after the fire it was an inescapable deduction that Fox had put them there after they had fallen from his murdered mother's mouth. Mr James D. Cassels, KC (as he then was), in defence of the prisoner fought valiantly and did all that could possibly be done to exploit the evidence of his expert pathologists who sought in vain to throw doubt upon that of Sir Bernard. But it was no use. The jury's verdict was a foregone conclusion. Fox was condemned to death and hanged.

* * *

It was always my belief – strange as it may seem – that Sidney Fox had a deep affection for his mother. Good-looking in her youth and middle age, she had enjoyed to the full what is commonly called a 'gay time'. Old age, failing health and abject poverty put an end to all that and left her nothing worth living for. It may well be that her son, keenly appreciating the tragedy of this decline, thought a quick death would be better for her than endurance of the miseries ahead. Having reached that conclusion he may have argued that the old lady would have wished her death to enrich him. Hence the insurances. This speculation may appear to be illogical, but when some years later I had the chance of putting the theory to the learned King's Counsels who had prosecuted and defended Fox at his trial, neither found it wholly untenable. The criminal who regards his own crimes as quite inexcusable is indeed a rarity. Even had the prosecution of Fox failed, his policies would have proved worthless. They were issued on a warranty that Rosaline Fox was in good health. She was in fact a paralytic, and only able to walk with great difficulty. Sidney Fox's own silent agreement with the jury's verdict is, I suggest, implicit in the fact that he did not appeal.

WILLIAM CHARLES CROCKER
Far from Humdrum
(1967), pp. 102–110

VII
Salvage

1 The Judea

This could have occurred nowhere but in England, where men and sea interpenetrate, so to speak – the sea entering into the life of most men, and the men knowing something or everything about the sea, in the way of amusement, of travel or of breadwinning.

We were sitting round a mahogany table that reflected the bottle, the claret-glasses, and our faces as we leaned on our elbows. There was a director of companies, an accountant, a lawyer, Marlow, and myself. The director had been a *Conway* boy, the accountant had served four years at sea, the lawyer – a fine crusted Tory, High Churchman, the best of old fellows, the soul of honour – had been chief officer in the P & O service in the good old days when mail-boats were square-rigged at least on two masts, and used to come down the China Sea before a fair monsoon with stun'-sails set alow and aloft. We all began life in the merchant service. Between the five of us there was the strong bond of the sea, and also the fellowship of the craft, which no amount of enthusiasm for yachting, cruising, and so on can give, since one is only the amusement of life and the other is life itself.

Marlow (at least, I think that is how he spelt his name) told the story, or rather the chronicle, of a voyage:

Yes, I have seen a little of the Eastern seas; but what I remember best is my first voyage there. You fellows know there are those voyages that seem ordered for the illustration of life, that might stand for a symbol of existence. You fight, work, sweat, nearly kill yourself, sometimes do kill yourself, trying to accomplish something – and you can't. Not from any fault of yours. You simply can do nothing, neither great nor little – not a thing in the world – not even marry an old maid, or get a wretched 600-ton cargo of coal to its port of destination.

It was altogether a memorable affair. It was my first voyage to the East, and my first voyage as second mate; it was also my skipper's first command. You'll admit it was time. He was sixty if a day; a little man, with a broad, not very straight back, with bowed shoulders and one leg more bandy than the other, he had the queer twisted-about appearance you see so often in men who work in the fields. He had a nut-cracker face, chin and nose trying to come together over a sunken mouth – and it was framed in iron-grey fluffy hair, that looked like a chin-strap of cotton-wool sprinkled with coal dust. And he had blue eyes in that old face of his, which were amazingly like a boy's, with that candid expression some quite common men preserve to the end of their days by a rare internal gift of simplicity of heart and rectitude of soul. What induced him to accept me was a wonder. I had come out of a crack Australian clipper, when I had been third officer, and he seemed to have a prejudice against crack clippers as aristocratic and high-toned. He said to me, 'You know, in this ship you will have to work'. I said I had to work in every ship I had ever been in. 'Ah, but this is different, and you gentlemen out of them big ships; . . . but there! I dare say you will do. Join tomorrow.'

I joined tomorrow. It was twenty-two years ago; and I was just twenty. How time passes! It was one of the happiest days of my life. Fancy! Second mate for the first time – a really responsible officer! I wouldn't have thrown up my new billet for a fortune. The mate looked me over carefully. He was an old chap, but of another stamp. He had a Roman nose, a snow-white, long beard and his name was Mahon, but he insisted that it should be pronounced Mann. He was well connected; yet there was something wrong with his luck, and he had never got on.

As to the captain, he had been for years in coasters, then in the Mediterranean, and last in the West Indian trade. He had never been round the Capes. He could just write a kind of sketchy hand, and didn't care for writing at all. Both were thorough good seamen of course, and between those two old chaps I felt like a small boy between two grandfathers.

The ship also was old. Her name was the *Judea*. Queer name, isn't it? She belonged to a man Wilmer, Willcox – some name like that; but he has been bankrupt and dead these twenty years or more, and his name don't matter. She had been laid up in Shadwell basin for ever so long. You may imagine her state. She was all rust, dust, grime – soot aloft, dirt on deck. To me it was like coming out of a palace into a ruined cottage. She was about 400 tons, had a primitive windlass, wooden latches to the doors, not a bit of brass about her, and a big square stern. There was on it, below her name in big letters, a lot of scroll-work, with the gilt off, and some sort of a coat of arms, with the motto 'Do or Die' underneath. I remember it took my fancy immensely. There was a touch of romance in it, something that made me love the old thing – something that appealed to my youth!

We left London in ballast – sand ballast – to load a cargo of coal in a northern port for Bangkok. Bangkok! I thrilled. I had been six years at sea, but had only seen Melbourne and Sydney, very good places, charming places in their way – but Bangkok!

We worked out of the Thames under canvas, with a North Sea pilot on board. His name was Jermyn, and he dodged all day long about the galley drying his handkerchief before the stove. Apparently he never slept. He was a dismal man, with a perpetual tear sparkling at the end of his nose, who either had been in trouble, or was in trouble, or expected to be in trouble – couldn't be happy unless something went wrong. He mistrusted my youth, my common-sense, and my seamanship, and made a point of showing it in a hundred little ways. I dare say he was right. It seems to me I knew very little then, and I know not much more now; but I cherish a hate for that Jermyn to this day.

We were a week working up as far as Yarmouth Roads, and then we got into a gale – the famous October gale of twenty-two years ago. It was wind, lightning, sleet, snow, and a terrific sea. We were flying light, and you may imagine how bad it was when I tell you we had smashed bulwarks and a flooded deck. On the second night she shifted her ballast into the lee bow, and by that time we had been blown off somewhere on the Dogger Bank. There was nothing for it but go below with shovels and try to right her, and there we were in that vast hold, gloomy like a cavern, the tallow dips stuck and flickering on the beams, the gale howling above, the ship tossing about like mad on her side; there we all were, Jermyn, the captain, every one, hardly able to keep our feet, engaged on that grave-digger's work, and trying to toss shovelsful of wet sand up to windward. At every tumble of the ship you could see vaguely in the dim light men falling down with a great flourish of shovels. One of the ship's boys (we had two), impressed by the weirdness of the scene, wept as if his heart would break. We could hear him blubbering somewhere in the shadows.

On the third day the gale died out, and by-and-by a north-country tug picked us up. We took sixteen days in all to get from London to the Tyne! When we got into dock we had lost our turn for loading, and they hauled us off to a tier where we remained for a month. Mrs Beard (the captain's name was Beard) came from Colchester to see the old man. She lived on board. The crew of runners had left, and there remained only the officers, one boy and the steward, a mulatto who answered to the name of Abraham. Mrs Beard was an old woman, with a face all wrinkled and ruddy like a winter apple, and the figure of a young girl. She caught sight of me once, sewing on a button, and insisted on having my shirts to repair. This was something different from the captains' wives I had known on board crack clippers. When I brought her the shirts, she said: 'And the socks? They want mending, I am sure, and John's – Captain Beard's – things are all in order now. I would be glad of something to do.' Bless the old woman. She overhauled my outfit for me, and meantime I read for the first time *Sartor Resartus* and Burnaby's *Ride to Khiva*. I didn't understand much of the first then; but I remember I preferred the soldier to the philosopher at the time; a preference which life has only confirmed. One was a man, and the other was either more – or less. However, they are both dead and Mrs Beard is dead, and youth, strength, genius, thoughts, achievements, simple hearts – all die. . . . No matter.

They loaded us at last. We shipped a crew. Eight able seamen and two boys. We hauled off one evening to the buoys at the dock-gates, ready to go out, and with a fair prospect of beginning the voyage next day. Mrs Beard was to start for home by a late train. When the ship was fast we went to tea. We sat rather silent through the meal – Mahon, the old couple, and I. I finished first, and slipped away for a smoke, my cabin being in a deck-house just against the poop. It was high water, blowing fresh with a drizzle; the double dock-gates were opened, and the steam-colliers were going in and out in the darkness with their lights burning bright, a great plashing of propellers, rattling of winches, and a lot of hailing on the pier-heads. I watched the procession of head-lights gliding high and of green lights gliding low in the night, when suddenly a red gleam flashed at me, vanished, came into view again, and remained. The fore-end of a steamer loomed up close. I shouted down the cabin, 'Come up, quick!' and then heard a startled voice saying afar in the dark, 'Stop her, sir.' A bell jingled. Another voice cried warningly, 'We are going right into that barque, sir'. The answer to this was a gruff 'All right', and the next thing was a heavy crash as the steamer struck a glancing blow with the bluff of her bow about our fore-rigging. There was a moment of confusion, yelling, and running about. Steam roared. Then somebody was heard saying, 'All clear, sir' . . . 'Are you all right?' asked the gruff voice. I had jumped forward to see the damage, and hailed back, 'I think so'. 'Easy astern', said the gruff voice. A bell jingled. 'What steamer is that?' screamed Mahon. By that time she was no more to us than a bulky shadow manoeuvring a little way off. They shouted at us some name – a woman's name, Miranda or Melissa – or some such thing. 'This means another month in this beastly hole', said Mahon to me, as we peered with lamps about the splintered bulwarks and broken braces. 'But where's the captain?'

We had not seen anything of him all that time. We went aft to look. A doleful voice arose hailing somewhere in the middle of the dock, '*Judea* ahoy!' How the devil did he get there? 'Hallo!' we shouted. 'I am adrift in our boat without oars', he cried. A belated water-man offered his services, and Mahon struck a bargain with him for half-a-crown to tow our skipper alongside; but it was Mrs Beard that came up the ladder first. They had been floating about the dock in that mizzly cold rain for nearly an hour. I was never so surprised in my life.

It appears that when he heard my shout 'Come up' he understood at once what was the matter, caught up his wife, ran on deck, and across, and down into our boat, which was fast to the ladder. Not bad for a sixty-year-old. Just imagine that old fellow saving heroically in his arms that old woman – the woman of his life. He set her down on a thwart, and was ready to climb back on board when the painter came adrift somehow, and away they went together. Of course in the confusion we did not hear him shouting. He looked abashed. She said cheerfully, 'I suppose it does not matter my losing the train now?' – 'No, Jenny – you go below and get warm', he growled. Then to us: 'A sailor has not business with a wife – I say. There I was, out of the ship. Well, no harm done this time. Let's go and look at what that fool of a steamer smashed.'

It wasn't much, but it delayed us three weeks. At the end of that time, the captain being engaged with his agents, I carried Mrs Beard's bag to the railway station and put her all comfy into a third-class carriage. She lowered the window to say, 'You are a good young man. If you see John – Captain Beard – without his muffler at night, just remind him from me to keep his throat well wrapped up.' 'Certainly, Mrs Beard', I said. 'You are a good young man; I noticed how attentive you are to John – to Captain——' The train pulled out suddenly; I took my cap off to the old woman: I never saw her again. . . . Pass the bottle.

We went to sea next day. When we made that start for Bangkok we had been already three months out of London. We had expected to be a fortnight or so – at the outside.

It was January, and the weather was beautiful – the beautiful sunny winter weather that has more charm than in the summertime, because it is unexpected, and crisp, and you know it won't, it can't, last long. It's like a windfall, like a godsend, like an unexpected piece of luck.

It lasted all down the North Sea, all down Channel; and it lasted till we were three hundred miles or so to the westward of the Lizards: then the wind went round to the sou'-west and began to pipe up. In two days it blew a gale. The *Judea* hove to, wallowed on the Atlantic like an old candle-box. It blew day after day: it blew with spite, without interval, without mercy, without rest. The world was nothing but an immensity of great foaming waves rushing at us, under a sky low enough to touch with the hand and dirty like a smoked ceiling. In the stormy space surrounding us there was as much flying spray as air. Day after day and night after night there was nothing round the ship but the howl of the wind, the tumult of the sea, the noise of water pouring over her deck. There was no rest for her and no rest for us. She tossed, she pitched, she stood on her head, she sat on her tail, she rolled, she groaned, and we had to hold on while on deck and cling to our bunks when below, in a constant effort of body and worry of mind.

One night Mahon spoke through the small window of my berth. It opened right into my very bed, and I was lying there sleepless, in my boots, feeling as though I had not slept for years, and could not if I tried. He said excitedly:

'You got the sounding-rod in here, Marlow? I can't get the pumps to suck. By God! it's no child's play.'

I gave him the sounding-rod and lay down again, trying to think of various things – but I thought only of the pumps. When I came on deck they were still at it, and my watch relieved at the pumps. By the light of the lantern brought on deck to examine the sounding-rod I caught a glimpse of their weary, serious faces. We pumped all the four hours. We pumped all night, all day, all the week – watch and watch. She was working herself loose, and leaked badly – not enough to drown us at once, but enough to kill us with the work at the pumps. And while we pumped the ship was going from us piecemeal: the bulwarks went, the stanchions were torn out, the ventilators smashed, the cabin-door burst in. There was not a dry spot in the ship. She was being gutted bit by bit. The long-boat changed, as if by magic, into matchwood where she stood in her gripes. I had lashed her myself, and was rather proud of my handiwork, which had withstood so long the malice of the sea. And we pumped. And there was no break in the weather. The sea was white like a sheet of foam, like a caldron of boiling milk; there was not a break in the clouds, no – not the size of a man's hand – no, not for so much as ten seconds. There was for us no sky, there were for us no stars, no sun, no universe –

nothing but angry clouds and an infuriated sea. We pumped watch and watch, for dear life; and it seemed to last for months, for years, for all eternity, as though we had been dead and gone to a hell for sailors. We forgot the day of the week, the name of the month, what year it was, and whether we had ever been ashore. The sails blew away, she lay broadside on under a weather-cloth, the ocean poured over her, and we did not care. We turned those handles and had the eyes of idiots. As soon as we had crawled on deck I used to take a round turn with a rope about the men, the pumps, and the mainmast and we turned, we turned incessantly, with the water to our waists, to our necks, over our heads. It was all one. We had forgotten how it felt to be dry.

And there was somewhere in me the thought: By Jove! this is the deuce of an adventure – something you read about; and it is my first voyage as second mate – and I am only twenty – and here I am lasting it out as well as any of these men, and keeping my chaps up to the mark. I was pleased. I would not have given up the experience for worlds. I had moments of exultation. Whenever the old dismantled craft pitched heavily with her counter high in the air, she seemed to me to throw up, like an appeal, like a defiance, like a cry to the clouds without mercy, the words written on her stern: *Judea*, London. Do or die.

'O youth! The strength of it, the faith of it, the imagination of it! To me she was not an old rattle-trap carting about the world a lot of coal for a freight – to me she was the endeavour, the test, the trial of life. I think of her with pleasure, with affection, with regret – as you would think of someone dead you have loved. I shall never forget her . . . Pass the bottle.

One night when tied to the mast, as I explained, we were pumping on, deafened with the wind, and without spirit enough in us to wish ourselves dead, a heavy sea crashed aboard and swept clean over us. As soon as I got my breath I shouted, as in duty bound, 'Keep on, boys!' when suddenly I felt something hard floating on deck strike the calf of my leg. I made a grab at it and missed. It was so dark we could not see one another's faces within a foot – you understand.

After that thump the ship kept quiet for a while, and the thing, whatever it was, struck my leg again. This time I caught it – and it was a saucepan. At first being stupid with fatigue and thinking of nothing but the pumps, I did not understand what I had in my hand. Suddenly it dawned upon me, and I shouted, 'Boys, the house on deck is gone. Leave this, and let's look for the cook.'

There was a deck-house forward, which contained the galley, the cook's berth, and the quarters of the crew. As we had expected for days to see it swept away, the hands had been ordered to sleep in the cabin – the only safe place in the ship. The steward, Abraham, however, persisted in clinging to his berth, stupidly, like a mule – from sheer fright, I believe, like an animal that won't leave a stable falling in an earthquake. So we went to look for him. It was chancing death, since once out of our lashings we were as exposed as if on a raft. But we went. The house was shattered as if a shell had exploded inside. Most of it had gone overboard – stove, men's quarters, and their property, all was gone; but two posts, holding a portion of the bulkhead to which Abraham's bunk was attached, remained as if by a miracle. We groped in the ruins and came upon this, and there he was, sitting in his bunk, surrounded by foam and wreckage, jabbering cheerfully to himself. He was out of his mind; completely and for ever mad, with this sudden shock coming upon the fag-end of his endurance. We snatched him up, lugged him aft, and pitched him head-first down the cabin companion. You understand there was no time to carry him down with infinite precautions and wait to see how he got on. Those below would pick him up at the bottom of the stairs all right. We were in a hurry to go back to the pumps. That business could not wait. A bad leak is an inhuman thing.

One would think that the sole purpose of that fiendish gale had been to make a lunatic of that poor devil of a mulatto. It eased before morning, and the next day the sky cleared, and as the sea went down the leak took up. When it came to bending a fresh set of sails the crew demanded to put back – and really there was nothing else to do. Boats gone, decks swept clean, cabin gutted, men without a stitch but what they stood in, stores spoiled, ship strained. We put her head for home, and – would you believe it? The wind came east right in our teeth. It blew fresh, it blew continuously. We had to beat up every inch of the way, but she did not leak so badly, the water keeping comparatively smooth. Two hours' pumping in every four is no joke – but it kept her afloat as far as Falmouth.

The good people there live on casualties of the sea, and no doubt were glad to see us. A hungry crowd of shipwrights sharpened their chisels at the sight of that carcass of a ship. And, by Jove! they had pretty pickings off us before they were done. I fancy the owner was already in a tight place. There were delays. Then it was decided to take part of the cargo out and caulk her topsides. This was done, the repairs finished, cargo reshipped; a new crew came on board, and we went out – for Bangkok. At the end of a week we were back again. The crew said they weren't going to Bangkok – a hundred and fifty days' passage – in a something hooker that wanted pumping eight hours out of the twenty-four; and the nautical papers inserted again the little paragraph: '*Judea.* Barque, Tyne to Bangkok; coals; put back to Falmouth leaky and with crew refusing duty.'

There were more delays – more tinkering. The owner came down for a day, and said she was as right as a little fiddle. Poor old Captain Beard looked like the ghost of a Geordie skipper – through the worry and humiliation of it. Remember he was sixty and it was his first command. Mahon said it was a foolish business, and would end badly. I loved the ship more than ever, and wanted awfully to get to Bangkok. To Bangkok! Magic name, blessed name. Mesopotamia wasn't a patch on it. Remember I was twenty, and it was my first second-mate's billet, and the East was waiting for me.

We went out and anchored in the outer roads with a fresh crew – the third. She leaked worse than ever. It was as if those confounded shipwrights had actually made a hole in her. This time we did not even go outside. The crew simply refused to man the windlass.

They towed us back to the inner harbour, and we became a fixture, a feature, an institution of the place. People pointed us out to visitors as 'That 'ere barque that's going to Bangkok – has been here six months – put back three times.' On holidays the small boys pulling about in boats would hail, '*Judea*, ahoy!' and if a head showed above the rail shouted, 'Where are you bound to? – Bangkok?' and jeered. We were only three on board. The poor old skipper mooned in the cabin. Mahon undertook the cooking, and unexpectedly developed all a Frenchman's genius for preparing nice little messes. I looked languidly after the rigging. We became citizens of Falmouth. Every shopkeeper knew us. At the barber's or tobacconist's they asked familiarly, 'Do you think you will ever get to Bangkok?' Meantime the owner, the underwriters, and the charterers squabbled amongst themselves in London, and our pay went on . . . Pass the bottle.

It was horrid. Morally it was worse than pumping for life. It seemed as though we had been forgotten by the world, belonged to nobody, would get nowhere; it seemed that, as if bewitched, we would have to live for ever and ever in that inner harbour, a derision and a byword to generations of longshore loafers and dishonest boatmen. I obtained three months' pay and a five days' leave, and made a rush for London. It took me a day to get there and pretty well another to come back – but three months' pay went all the same. I don't know what I did with it. I went to a music-hall, I believe, lunched, dined, and supped in a swell place in Regent Street, and was back to time, with nothing but a complete set of Byron's works. The boatman who pulled me off to the ship said: 'Hallo! I thought you had left the old thing. *She* will never get to Bangkok'. 'That's all *you* know about it', I said scornfully – but I didn't like that prophecy at all.

Suddenly a man, some kind of agent to somebody, appeared with full powers. He had grog-blossoms all over his face, an indomitable energy, and was a jolly soul. We leaped into life again. A hulk came alongside, took our cargo, and then we went into dry dock to get our copper stripped. No wonder she leaked. The poor thing, strained beyond endurance by the gale, had, as if in disgust, spat out all the oakum of her lower seams. She was recaulked, new coppered, and made as tight as a bottle. We went back to the hulk and reshipped our cargo.

Then on a fine moonlight night, all the rats left the ship.

We had been infested with them. They had destroyed our sails, consumed more stores than the crew, affably shared our beds and our dangers, and now, when the ship was made seaworthy, concluded to clear out. I called Mahon to enjoy the spectacle. Rat after rat appeared on our rail, took a last look over his shoulder, and leaped with a hollow thud into the empty hulk. We tried to count them, but soon lost the tale. Mahon said: 'Well, well! don't talk to me about the intelligence of rats. They ought to have left before, when we had that narrow squeak from foundering. There you have the proof how silly is the superstition about them. They leave a good ship for an old rotten hulk, where there is nothing to eat, too, the fools! . . . I don't believe they know what is safe or what is good for them, any more than you or I.'

And after some more talk we agreed that the wisdom of rats had been grossly overrated, being in fact no greater than that of men.

The story of the ship was known, by this, all up the Channel from Land's End to the Forelands, and we could get no crew on the south coast. They sent us one all complete from Liverpool, and we left once more – for Bangkok.

We had fair breezes, smooth water right into the tropics, and the old *Judea* lumbered along in the sunshine. When she went eight knots everything cracked aloft, and we tied our caps to our heads; but mostly she strolled on at the rate of three miles an hour. What could you expect? She was tired – that old ship. Her youth was where mine is – where yours is – you fellows who listen to this yarn; and what friend would throw your years and your weariness in your face? We didn't grumble at her. To us aft, at least, it seemed as though we had been born in her, reared in her, and lived in her for ages, had never known any other ship. I would just as soon have abused the old village church at home for not being a cathedral.

And for me there was also my youth to make me patient. There was all the East before me, and all life, and the thought that I had been tried in that ship and had come out pretty well. And I thought of men of old who, centuries ago, went that road in ships that sailed no better, to the land of palms, and spices, and yellow sands, and of brown nations ruled by kings more cruel than Nero the Roman, and more splendid than Solomon the Jew. The old bark lumbered on, heavy with her age and the burden of her cargo, while I lived the life of youth in ignorance and hope. She lumbered on through an interminable procession of days; and the fresh gilding flashed back at the setting sun, seemed to cry out over the darkening sea the words painted on her stern, '*Judea*. London. Do or Die'.

Then we entered the Indian Ocean and steered northerly for Java Head. The winds were light. Weeks slipped by. She crawled on, do or die, and people at home began to think of posting us as overdue.

One Saturday evening, I being off duty, the men asked me to give them an extra bucket of water or so – for washing clothes. As I did not wish to screw on the fresh-water pump so late, I went forward whistling, and with a key in my hand to unlock the forepeak scuttle, intending to serve the water out of a spare tank we kept there.

The smell down below was as unexpected as it was frightful. One would have thought hundreds of paraffin lamps had been flaring and smoking in that hole for days. I was glad to get out. The man with me coughed and said, 'Funny smell, sir'. I answered negligently, 'It's good for the health; they say', and walked aft.

The first thing I did was to put my head down the square of the midship ventilator. As I lifted the lid a visible breath, something like a thin fog, a puff of faint haze, rose from the opening. The ascending air was hot, and had a heavy sooty, paraffiny smell. I gave one sniff, and put down the lid gently. It was no use choking myself. The cargo was on fire.

Next day she began to smoke in earnest. You see it was to be expected, for though the coal was of a safe kind, that cargo had been so handled, so broken up with handling, that it looked more like smithy coal than anything else. Then it had been wetted – more than once. It rained all the time we were taking it back from the hulk, and now with this long passage it got heated, and there was another case of spontaneous combustion.

The captain called us into the cabin. He had a chart spread on the table, and looked unhappy. He said, 'The coast of West Australia is near, but I mean to proceed to our destination. It is the hurricane month, too; but we will just keep her head for Bangkok, and fight the fire. No more putting back anywhere, if we all get roasted. We will try first to stifle this 'ere damned combustion by want of air.'

We tried. We battened down everything, and still she smoked. The smoke kept coming out through imperceptible crevices; it forced itself through bulkheads and covers; it oozed here and there and everywhere in slender threads, in an invisible film, in an incomprehensible manner. It made its way into the cabin, into the forecastle; it poisoned the sheltered places on the deck, it could be sniffed as high as the mainyard. It was clear that if the smoke came out the air came in. This was disheartening. This combustion refused to be stifled.

We resolved to try water, and took the hatches off. Enormous volumes of smoke, whitish, yellowish, thick, greasy, misty, choking, ascended as high as the trucks. All hands cleared out aft. Then the poisonous cloud blew away, and we went back to work in a smoke that was no thicker now than that of an ordinary factory chimney.

We rigged the force-pump, got the hose along, and by-and-by it burst. Well, it was as old as the ship – a prehistoric hose, and past repair. Then we pumped with the feeble head-pump, drew water with buckets, and in this way managed in time to pour lots of Indian Ocean into the main hatch. The bright stream flashed in sunshine, fell into a layer of white crawling smoke, and vanished on the black surface of coal. Steam ascended mingling with the smoke. We poured salt water as into a barrel without a bottom. It was our fate to pump in that ship, to pump out of her, to pump into her; and after keeping water out of her to save ourselves from being drowned, we frantically poured water into her to save ourselves from being burnt.

And she crawled on, do or die, in the serene weather. The sky was a miracle of purity, a miracle of azure. The sea was polished, was blue, was pellucid, was sparkling like a precious stone, extending on all sides, all round to the horizon – as if the whole terrestrial globe had been one jewel, one colossal sapphire, a single gem fashioned into a planet. And on the lustre of the great calm waters the *Judea* glided imperceptibly, enveloped in languid and unclean vapours, in a lazy cloud that drifted to leeward, light and slow; a pestiferous cloud defiling the splendour of sea and sky.

All this time of course we saw no fire. The cargo smouldered at the bottom somewhere. Once Mahon, as we were working side by side, said to me with a queer smile: 'Now, if she only would spring a tidy leak – like that time when we first left the Channel – it would put a stopper on this fire. Wouldn't it?' I remarked irrelevantly, 'Do you remember the rats?'

We fought the fire, and sailed the ship as carefully as though nothing had been the matter. The steward cooked and attended on us. Of the other twelve men, eight worked while four rested. Everyone took his turn, captain included. There was equality, and if not exactly fraternity, then a deal of good feeling. Sometimes a man, as he dashed a bucketful of water down the hatchway, would yell out, 'Hurrah for Bangkok!' and the rest laughed. But generally we were taciturn and serious – and thirsty. Oh! how thirsty! And we had to be careful with the water. Strict allowance. The ship smoked, the sun blazed . . . Pass the bottle.

We tried everything. We even made an attempt to dig down to the fire. No good, of course. No man would remain more than a minute below. Mahon, who went first, fainted there, and the man who went to fetch him out did likewise. We lugged them out on deck. The I leaped down to show how easily it could be done. They had learned wisdom by that time, and contented themselves by fishing for me with a chain-hook tied to a broom-handle, I believe. I did not offer to go and fetch up my shovel, which was left down below.

Things began to look bad. We put the long-boat into the water. The second boat was ready to swing out. We had also another, a 14-foot thing, on davits aft, where it was quite safe.

Then, behold, the smoke suddenly decreased. We redoubled our efforts to flood the bottom of the ship. In two days there was no smoke at all. Everybody was on the broad grin. This was on a Friday. On Saturday no work, but sailing the ship of course, was done. The men washed their clothes and their faces for the first time in a fortnight, and had a special dinner given them. They spoke of spontaneous combustion with contempt, and implied *they* were the boys to put out combustions. Somehow we all felt as though we each had inherited a large fortune. But a beastly smell of burning hung about the ship. Captain Beard had hollow eyes and sunken cheeks. I had never noticed so much before how twisted and bowed he was. He and Mahon prowled soberly about hatches and ventilators, sniffing. It struck me suddenly poor Mahon was a very, very old chap. As to me, I was as pleased and proud as though I had helped to win a great naval battle. O! Youth!

The night was fine. In the morning a homeward-bound ship passed us hull down – the first we had seen for months; but we were nearing the land at last, Java Head being about 190 miles off, and nearly due north.

Next day it was my watch on deck from eight to twelve. At breakfast the captain observed, 'It's wonderful how that smell hangs about the cabin'. About ten, the mate being on the poop, I stepped down on the main-deck for a moment. The carpenter's bench stood abaft the mainmast: I leaned against it sucking at my pipe, and the carpenter, a young chap, came to talk to me. He remarked, 'I think we have done very well haven't we?' and then I perceived with annoyance the fool was trying to tilt the bench. I said curtly, 'Don't Chips,' and immediately became aware of a queer sensation of an absurd delusion – I seemed somehow to be in the air. I heard all round me like a pent-up breath released – as if a thousand giants simultaneously had said Phoo! – and felt a dull concussion which made by ribs ache suddenly. No doubt about it – I was in the air, and my body was describing a short parabola. But short as it was, I had the time to think several thoughts in, as far as I can remember, the following order: 'This can't be the carpenter – What is it? – Some accident – Submarine volcano? – Coals, gas! – By Jove! we are being blown up – Everybody's dead – I am falling into the afterhatch – I see fire in it.'

The coal-dust suspended in the air of the hold had glowed dull-red at the moment of the explosion. In the twinkling of an eye, in an infinitesimal fraction of a second since the first tilt of the bench, I was sprawling full length on the cargo. I picked myself up and scrambled out. It was quick like a rebound. The deck was a wilderness of smashed timber, lying crosswise like trees in a wood after a hurricane; an immense curtain of solid rags waved gently before me – it was the mainsail blown to strips. I thought: The masts will be toppling over directly; and to get out of the way bolted on all-fours towards the poop-ladder. The first person I saw was Mahon, with eyes like saucers, his mouth open, and the long white hair standing straight on end round his head like a silver halo. He was just about to go down when the sight of the main-deck stirring, heaving up, and changing into splinters before his eyes, petrified him on the top step. I stared at him in unbelief, and he stared at me with a queer kind of shocked curiosity. I did not know that I had no hair, no eyebrows, no eyelashes, that my young moustache was burnt off, that my face was black, one cheek laid open, my nose cut, and my chin bleeding. I had lost my cap, one of my slippers, and my shirt was torn to rags. Of all this I was not aware. I was amazed to see the ship still afloat, the poop-deck whole – and, most of all to see anybody alive. Also the peace of the sky and the serenity of the sea were distinctly surprising. I suppose I expected to see them convulsed with horror . . . Pass the bottle.

There was a voice hailing the ship from somewhere – in the air, in the sky – I couldn't tell. Presently I saw the captain – and he was mad. He asked me eagerly, 'Where's the cabin-table?' and to hear such a question was a frightful shock. I had just been blown up, you understand, and vibrated with that experience – I wasn't quite sure whether I was alive. Mahon began to stamp with both feet and yelled at him, 'God God! don't you see the deck's blown out of her?' I found my voice, and stammered out as if conscious of some gross neglect of duty, 'I don't know where the cabin-table is'. It was like an absurd dream.

Do you know what he wanted next? Well, he wanted to trim the yards. Very placidly, and as if lost in thought, he insisted on having the foreyard squared. 'I don't know if there's anybody alive', said Mahon, almost tearfully. 'Surely', he said, gently, 'there will be enough left to square the foreyard.'

The old chap, it seems, was in his own berth winding up the chronometers, when the shock sent him spinning. Immediately it occurred to him – as he said afterwards – that the ship had struck something, and ran out into the cabin. There, he saw, the cabin-table had vanished somewhere. The deck being blown up it had fallen down into the lazerette of course. Where we had our breakfast that morning he saw only a great hole in the floor. This appeared to him so awfully mysterious, and impressed him so immensely, that what he saw and heard after he got on deck were mere trifles in comparison. And, mark, he noticed directly the wheel deserted and this barque off her course – and his only thought was to get that miserable, stripped, undecked, smouldering shell of a ship back again with her head pointing at her port of destination. Bangkok! That's what he was after. I tell you this quiet, bowed, bandy-legged, almost deformed little man was immense in the singleness of his idea and in his placid ignorance of our agitation. He motioned us forward with a commanding gesture, and went to take the wheel himself.

Yes, that was the first thing we did – trim the yards of that wreck! No one was killed, or even disabled, but everyone was more or less hurt. You should have seen them! Some were in rags; with black faces, like coal-heavers, like sweeps, and had bullet heads that seemed closely cropped, but were in fact singed to the skin. Others, of the watch below, awakened by being shot out from their collapsing bunks, shivered incessantly, and kept on groaning even as went about our work. But they all worked. That crew of Liverpool hard cases had in them the right stuff. It's my experience they always have. It is the sea that gives it – the vastness, the loneliness surrounding their dark stolid souls. Ah! Well! we stumbled, we crept, we fell, we barked our shins on the wreckage, we hauled. The masts stood, but we did not know how much they might be charred down below. It was nearly calm, but a long swell ran from the west and made her roll. They might go at any moment. We looked at them with apprehension. One could not foresee which way they would fall.

Then we retreated aft and looked about us. The deck was a tangle of planks on edge, of planks on end, of splinters, of ruined woodwork. The masts rose from that chaos like big trees above a matted undergrowth. The interstices of that mass of wreckage were full of something whitish, sluggish, stirring – of something that was like a greasy fog. The smoke of the invisible fire was coming up again, was trailing, like a poisonous thick mist in some valley choked with dead wood. Already lazy wisps were beginning to curl upwards amongst the mass of splinters. Here and there a piece of timber, stuck upright, resembled a post. Half of a fife-rail had been shot through the foresail, and the sky made a patch of glorious blue in the ignobly soiled canvas. A portion of several boards holding together had fallen across the rail, and one end protruded overboard, like a gangway leading over the deep sea, leading to death – as if inviting us to walk the plank at once and be done with our ridiculous troubles. And still the air, the sky – a ghost, something invisible was hailing the ship.

Someone had the sense to look over, and there was the helmsman, who had impulsively jumped overboard, anxious to come back. He yelled and swam lustily like a merman, keeping up with the ship. We threw him a rope, and presently he stood amongst us streaming with water and very crestfallen. The captain had surrendered the wheel, and apart, elbow on rail and chin in hand, gazed at the sea wistfully. We asked ourselves, What next? I thought, Now, this is something like. This is great. I wonder what will happen. O youth!

Suddenly Mahon sighted a steamer far astern. Captain Beard said, 'We may do something with her yet'. We hoisted two flags, which said in the international language of the sea, 'On fire. Want immediate assistance.' The steamer grew bigger rapidly, and by-and-by spoke with two flags on her foremast, 'I am coming to your assistance'.

In half an hour she was abreast, to windward, within hail, and rolling slightly with her engines stopped. We lost our composure, and yelled all together with excitement, 'We've been blown up'. A man in a white helmet, on the bridge, cried, 'Yes! All right! all right!' and he nodded his head, and smiled, and made soothing motions with his hand as though at a lot of frightened children. One of the boats dropped in the water, and walked towards us upon the sea with her long oars. Four Calashes pulled a swinging stroke. This was my first sight of Malay seamen. I've known them since, but what struck me then was their unconcern: they came alongside, and even the bowman standing up and holding to our main-chains with the boat-hook did not deign to lift his head for a glance. I thought people who had been blown up deserved more attention.

A little man, dry like a chip and agile like a monkey, clambered up. It was the mate of the steamer. He gave one look, and cried, 'O boys – you had better quit'.

We were silent. He talked apart with the captain for a time – seemed to argue with him. Then they went away together to the steamer.

When our skipper came back we learned that the steamer was the *Somerville*, Captain Nash, from West Australia to Singapore *via* Batavia with mails, and that the agreement was she should tow us to Anjer or Batavia, if possible, where we could extinguish the fire by scuttling, and then proceed on our voyage – to Bangkok! The old man seemed excited. 'We will do it yet', he said to Mahon, fiercely. He shook his fist at the sky. Nobody else said a word.

At noon the steamer began to tow. She went ahead slim and high, and what was left of the *Judea* followed at the end of seventy fathom of tow-rope – followed her swiftly like a cloud of smoke with mast-heads protruding above. We went aloft to furl the sails. We coughed on the yards, and were careful about the bunts. Do you see the lot of us there, putting a neat furl on the sails of that ship doomed to arrive nowhere? There was not a man who didn't think that at any moment the masts would topple over. From aloft we could not see the ship for smoke, and they worked carefully, passing the gaskets with even turns. 'Harbour furl – aloft there!' cried Mahon from below.

You understand this? I don't think one of those chaps expected to get down in the usual way. When we did I heard them saying to each other, 'Well, I thought we would come down overboard, in a lump – sticks and all – blame me if I didn't' 'That's what I was thinking to myself', would answer wearily another battered and bandaged scarecrow. And, mind, these were men without the drilled-in habit of obedience. To an onlooker they would be a lot of profane scallywags without a redeeming point. What made them do it – what made them obey me when I, thinking consciously how fine it was, made them drop the bunt of the foresail twice to try and do it better? What? They had no professional reputation – no examples, no praise. It wasn't a sense of duty; they all knew well enough how to shirk, and laze, and dodge – when they had a mind to it – and mostly they had. Was it the two pounds ten a-month that sent them there? They didn't think their pay half good enough. No; it was something in them, something inborn and subtle and everlasting. I don't say positively that the crew of a French or German merchantman wouldn't have done it, but I doubt whether it would have been done in the same way. There was a completeness in it, something solid like a principle, and masterful like an instinct – a disclosure of something secret – of that hidden something, that gift of good or evil that makes racial difference, that shapes the fate of nations.

It was that night at ten, for the first time since we had been fighting it, we saw the fire. The speed of the towing had fanned the smouldering destruction. A blue gleam appeared forward, shining below the wreck of the deck. It wavered in patches, it seemed to stir and creep like the light of a glowworm. I saw it first, and told Mahon. 'Then the game's up', he said. 'We had better stop this towing, or she will burst out suddenly fore and aft before we can clear out.' We set up a yell; rang bells to attract their attention; they towed on. At last Mahon and I had to crawl forward and cut the rope with an axe. There was no time to cast off the lashings. Red tongues could be seen licking the wilderness of splinters under our feet as we made our way back to the poop.

Of course they very soon found out in the steamer that the rope was gone. She gave a loud blast of her whistle, her lights were seen sweeping in a wide circle, she came up ranging close alongside, and stopped. We were all in a tight group on the poop looking at her. Every man had saved a little bundle or bag. Suddenly a conical flame with a twisted top shot up forward and threw upon the black sea a circle of light, with the two vessels side by side and heaving gently in its centre. Captain Beard had been sitting on the grating still and mute for hours, but now he rose slowly and advanced in front of us, to the mizzen-shrouds. Captain Nash hailed: 'Come along! Look sharp. I have mail-bags on board, I will take you and your boats to Singapore.'

'Thank you! No!' said our skipper. 'We must see the last of the ship.'

'I can't stand by any longer', shouted the other. 'Mails – you know.'

'Ay! ay! We are all right.'

'Very well! I'll report you in Singapore . . . Goodbye!'

He waved his hand. Our men dropped their bundles quietly. The steamer moved ahead, and passing out of the circle of light, vanished at once from our sight, dazzled by the fire which burned freely. And then I knew that I would see the East first as commander of a small boat. I thought it fine; and the fidelity to the old ship was fine. We should see the last of her. Oh, the glamour of youth! Oh, the fire of it, more dazzling than the flames of the burning ship, throwing a magic light on the wide earth, leaping audaciously to the sky, presently to be quenched by time, more cruel, more pitiless, more bitter than the sea – and like the flames of the burning ship surrounded by an impenetrable night.

The old man warned us in his gentle and inflexible way that it was part of our duty to save for the underwriters as much as we could of the ship's gear. Accordingly we went to work aft, while she blazed forward to give us plenty of light. We lugged out a lot of rubbish. What didn't we save? An old barometer fixed with an absurd quantity of screws nearly cost me my life: a sudden rush of smoke came upon me, and I just got away in time. There were various stores, bolts of canvas, coils of rope; the poop looked like a maritime bazaar, and the boats were lumbered to the gunwales. One would have thought the old man wanted to take as much as he could of his first command with him. He was very very quiet, but off his balance evidently. Would you believe it? He wanted to take a length of old stream-cable and a kedge-anchor with him in the long-boat. We said 'Ay, ay, sir,' deferentially, and on the quiet let the things slip overboard. The heavy medicine-chest went that way, two bags of green coffee, tins of paint – fancy, paint! – a whole lot of things. Then I was ordered with two hands into the boats to make a stowage and gave them ready against the time it would be proper for us to leave the ship.

We put everything straight, stepped the long-boat's mast for our skipper, who was to take charge of her, and I was not sorry to sit down for a moment. My face felt raw, every limb ached as if broken, I was aware of all my ribs, and would have sworn to a twist in the backbone. The boats, fast astern, lay in a deep shadow, and all around I could see the circle of the sea lighted by the fire. A gigantic flame arose forward straight and clear. It flared fierce, with noises like the whirr of wings, with rumbles as of thunder. There were cracks, detonations, and from the cone of flame the sparks flew upwards, as man is born to trouble, to leaky ships, and to ships that burn.

What bothered me was that the ship, lying broadside to the swell and to such wind as there was – a mere breath – the boats would not keep astern where they were safe, but persisted, in a pig-headed way boats have, in getting under the counter and then swinging alongside. They were knocking about dangerously and coming near the flame, while the ship rolled on them, and, of course, there was always the danger of the masts going over the side at any moment. I and my two boat-keepers kept them off as best we could, with oars and boathooks; but to be constantly at it became exasperating, since there was no reason why we should not leave at once. We could not see those on board, nor could we imagine what caused the delay. The boat-keepers were swearing feebly, and I had not only my share of the work but also had to keep at it two men who showed a constant inclination to lay themselves down and let things slide.

At last I hailed, 'On deck there', and someone looked over. 'We're ready here', I said. The head disappeared, and very soon popped up again 'The captain says, All right, sir, and to keep the boats well clear of the ship.'

Half an hour passed. Suddenly there was a frightful racket, rattle, clanking of chain, hiss of water, and millions of sparks flew up into the shivering column of smoke that stood leaning slightly over the ship. The cat-heads had burned away, and the two red-hot anchors had gone to the bottom, tearing out after them two hundred fathom of red-hot chain. The ship trembled, the mass of flame swayed as if ready to collapse, and the fore top-gallant-mast fell. It darted down like an arrow of fire, shot under, and instantly leaping up within an oar's length of the boats, floated quietly, very black on the luminous sea. I hailed the deck again. After some time a man in an unexpectedly cheerful but also muffled tone, as though he had been trying to speak with his mouth shut, informed me, 'Coming directly, sir', and vanished. For a long time I heard nothing but the whirr and roar of the fire. There were also whistling sounds. The boats jumped, tugged at the painters, ran at each other playfully, knocked their sides together, or, do what we would, swung in a bunch against the ship's side. I couldn't stand it any longer, and swarming up a rope, clambered aboard over the stern.

It was a bright as day. Coming up like this, the sheet of fire facing me was a terrifying sight, and the heat seemed hardly bearable at first. On a settee cushion dragged out of the cabin Captain Beard, his legs drawn up and one arm under his head, slept with the light playing on him. Do you know what the rest were busy about? They were sitting on deck right aft, round an open case eating bread and cheese and drinking bottled stout.

On the background of flames twisting in fierce tongues above their heads they seemed at home like salamanders, and looked like a band of desperate pirates. The fire sparkled in the whites of their eyes, gleamed on patches of white skin seen through the torn shirts. Each had the marks as of a battle about him – bandaged heads, tied-up arms, a strip of dirty rag round a knee – and each man had a bottle between his legs and a chunk of cheese in his hand. Mahon got up. With his handsome and disreputable head, his hooked profile, his long white beard, and with an uncorked bottle in his hand, he resembled one of those reckless sea-robbers of old making merry amidst violence and disaster. 'The last meal on board', he explained solemnly. 'We had nothing to eat all day, and it was no use leaving all this.' He flourished the bottle and indicated the sleeping skipper. 'He said he couldn't swallow anything, so I got him to lie down', he went on; and as I stared, 'I don't know whether you are aware young fellow, the man had no sleep to speak of for days – and there will be dam' little sleep in the boats'. 'There will be no boats by-and-by if you fool about much longer', I said, indignantly. I walked up to the skipper and shook him by the shoulder. At last he opened his eyes, and did not move. 'Time to leave her, sir', I said quietly.

He got up painfully, looked at the flames, at the sea sparkling round the ship, and black, black as ink farther away; he looked at the stars shining dim through a thin veil of smoke in a sky black, black as Erebus.

'Youngest first', he said.

And the ordinary seaman, wiping his mouth with the back of his hand, got up, clambered over the taffrail, and vanished. Others followed. One, on the point of going over, stopped short to drain his bottle, and with a great swing of his arm flung it at the fire. 'Take this!' he cried.

The skipper lingered disconsolately, and we left him to commune alone for a while with his first command. Then I went up again and brought him away at last. It was time. The ironwork on the poop was hot to the touch.

Then the painter of the long-boat was cut, and the three boats, tied together, drifted clear of the ship. It was just sixteen hours after the explosion when we abandoned her. Mahon had charge of the second boat, and I had the smallest – the 14-foot thing. The long-boat would have taken the lot of us; but the skipper said we must save as much property as we could – for the underwriters – and so I got my first command. I had two men with me, a bag of biscuits, a few tins of meat, and a beaker of water. I was ordered to keep close to the long-boat, that in bad weather we might be taken into her.

And do you know what I thought? I thought I would part company as soon as I could. I wanted to have my first command all to myself. I wasn't going to sail in a squadron if there were a chance for independent cruising. I would make land by myself. I would beat the other boats. Youth! All youth! The silly, charming, beautiful youth.

But we did not make a start at once. We must see the last of the ship. And so the boats drifted about that night, heaving and setting on the swell. The men dozed, waked, sighed, groaned. I looked at the burning ship.

Between the darkness of earth and heaven she was burning fiercely upon a disc of purple sea shot by the blood-red play of gleams; upon a disc of water glittering and sinister. A high, clear flame, an immense and lonely flame, ascended from the ocean, and from its summit the black smoke poured continuously at the sky. She burned furiously; mournful and imposing like a funeral pile kindled in the night, surrounded by the sea, watched over by the stars. A magnificent death had come like a grace, like a gift, like a reward to that old ship at the end of her laborious days. The surrender of her weary ghost to the keeping of stars and sea was stirring like the sight of a glorious triumph. The masts fell just before daybreak, and for a moment there was a burst and turmoil of sparks that seemed to fill with flying fire the night patient and watchful, the vast night lying silent upon the sea. At daylight she was only a charred shell, floating still under a cloud of smoke and bearing a glowing mass of coal within.

Then the oars were got out, and the boats forming in a line moved round her remains as if in procession – the long-boat leading. As we pulled across her stern a slim dart of fire shot out viciously at us, and suddenly she went down, head first, in a great hiss of steam. The unconsumed stern was the last to sink; but the paint had gone, had cracked, had peeled off, and there were no letters, there was no word, no stubborn device that was like her soul, to flash at the rising sun her creed and her name.

We made our way north. A breeze sprang up, and about noon all the boats came together for the last time. I had no mast or sail in mine, but I made a mast out of a spare oar and hoisted a boat-awning for a sail, with a boat-hook for a yard. She was certainly over-masted, but I had the satisfaction of knowing that with the wind aft I could beat the other two. I had to wait for them. Then we all had a look at the captain's chart, and, after a sociable meal of hard bread and water, got our last instructions. These were simple; steer north, and keep together as much as possible. 'Be careful with that jury-rig, Marlow', said the captain; and Mahon, as I sailed proudly past his boat, wrinkled his curved nose and hailed, 'You will sail that ship of yours under water, if you don't look out, young fellow'. He was a malicious old man – and may the deep sea where he sleeps now rock him gently, rock him tenderly to the end of time!

Before sunset a thick rain-squall passed over the two boats, which were far astern, and that was the last I saw of them for a time. Next day I sat steering my cockle-shell – my first command – with nothing but water and sky around me. I did sight in the afternoon the upper sails of a ship far away, but said nothing, and my men did not notice her. You see I was afraid she might be homeward bound, and I had no mind to turn back from the portals of the East. I was steering for Java – another blessed name – like Bangkok, you know. I steered many days.

I need not tell you what it is to be knocking about in an open boat. I remembered nights and days of calm, when we pulled, we pulled, and the boat seemed to stand still, as if bewitched within the circle of the sea horizon. I remember the heat, the deluge of rain-squalls that kept us baling for dear life (but filled our water-cask), and I remember sixteen hours on end with a mouth dry as a cinder and a steering-oar over the stern to keep my first command head on to a breaking sea. I did not know how good a man I was till then. I remember the drawn faces, the dejected figures of my two men, and I remember my youth and the feeling that will never come back any more – the feeling that I could last for ever, outlast the sea, the earth, and all men; the deceitful feeling that lures us on to joys, to perils, to love, to vain effort – to death; the triumphant conviction of strength, the heat of life in the handful of dust, the glow in the heart that with every year grows dim, grows cold, grows small, and expires – and expires, too soon, too soon – before life itself.

And this is how I see the East. I have seen its secret places and have looked into its very soul; but now I see it always from a small boat, a high outline of mountains, blue and afar in the morning; like faint mist at noon; a jagged wall of purple at sunset. I have the feel of the oar in my hand, the vision of a scorching blue sea in my eyes. And I see a bay, a wide bay, smooth as glass and polished like ice, shimmering in the dark. A red light burns far off upon the gloom of land, and the night is soft and warm. We drag at the oars with aching arms, and suddenly a puff of wind, a puff faint and tepid and laden with strange odours of blossoms, of aromatic wood, comes out of the still night – the first sigh of the East on my face. That I can never forget. It was impalpable and enslaving, like a charm, like a whispered promise of mysterious delight.

We had been pulling this finishing spell for eleven hours. Two pulled, and he whose turn it was to rest sat at the tiller. We had made out the red light in that bay and steered for it, guessing it must mark some small coasting port. We passed two vessels, outlandish and high-sterned, sleeping at anchor, and approaching the light, now very dim, ran the boat's nose against the end of a jutting wharf. We were blind with fatigue. My men dropped the oars and fell off the thwarts as if dead. I made fast to a pile. A current rippled softly. The scented obscurity of the shore was grouped into vast masses, a density of colossal clumps of vegetation, probably – mute and fantastic shapes. And at their foot the semicircle of a beach gleamed faintly, like an illusion.

There was not a light, not a stir, not a sound. The mysterious East faced me, perfumed like a flower, silent like death, dark like a grave.

And I sat weary beyond expression, exulting like a conqueror, sleepless and entranced as if before a profound, a fateful enigma.

A splashing of oars, a measured dip reverberating on the level of water, intensified by the silence of a shore into loud claps, made me jump up. A boat, a European boat, was coming in. I invoked the name of the dead; I hailed: *Judea* ahoy! A thin shout answered.

It was the captain. I had beaten the flagship by three hours, and I was glad to hear the old man's voice again, tremulous and tired. 'Is it you, Marlow?' – 'Mind the end of that jetty, sir,' I cried.

He approached cautiously, and brought up with the deep-sea lead-line which we saved – for the underwriters. I eased my painter and fell alongside. He sat, a broken figure at the stern, wet with dew, his hands clasped in his lap. His men were asleep already. 'I had a terrible time of it', he murmured. 'Mahon is behind – not very far.' We conversed in whispers, in loud whispers, as if afraid to wake up the land. Guns, thunder, earthquakes would not have awakened the men just then.

Looking around as we talked, I saw away at sea a bright light travelling in the night. 'There's a steamer passing the bay', I said. She was not passing, she was entering, and she even came close and anchored. 'I wish', said the old man, 'you would find out whether she is English. Perhaps they could give us a passage somewhere.' He seemed nervously anxious. So by dint of punching and kicking I started one of my men into a state of somnambulism, and giving him an oar, took another and pulled towards the lights of the steamer.

There was a murmur of voices in her, metallic hollow clangs of the engine-room, footsteps on the deck. Her ports shone, round with dilated eyes. Shapes moved about, and there was a shadowy man high up on the bridge. He heard my oars.

And then, before I could open my lips, the East spoke to me, but it was a Western voice. A torrent of words was poured into the enigmatical, the fateful silence; outlandish, angry words, mixed with words and even whole sentences of good English, less strange but even more surprising. The voice swore and cursed violently; it riddled the solemn peace of the bay by a volley of abuse. It began by calling me Pig, and from that went crescendo into unmentionable adjectives – in English. The man up there raged aloud in two languages, and with a sincerity in his fury that almost convinced me I had, in some way, sinned against the harmony of the universe. I could hardly see him, but began to think he would work himself into a fit.

Suddenly he ceased, and I could hear him snorting and blowing like a porpoise. I said:

'What steamer is this pray?'

'Eh? What's this? And who are you?'

'Castaway crew of an English barque burnt at sea. We came here to-night. I am the second mate. The captain is in the long-boat and wishes to know if you would give us a passage somewhere.'

'Oh, my goodness! I say . . . This is the *Celestial* from Singapore on her return trip. I'll arrange with your captain in the morning, . . . and, . . . I say, . . . did you hear me just now?'

'I should think the whole bay heard you.'

'I thought you were a short-boat. Now, look here – this infernal lazy scoundrel of a caretaker has gone to sleep again – curse him. The light is out, and I nearly ran foul of the end of this damned jetty. This is the third time he plays me this trick. Now, I ask you, can anybody stand this kind of thing? It's enough to drive a man out of his mind. I'll report him. . . . I'll get the Assistant Resident to give him the sack, by . . . ! See –

there's no light. It's out isn't it? I take you to witness the light's out. There should be a light, you know. A red light on the——'

'There was a light', I said, mildly.

'But it's out, man! What's the use of talking like this? You can see for yourself it's out – can't you? If you had to take a valuable steamer along this God-forsaken coast you would want a light too. I'll kick him from end to end of his miserable wharf. You'll see if I don't. I will——'

'So I may tell my captain you'll take us?' I broke in.

'Yes, I'll take you. Good night', he said, brusquely.

I pulled back, made fast again to the jetty, and then went to sleep at last:. I had faced the silence of the East. I had heard some of its language. But when I opened my eyes again the silence was as complete as though it had never been broken. I was lying in a flood of light, and the sky had never looked so far, so high, before I opened my eyes and lay without moving.

And then I saw the men of the East – they were looking at me. The whole length of the jetty was full of people. I saw brown, bronze, yellow faces, the black eyes, the glitter, the colour of an Eastern crowd. And all these beings stared without a murmur, without a sigh, without a movement. They stared down at the boats, at the sleeping men who at night had come to them from the sea. Nothing moved. The fronds of palms stood still agains the sky. Not a branch stirred along the shore, and the brown roofs of hidden houses peeped through the green foliage, through the big leaves that hung shining and still like leaves forged of heavy metal. This was the East of the ancient navigators, so old, so mysterious, resplendent and sombre, living and unchanged, full of danger and promise. And these were the men. I sat up suddenly. A wave of movement passed through the crowd from end to end, passed along the heads, swayed the bodies, ran along the jetty like a ripple on the water, like a breath of wind on a field – and all was still again. I see it now – the wide sweep of the bay, the glittering sands, the wealth of green infinite and varied, the sea blue like the sea of a dream, the crowd of attentive faces, the blaze of vivid colour – the water reflecting it all, the curve of the shore, the jetty, the high-sterned outlandish craft floating still, and the three boats with the tired men from the West sleeping, unconscious of the land and the people and of the violence of sunshine. They slept thrown across the thwarts, curled on bottom-boards, in the careless attitudes of death. The head of the old skipper, leaning back in the stern of the long-boat, had fallen on his breast, and he looked as though he would never wake. Farther out old Mahon's face was upturned to the sky, with the long white beard spread out on his breast, as though he had been shot where he sat at the tiller; and a man, all in a heap in the bows of the boat, slept with both arms embracing the stem-head and with his cheek laid on the gunwale. The East looked at them without a sound.

I have known its fascination since; I have seen the mysterious shores, the still water, the lands of brown nations, where a stealthy Nemesis lies in wait, pursues, overtakes so many of the conquering race, who are proud of their wisdom, of their knowledge, of their strength. But for me all the East is contained in that vision of my youth. It is all in that moment when I opened my young eyes on it. I came upon it from a tussle with the sea – and I was young – I saw it looking at me. And this is all that is left of it! Only a moment of strength, of romance, of glamour – of youth! . . . A flick of sunshine upon a strange shore, the time to remember, the time for a sigh, and – goodbye! – Night – Good-bye . . . !

He drank

Ah! The good old time – the good old time. Youth and the sea. Glamour and the sea!

The good, strong sea, the salt, bitter sea, that could whisper to you and roar at you and knock your breath out of you.

He drank again

By all that's wonderful it is the sea, I believe, the sea itself – or is it youth alone? Who can tell? But you here – you all had something out of life: money, love – whatever one gets on shore – and, tell me, wasn't that the best time, that time when we were young at sea; young and had nothing, on the sea that gives nothing, except hard knocks – and sometimes a chance to feel your strength – that only – what you all regret?

And we all nodded at him: the man of finance, the man of accounts, the man of law, we all nodded at him over the polished table that like a still sheet of brown water reflected our faces lined, wrinkled; our faces marked by toil, by deceptions, by success, by love; our weary eyes looking still, looking always, looking anxiously for something out of life, that while it is expected is already gone – has passed unseen, in a sigh, in a flash – together with the youth, with the strength, with the romance of illusions.

JOSEPH CONRAD
Youth
(1902), pp. 17–47

2 *Diamonds in the Desert*

My investigations in Palestine showed that the non-arrival of registered diamond packages posted in Jerusalem (and ultimately paid for by Lloyd's) had been due to theft at the Jerusalem end. It was fairly easy to pin-point the leak and so soon as this was plugged by a slight change of postal routine the losses ceased.

But among the diamond losses which fell on underwriters a heavy one had arisen when, according to a top-secret certificate from the Jerusalem Postmaster General, a consignment was destroyed by an accident to the aeroplane carrying it.

My clients, mildly curious to know when, where and how that accident had happened, invited me while in the Middle East to make a few enquiries about it 'without going to a lot of trouble'!

In Cairo I learned unofficially that the mail-carrying plane, the subject of the Postmaster General's certificate, had crashed in the desert about four miles from Khartoum. Air Force and British Overseas Airways personnel and Sudanese soldiery, on the spot almost immediately, had taken charge. In spite of the terrific heat of the flaming wreckage they had recovered the bodies of the twenty men who were aboard and had salvaged from the vicinity of the craft a quarter of a ton of mail. Such of it as was decipherable dribbled back to the senders *via* the various post offices concerned. Only part of one package of our diamonds, however, got back to Jerusalem. The remaining gems (some

23,000 in all) were generally thought to have adhered somewhere among the multitude of sticky fingers between the Blue Nile and the Jordan.

This ungenerous view did not seem to tune in with some of the known facts. Nearly 1,500 £1 notes, gathered from a wide area around the wreck, had been passed to the local RAF and through them had reached Cairo safely. This alone would have warned me not to accept the 'sticky fingers' idea without proper enquiry.

* * *

In Cairo the BOAC engineers who had studied the accident on the spot told me that the forces developed by the plane hitting earth at terrific speed were unimaginable. Sheet steel used in its construction was torn to ribbons. Stout mail-bag canvas disintegrated as though it had been muslin.

Diamonds for mailing are made up into flat paper packets which resemble Seidlitz powders. Covered with extra paper wrappings or put into tough cardboard boxes they go into ordinary registered envelopes. All these envelopes travel in a small sealed 'registered' canvas sack which in turn goes into a mail-sack of ordinary size.

* * *

A paper bag of marbles will burst if dropped a few feet. Substitute canvas for the paper and the bag will survive such a fall intact. Increase the drop sufficiently and even the canvas will infallibly burst. Could I assume that my diamonds had been thrown far enough and hard enough to cut through the several layers of paper and cardboard and canvas which confined them and so to escape? My friendly BOAC expert, instead of laughing, accepted this as quite within the bounds of possibility. Any theory which allowed for the missing diamonds being still in the Sudan desert attracted me strongly. However far-fetched this one was, it seemed reasonably clear that since diamonds are well-nigh indestructible, there were, in fact, only two possibilities: either the gems had been stolen (which I refused to believe) or they were still resting in the sand.

I decided to fly down the Nile from Cairo for a personal survey of the *locus in quo*. The young BOAC station manager at Khartoum, Mr Ogilvie, was used to dealing with all sorts of odd situations and passengers. A polite man, if ever there was one, he smiled hardly at all when I asked to be driven to the scene of the six months' old accident for the purpose of recovering any diamonds which might yet be lying there. He reddened a little when I asked him to provide me with a shovel and rake, and a haversack (which he assumed was to carry the catch!).

* * *

Khartoum sits at the edge of a hard-packed and immense sandy tract on the surface of which a motor vehicle can run almost without leaving a wheel mark. To the newcomer any one part of this terrain looks like any other part. At the end of an hour's driving the place we wanted, four miles out, still eluded us. The district, as one would expect, is not thickly populated and it was by the merest chance that we met an elderly native to whom we turned for help. He had no English. Neither Ogilvie nor his aide Lloyd (who was with us) had adequate Arabic. I resorted to pantomime and did sketches of a crashed aeroplane with crumpled wings. With a long 'Ah!' of understanding the native climbed into our car and had led us for some miles before an Arabic-speaking army officer, encountered in a Jeep, put a few questions for us. He learned that our guide thought it was our wish to see a flying boat alight on the water and was accordingly steering us to the BOAC 'landing' area on the Blue Nile. Our interpreter put the guide right and within ten minutes we were examining the unpromising rumpled circle of earth – twelve yards across – for which we had been looking. The carcass of the aeroplane had long since been removed and all that remained to mark the accident was a pencil-sized scrap or so of metal, an odd piece of paper here and there, and a few handfuls of rag or cotton waste, vestiges of what had once been sturdy mail-bags. Ogilvie, who had already given up more time than he could well spare from his duties, left Lloyd and me to our own devices and, promising to come back for us in an hour, drove off to Khartoum smiling.

'What do we do now?' asked Lloyd.

I explained my notion that if diamonds were there they would glitter if the sand above them were stroked away. Lloyd, although patently embarrassed and sceptical, joined me in scraping and scanning as though we might, in truth, be standing over all the wealth of Sheba's queen. Alas! My glitter theory proved a failure. The sand was heavy with quartz particles and everything glittered. We were not a very happy pair. At the end of thirty-five minutes Lloyd's boredom was hidden with difficulty. So would mine have been but for the novelty of the situation. The desert shimmered under a grilling sun, a distant lake was ringed and dotted with waving palm trees. In the middle distance a Sudanese pony patrol rode curiously by, no doubt wondering what madness impelled a young British officer and a big man in London clothes to play like children in the wastes so far from town. We went on with our sand-stroking, but the glare taxed my eyes and I rested them for a while on the hazy horizon.

'How far off is that lake?' I asked.

Lloyd straightened his back and replied patiently: 'There is no lake, there are no palms. That is a mirage', and perhaps added *sotto voce*, 'like your diamonds'.

Any faith he had in me went when my 'glitter' idea blew up. Reaching a stage of ennui in which I was ready to pick up anything other than dirt, I idly collected what I thought was a bit of green beer-bottle glass. I dusted it off, looked again and saw it was a good-sized square-cut emerald, but I kept an outward calm, and showed Lloyd my find without comment. Making a brave effort to believe the unbelievable, he asked me, 'What is it?' I told him. His attitude changed completely. All his doubts vanished. He resumed work with a will. A moment later he took something from the ground, examined it and passed it to me with a diffident 'I suppose this wouldn't be anything would it, sir?' It was a small ruby. Then, by merely stroking away the surface of the dry earth, we uncovered ruby after ruby. In half an hour we had found fifty.

* * *

Ogilvie, returning with the car to rescue us at lunchtime, asked politely, 'Any luck, sir?' The chance of a leg-pull was too good to miss. Glumly I replied, 'No, we've searched most assiduously ever since you left us and we've seen nothing that even begins to look like a diamond [pause]. All we can find is emeralds and rubies.' 'You're joking, sir!' he said. I handed him our collection of gems in a matchbox. Gulping down his astonishment he enthusiastically joined the treasure-hunt. Within a minute he dropped into my hand a little split pea which I took to be a blob of melted paint from the plane's fuselage. In almost the words which Lloyd had used about the first ruby, he asked, 'This isn't anything, sir, is it?' I dusted it, looked at it again and said, 'This, Ogilvie, is a cabuchon emerald. What I want is *diamonds!*' By this time we were a really gay team, laughing, excited and determined to extract from this hidden hoard at least one of the diamonds I now knew *must* be there. Finally I found it myself by the tedious process of concentrating on a square foot of soil pinching it up millimetre by millimetre and examining everything which was larger than a grain of soil and glittered.

* * *

On reaching my hotel with a haversack full of sand I confirmed the richness of the 'lode' by washing a few ounces of it in a saucer under a gentle stream from my bedroom tap until all the soluble matter had been carried away. In the small residue of clean hard sand which remained I found a few more diamonds and several rubies. It seemed probable, therefore, that the site from which the sample came was, in mining parlance, 'rich pay-dirt'.

My chief concern now was to bring the whole of that 'dirt' into Khartoum for safe custody and scientific sifting. The Provincial Governor, to whom I appealed, blessed my project and appointed to carry it out his municipal engineer, whose name was Watson! Two days later the mound, brought away in 1,600 linen sacks, was under lock and key. During the months which followed, 'my dear Watson' washed and sifted and re-sifted it. In the final count it yielded nearly all my clients' diamonds, thirty-two emeralds and 1,000 carats of Burmese rubies. In spite of world-wide publicity the owners of the emeralds and rubies were never traced. The Sudan Government in my case rejected the time-honoured legal principle 'findings is keepings'. On the other hand, Lloyd's treated me with such princely generosity (they gave me 25 per cent of the net salvage recovery) that I felt it within my means to buy back from that government my good fat square-cut emerald and a few dozen of the rubies. These gems, with some of the Lloyd's diamonds, adorn the saddlecloth and neck-band of a disdainful Sudanese camel in gold and platinum which I designed as a present for my wife.

WILLIAM CHARLES CROCKER
Far from Humdrum
(1967), pp. 229–234

3 *Who Owns the* Titanic?

No other doomed vessel has had such an emotional and romantic hold over the public imagination and even the faintest prospect that some of the *Titanic*'s 73-year-old secrets may be revealed – and commercially exploited – has excited lively interest from salvage operators, souvenir hunters and entrepreneurs out to make a quick buck.

The possibly, however remote, of the *Titanic* once again becoming an economic asset raises all sorts of complex legal issues which, if they ever surface, will have a phalanx of lawyers salivating at the prospect of another huge pay-day.

The legal wrangles and procedures that might arise could take many forms but they start from one basic question: who owns the *Titanic*?

There is no doubt who owned the 46,000 ton liner when it set out on its maiden voyage across the Atlantic on 10 April 1912, amid great publicity. The last word in size, opulence and up-to-date technology (one element of which was claimed to render it 'unsinkable') the *Titanic* and her sister ship the *Olympic* were to be the White Star Line's answer to its main competitor, Cunard.

It hit the world's most famous iceberg on the night of 14 April and sank within three hours. The final loss of life was (on the most persuasive figures) 1502, with just over 700 saved. Those facts are virtually the only ones not in dispute. Even after three-quarters of a century and countless inquiries, books and articles, exactly what happened and who was to blame – for the collision in the first place and the ensuing casualties – remain a subject of controversy. Myths have taken over where facts were scarce or ambiguous and it is often difficult to disentangle the two.

One of the most intriguing questions of them all has suddenly become relevant again: is the wreck of the *Titanic* a treasure trove, holding vast quantities of diamonds, jewellery and, some say, even gold or just a receptacle for the ordinary artefacts of voyage, from dinner plates to deck-quoits?

The liner itself was insured for £1 million, the insurance placed by brokers Willis Faber & Co and the White Star Line seems to have been paid promptly and without any difficulties. What happened after the claim was met is unclear yet crucial.

If White Star exercised its right of abandonment and the underwriters accepted title to the ship, the position, at first glance, is relatively clear. In 1912 ownership in the *Titanic* was vested in the original underwriters and, unless some relevant event occurred between 1912 and 1985, they still own it.

But if the underwriters did not accept White Star's attempt to transfer title or if nothing was said at all – remembering that at the time the *Titanic* was thought well and truly lost and no one conceived of it being raised – the White Star Line may have remained the ship's owners.

Who were the underwriters who may now have a stake in the *Titanic*'s revival? The 'Titanic' slip shows that the leading underwriter was the Indemnity Marine Insurance, now the Commercial Union, which took 7½ per cent (£75,000). The Royal Exchange (now Guardian Royal Exchange) and the Sea Insurance each took a similar percentage.

Two or three insurance companies subscribed for lesser amounts and the remainder was taken up by some 70 Lloyd's syndicates. Some of the signatures (or mere initials) on the slip are indecipherable from the copies available (the original has been lost) and even where they can be made out, it might prove impossible to trace exactly on whose behalf the signing agent was acting. Those 70 or so signatures probably represent hundreds of small participants. Moreover, many of the underwriters have ceased to exist or been swallowed up.

The task of tracing all the heirs and descendants who might be entitled to a share of any proceeds from the *Titanic* would be enormous and perhaps impossible. Some underwriters on the slip, however, are very much still in business and would clearly be entitled to their proportionate slice.

The first few days following the discovery of the wreck were confusing. The Commercial Union, the leading underwriters, were obviously taken by surprise and issued a series of not always consistent statements. Yes, we (and the other underwriters) own it. No, after we paid out we abandoned our right to it. No, we can't find any mention of the abandonment in our records. Yes, we probably do own it after all.

The Commercial Union's position is more relaxed now. 'Our best guess is that we probably never did anything about our right to abandon. We thought it inconceivable that it would ever be raised and clearly it wouldn't constitute a hazard, so we probably did nothing at all', their spokesman said. But there are no records to show whether or not they accepted title in the first place, after meeting the claim.

If title did not pass in 1912, the White Star Line remained the *Titanic*'s owners. But they merged with Cunard in 1934 and the *Titanic* was not listed or mentioned in any of the documents relating to the merger, which are now kept at Liverpool University. The sunken liner was obviously not considered an operating asset and seems to have been totally ignored, either because White Star did not believe it owned it or because it would not have been relevant to the merger. Eventually Cunard took over White Star completely and has in turn become part of the Trafalgar House group.

The possibility that Trafalgar House, as White Star's legal successors, might still own the liner is rejected by the company. 'We've never owned it, we don't own it and never will', is its uncompromising view. The law may say otherwise.

There remains the legally obscure and remote possibility that the wreck belongs to no one, a *res nullius*, legally speaking. If, for instance, the underwriters never owned it and White Star made some unequivocal statement of renunciation of title, it is just possible (though the law is vague) that the *Titanic* is, in effect, up for grabs as abandoned property. That option does not, however, fit what facts we know. There is no evidence of such abandonment by any of the possible owners. The mere fact that no one has done anything for 73 years to confirm their ownership is not evidence of an intention to discard title, especially as, for all practical purposes, the ship was considered permanently lost.

Could the *Titanic* belong to some third party? Yes, if the owner had validly sold or ceded his right to title. Since the late 1960s a Mr Douglas Woolley has made various claims to being the true owner of the liner and has unsuccessfully tried to launch a multi-million pound project to find and salvage it. But there is no evidence whatever to suggest that Commercial Union or any other underwriters, or Cunard or Trafalgar House, have ever had formal dealings with Mr Woolley and he has never publicly explained the grounds on which he bases his claim.

In the absence of any firm evidence either way, the *Titanic* is owned either by the heirs and descendants of the 1912 underwriters or by Trafalgar House as the legal successors to White Star. The contents of the ship are another matter. Cargo-owners and passengers, if they insured at all, did so with a large number of insurance companies, most of them American, some British. It is impossible at this stage to ascertain exactly how much was insured and how much was paid out. The American-based Titanic Historical Society has worked out that the total cargo insurance amounted to less than $500,000, most of it for perishables or other goods (like wine, textiles, furs, ostrich feathers, grandfather clocks and medicinal opium) which would not have withstood the ravages of 73 years.

The most valuable painting on board, a large canvas by the French painter Blondel (over-insured for a ludicrous $100,000) and an exquisitely bound volume of a translation of Omar Khayyam's Rubaiyat, would equally be unlikely to have survived.

Romantic claims about the wealth on board the ship (there were at least 10 millionaires among the passengers) do not, unfortunately, conform to the evidence. The £5m worth of uncut diamonds is almost certainly a myth. De Beers, the diamond company alleged to have owned those diamonds, have consistently denied all knowledge of them. Certainly no insurance was paid out.

The vast array of valuable personal jewellery that was said to be in the purser's safe or around the necks of millionaires' wives as they danced and dined was also highly exaggerated. If there was any real jewellery (the rich often wore paste replicas when travelling) it either accompanied its owners into the water or into the lifeboats and back to New York. There were stories of passengers queueing to get their valuables back from the purser but his own list of belongings left with him showed nothing worth more than $500.

Insurance claims for loss of valuables were comparatively small, though not everyone in those days would have insured even their most valuable possessions.

Legally, whatever property may be lying 13,000 feet below the surface still belongs to its owners – whether individuals or, if insurance claims were met, insurance companies. Tracing the descendents of the owners could become an administrative headache as well as a legal puzzle, especially as many of the insurance companies of the time are no longer in business, quite apart from the difficulties of identifying the property that would undoubtedly arise.

All indications are that the costs of bringing the *Titanic*'s contents to the surface (assuming the technology was there) would far exceed any possible material benefit. Raising the hull, with its even greater practical difficulties, would equally seem to be an economically fruitless operation. The lure of the *Titanic*, though, may prove more powerful than good sense and salvage operators are already flexing their underwater muscles, as much, perhaps, for the glory and the romance as for the money.

What rights would such potential salvors have? It is, of course, open to any owner of a wreck to enter into a salvage agreement. But with whom would the salvors deal? If the 1912 underwriters are the owners, is it enough to agree with the Commercial Union or would all or a majority of underwriters have to approve? And any agreement reached relating to the hull cannot include the right to fish for contents. In theory, though absurd in practice, salvors would have to reach separate deals with the owners of the articles they wish to bring back.

If salvage operators began their work without permission, the owners would have the right to restrain them. How they would *exercise* that right would present further legal complications. The wreck itself is in international waters, 500 miles from the nearest land-mass (Newfoundland) and therefore not within the jurisdiction of any national courts.

If the salvage company were English, it would be possible to apply for an injunction in our courts. But what if the salvors were European or American or Japanese or their company was registered in one of the legal havens? The international legal merry-go-round that could ensue – several countries might be involved – would be amusing to follow, the only certain winners being the lawyers on both sides of the Atlantic.

As soon as the ship or its contents is brought within territorial waters, more complications arise because it then becomes subject to the law of the country whose waters have been entered. Under English law, anything recovered from a wreck, whether it lay in or outside territorial waters, comes under the jurisdiction of a Receiver of Wrecks (a part-time office, usually held by a Customs and Excise official). The salvor then has to prove his right to the property, otherwise it is sold and a salvage award made out of the proceeds, the remainder going to the owners. In practice, it is probable that the *Titanic* or its contents would first reach the shores of the United States or Canada (Newfoundland) and those laws would then apply.

What is certain is that whatever country's jurisdiction becomes involved, it will not be just a case of 'finders keepers' for the salvors.

All this is, of course, hugely speculative. The *Titanic* is nowhere near being raised or explored or scavenged. But if ever the technology advances and the economic equation begins to make sense and the *Titanic* comes within reach, we can be sure that the lawyers will not be far behind.

MARCEL BERLINS
Lloyd's Log

4 *The* Torrey Canyon *and the Question of Salvage*

Just as the breakup of the tanker forced a decision upon Wijsmuller and Union Oil, so it also forced the government to act and simultaneously narrowed the choice of action. The Zuckerman committee, in its few frantic days of existence, had prepared technical evaluations of three courses. They were salvage of the ship, including cutting her in two and saving only part; pumping out the oil; burning the oil.

These alternatives have been discussed at length by the Zuckerman group in a government White Paper, 'The *Torrey Canyon*,' published by Her Majesty's Stationery Office at the end of 1967. While this forty-eight-page pamphlet probably presents the analysis with more refinement than was available to the Cabinet at the time, it evidently does reflect the advice coming from Sir Solly's hastily recruited team of fourteen experts. The report, incidentally, merits reading by the appropriate officials of every government whose waterways and harbours receive oil tankers.

The report put the committee on all sides of the salvage question. It said the government was right, in the light of previous success in salvage operations at sea, in attempting to 'save a stranded tanker and to avoid large-scale pollution'. That, the Zuckerman committee (really Sir Solly, the government's chief scientific adviser) wrote, 'was the first course which the government necessarily had to try in the light of the professional advice it had been given'. Then the report added, 'The stranding of the *Torrey Canyon*, however, was no ordinary accident', and it explained how badly the tanker was impaled.

As for the salvors' expectation that the tanker could be refloated on the Easter week-end tides, the report said, 'Although the Committee of Scientists and the Chief Naval Salvage Officer [Peter Flett] agreed that this was a reasonable possibility, they took a less optimistic view of the chances of success'. The committee managed that blindingly subtle distinction on the basis of the tanker's speed at impact – 16 knots – and her position on Pollard Rock.

Finally, the committee said it was not given enough information. Specifically, it lacked 'a quantitative estimate of the extra buoyancy which would be required to lift the ship clear at high tide, and how this might be obtained without deliberately discharging an excessive amount of oil'. That statement in the report followed by two paragraphs the committee's observation that pinnacles of the reef had penetrated about 15 feet into the first row of tanks and from 5 to 10 feet into the fifth row.

Deliberately breaking the *Torrey Canyon* in half so that the afterpart could be towed away looked feasible, but only at first glance. The demolitions experts, D. J. Lyons and E. C. Williams of the Ministry of Transport, both of whom had once held senior military research-development posts, were confident that linear-shaped plastic charges would sever the deck and hull plates tidily. But it was discovered, the committee reported, that the 'robust internal structure,' that is, the bulkheads and longitudinal stiffeners, 'would defeat any attempt to tow away' the afterpart. There was no practical way to sever those internal members without exposing to the peril of explosion the men assigned to such a task.

Pumping the oil into another ship was theoretically possible. But to bring another ship close by the *Torrey Canyon* would have posed 'considerable risk' because of the rocks and the generally rough weather. The farther off a receiving ship might stand, the greater the difficulty of making the transfer. A pipeline along the ocean floor would have been the most reliable conduit but would have required a week to install. Hoses could have been fitted together and fastened to floats, but they 'would have been extremely vulnerable to weather'. With the pumps available, transferring the *Torrey Canyon*'s remaining 70,000 tons of oil to a ship a thousand feet away would have taken at least thirty days.

So, pumping out the oil, which oilmen, pump vendors and armchair sea dogs would tell each other over luncheon in London clubs was obviously the thing to have done, was ruled out.

On Monday morning, with the tanker's back broken, the government had little choice but to fire the remaining oil – or so it seems clear with hindsight.

Roy Jenkins called his Cabinet Standing Emergency Committee into session in London. Afterward, the Home Secretary announced several measures that had to do with protecting or cleaning up the beaches. As for firing the tanker, Jenkins told reporters that it would be extremely dangerous. He did not say more because he was awaiting a new evaluation from Maurice Foley.

Foley, in his ninth consecutive day of full-time *Torrey Canyon* duty, surveyed the tanker from a helicopter for the better part of two hours. Back in Plymouth, he told a news conference that 30,000 tons of crude had been released since the ship broke apart. The oil was 'a menace and a threat to Britain', Foley declared. 'Given the extra oil now floating off Cornwall, all the extra men and equipment in the world could not deal with this problem.'

'Neither the legal implications, which are pretty horrible, nor the financial implications will hinder us in our task of dealing with oil pollution', Foley said. As for blowing up the tanker, he observed that it was one of several possible alternatives and added, 'There is a legal problem involved'. Foley pointed out it was 'an American-owned tanker flying a Liberian flag, sailing on charter to a British company and resting outside Britain's territorial waters'.

'I think it is extremely important', said Roy Jenkins that same day, 'that it should be clear in everybody's mind what has been the governing factor in what we are doing. The overriding factor has been to minimise pollution. Legal and financial considerations have not been our concern. International law has not been considered from the time the ship foundered.'

Foley concluded from his aerial inspection that rescuing any part of the *Torrey Canyon* was impossible. He said as much to the press, and he conveyed that conclusion to the Home Secretary. Jenkins discussed it by telephone with the Prime Minister, still on St Mary's. In this conversation, they had the benefit of new information that had been unavailable to them during the Sunday afternoon meeting at Culdrose. On Sunday, under the direction of members of Sir Solly's committee, one thousand gallons of Kuwait crude oil spread about one inch thick were burned in an experimental firing on a pond at the Royal Armament Research and Development Establishment, Langhurst, Sussex. The pond had been agitated by air blown by a jet engine to simulate the turbulent conditions of the sea. Ignition was provided by an incendiary device known as an 'oxygen tile'. The scientists estimated the combustion of the oil at 99.5 per cent.

That was extremely important. It meant that Harold Wilson and his ministerial associates could attempt to fire the oil with a reasonable prospect of success – and now 'reasonable' seemed to signify a higher order of probability than it had when Maurice Foley was appraising the prospect of refloating the *Torrey Canyon*. For it would be infinitely embarrassing for the government to commit its warplanes and munitions to an assault on a stationary, helpless target and fail. Wilson and Jenkins decided to go ahead.

On Monday evening, Jenkins asked the Navy when it could start bombing. Within two hours came the reply: Tuesday morning.

The task was far more exacting than just plastering the *Torrey Canyon* with high-explosive bombs, smashing her hull and sinking her; to do so would release into the sea the remaining oil in her tanks, some 60,000 or 70,000 tons, half or more of her original cargo.

There was a good chance that the crude oil would burn well if it could be ignited while contained. Then the light, volatile fractions, such as petrol, would burn and generate enough heat to ignite the heavier hydrocarbon molecules, such as tar and paraffin, in much the way that kindling wood is necessary to set thick logs afire. But if the crude oil spread itself on the sea, the light fractions would soon be lost, either evaporated or mixed with the salt water. Moreover, the cooling effect of the sea would make burning the heavier components of the crude more difficult.

All of this argued for opening the tanker up as one opens a tin can, removing the top but not the sides. 'Explosive surgery', Sir Solly called it. The committee of scientists considered two methods. One was laying line charges that would open a hole over each tank, with subsequent ignition of the oil in each tank by a separate device. The second method was wholesale blasting of the deck plating by a massive charge and simultaneous ignition of the oil.

The first method, tidier and more exact than the other, had to be discarded. The deck supports were too strong and arranging the charges would have taken too long. The second method, with the explosives inside the tanks, looked more feasible. There was some thought of putting a thousand-pound bomb in each tank, but the Navy was not keen to deliver them by helicopter to the tanker. In the end, the breakup of the *Torrey Canyon* and the heavy seas precluded any type of explosive surgery.

Butchery was required. The bombing began on Tuesday, in the late afternoon at high tide, so that the oil in the tanks would be at its highest level. Royal Navy Buccaneer strike aircraft zoomed in at 2,500 feet and 500 miles an hour and dropped forty-one thousand-pound bombs. The high explosive inside them had been treated with aluminium to produce more flame and burn more of the oil. The bombs' fuses were set for a delay of 0.35 seconds so that the explosions would occur after the bombs had broken through the deck, whose steel plates had a thickness of 1.25 to 1.43 inches. By forcing oil and water up against the plates, the scientists hoped to open bigger holes than external explosions would have produced.

Forty-one bombs may seem like a great many for opening sixteen tanks. The only hope of getting each of the tanks, one of the experts explained, was 'pure statistics – dropping enough bombs'. The Zuckerman committee report put it more formally: 'Bearing in mind the small target each tank presented, and the difficulty of recognising its exact position, it was clear that multiple attacks were called for.'

The Buccaneers attacked in pairs, dropping their payloads first on the forepart of the *Torrey Canyon*. 'After the first four hits', the report said, 'the flame and smoke of the burning made it difficult to aim subsequent bombs but, nevertheless, it was estimated that thirty hits were scored.' The estimates came from the pilots.

Hunter fighters of the Royal Air Force followed the first phase of the bombing and dropped underwing fuel tanks containing aviation petrol to feed the fires and make sure the oil burned. As daylight started to fade, another round of Buccaneers and Hunters assaulted the *Torrey Canyon*. In all 5,400 gallons of aviation fuel were used. Fires burned for two hours after the last drop.

Dennis Barker of *The Guardian* viewed the attack from a Royal Navy helicopter. He probably had the best view of any civilian that day. He wrote:

> From just over a mile, the fierce orange flame could be seen ringing the pillars of smoke, as if a magnified domestic hearth had been towed into the middle of the sea.
>
> Then the Buccaneers glided down, almost leisurely, like tiny birds against the background of the huge smoke pillar, glinting silver in the sun. More and more puffs of black smoke went up from the sea as the Buccaneers dropped their bombs. Areas of flame sprang up on the sea and merged themselves as the linking oil surface flashed fire. The fires eased their way towards each other and became one creeping orange circle of flames. There was still no sight of the ship itself, lost somewhere within this shifting funeral pyre.

Photographs later showed nearly all the smoke billowing up from the sea, caused presumably by the burning mixture of oil and aviation fuel, and not from the *Torrey Canyon*. But the tanker was hit. That evening, at Lossiemouth (Scotland) Royal Navy Air Station, Lieutenant Commander David Howard, the strike leader, recounted the attack this way:

> I went down fast and did one attack – one of my two bombs striking the starboard side but failing to explode. I was followed in by Lieutenant Commander David Meare, senior pilot of 800 Squadron, who put two bombs into the middle of the rear section. These were direct hits.
>
> Immediately, a fire started. It spread very quickly indeed, burning fiercely and giving off a lot of black smoke. One my next run I dropped two bombs on target. After the first four hits there was so much flame and smoke that it was difficult to see anything of the stern section at all.
>
> It got worse as we pumped more bombs into it. Smoke shot up to 8,000 feet and continued to rise rapidly. It got very black and dense and we had to alter the line of our attack to avoid firing through the smoke – and I was also rather worried in case the thing blew up.

The aviation fuel was intended to promote the burning of the oil both in the *Torrey Canyon* and near the ship, for, presumably, the bombing was causing some of the tanker's remaining cargo to spill. An experiment Tuesday morning before the bombing began had demonstrated that oil did not burn well on the open sea. On an oily patch of sea near Wolf Rock, the Navy and scientists from the Royal Armament Research and Development Establishment at Langhurst, Sussex, had tested an oxygen tile. The tile is a plastic-coated block containing sodium chlorate, which is highly flammable. The block was dangled by cable from a helicopter into the oil. When an electric current was passed down the cable to the block it burst into flame.

The Guardian's Dennis Barker, who reported all this, quoted a Ministry of Technology engineer, Stanley Bridges, as saying the device had been perfected shortly after World War II for following up bombing attacks on enemy fuel storage tanks.

Navy officers planned to use the incendiary brick to burn the oil on the sea backwards to the *Torrey Canyon* – if it worked. It didn't. The oil didn't catch fire. Bridges said that the trouble was the oil on the ocean had been churned by waves and had lost its inflammable elements. Had the use of the sodium device succeeded, the spectacular bombing mission might have been called off. During the bombing, five attempts to ignite oil with oxygen tiles were made, but only one was successful, according to British Petroleum's own account, 'The Torrey Canyon Incident', written by L. R. Beynon.

The next morning, Wednesday, March 29, oil was seen escaping from the *Torrey Canyon*. The bombardment resumed at noon. RAF Hunters fired rockets at the tanker to see if they would do a better job of opening her up. High-explosive bombs and 6,200 gallons of aviation fuel were again dropped, and – the government having put down its fears of political backlash in Vietnam-conscious Britain – napalm was used.

The results were less spectacular than on Tuesday. But the air sorties still produced fire and smoke – a column clearly visible in mid-afternoon 40 miles to the east at the Helford River where workmen were trying to protect oyster beds from oil pollution. The afternoon fires died down. An evening assult by Buccaneers started no new fires.

The napalm was particularly disappointing to the military. The *Western Morning News*, Plymouth, reported the following account by RAF Squadron Leader Granville (Spike) Jones, who led the first trio of Hunters, each carrying two napalm bombs: 'I dropped mine at 420 knots [about 480 m.p.h.] at fifty feet but they failed to ignite the slick. The other two dropped theirs on the ship and they also dropped them on the slick but here again it failed to ignite.'

Other aerial reconnaissance was provided by one Harold Wilson, as he flew from St Mary's to Penzance in a BEA helicopter. The Prime Minister, who had been watching the bombing from Telegraph Hill on St Mary's, said he had clearly discerned from the helicopter two fires on the tanker. 'Obviously one of the main oil seams had been struck again', he told reporters at Penzance.

By Thursday morning, the newspapers, although aware that the object of the exercise was to burn the oil without destroying the remains of the tanker, couldn't resist playing up what appeared to be military ineptitude. 'The

Torrey Canyon was still there last night', *The Guardian* announced. 'The *Torrey Canyon* is a long time dying', began the *Financial Times* story.

The Home Office, piqued, issued a statement which pointed out that the fliers' mission was to open the top of the tanker, not sink her.

On Thursday, a sunny, brisk day worthy of the transitional season, Navy Vixens and Buccaneers and RAF Hunters let loose some hundred thousand pounds of bombs on the *Torrey Canyon.* From the grassy slopes in front of the parking lot at Land's End, and from the glass-walled bar of the adjacent hotel, Cornishmen and tourists watched the bombing for the third day in a row. Some of these people knew the sound of bursting bombs, even the tremors. But none had watched serenely, as if on a family outing to see the Guy Fawkes Day fireworks, strike aircraft rain destruction from the skies.

From Land's End the naked eye could discern the *Torrey Canyon* as a blotch on the horizon. Without smoke and fire the third day's bombing lacked something for mainland spectators. The biggest excitement came from the bombs that missed; they sent geysers of water climbing toward the sky, and the youngsters and oldsters oohed and aahed.

Because no fires were started, the wreck was presumed to be oil free, according to the Zuckerman committee. Various military officers said as much during the afternoon. Roy Jenkins made it official that evening. 'The probability is that the bombing is over', said the Home Secretary. 'As a result of the sorties this afternoon, all the oil in the ship has probably been destroyed and the area around the ship is free from oil.'

That evening, the Seven Stones lightship, which had been taken off station for safety's sake, was towed back to her normal position.

It would appear that the bombing, which cost about £200,000 ($560,000), was largely successful. Precisely how successful may never be known. It was impossible to determine how much oil was left in the tanker's battered hull. From time to time during the following months, there were rumours that oil was escaping from the wreckage. Fishermen interviewed at the end of May on Newlyn pier, adjacent to Penzance, said they regularly sailed by the wreckage and had seen none.

It is probable, taking account of the scale and difficulty of the operation, that some small volume of crude oil went unburned, and perhaps some of the *Torrey Canyon*'s fuel oil. One might guess that such oil escaped within days or weeks, as the wreckage settled and slipped off Pollard Rock. It is also likely that the wave action of the sea washed loose oil deposits on the inside on the tanks, deposits which form in every tanker. In June, intrepid Royal Navy divers found such a coating of oil, about 1.5 inches thick, clinging to the underside of deck inspection plates which the divers removed to have a look inside some of the tanks. Occasionally, according to the officer in charge of the divers, Lieutenant Cyril Lafferty, a blob of oil would surface and break up into a film.

Lafferty led the Plymouth Command Clearance Diving Team, the only deep-diving team (to 250 feet; others were limited to 180 feet) in the Royal Navy. Its other members were Chief Petty Officer George Witherell, Petty Officers Len Woods and Dennis Williams, Leading Seamen Al Dalton, David Higginson and John Curran and Able Seaman Taff Sweeney. From June 7 through June 13, Lafferty and his seven ratings made a series of dangerous underwater inspections. They found no liquid oil and a bizarre assortment of consequences and nonconsequences of the bombing.

The team had been put on alert on March 21. The next day it left HMS *Drake*, a Navy base just west of Plymouth, by ship and sailed to the Seven Stones. The divers took with them their diving suits, breathing apparatus, Gemini rubber boats and other equipment. Their initial assignment was to determine whether diving was possible. A visual underwater survey of the damage might have facilitated the salvage effort.

Lafferty found that diving was out of the question. 'The oil was so thick', he recalled later, 'that you put your arm in the water and couldn't feel any water.'

The waves and the updraughts caused by helicopters soon covered most of the team's gear with crude oil. Within an hour or two, the rubber diving apparatus began to rot – possibly from the detergent as well as the oil. (On land, detergent ate through fire hoses.) Even without the corrosive effect, the oil would have acted as a blackout curtain in the face of any diver. And, Lafferty observed, a diver normally gets some sea water inside his face mask and in his eyes. Small quantities of sea water are tolerable but, as even a layman can imagine, a few drops of oil in the eyes are not.

Lafferty related the team's *Torrey Canyon* adventures during a long talk in his tiny office at HMS *Drake* in June. Alert, relaxed and affable, he is an impressive Navy officer. He joined the Navy in 1954 at the age of sixteen and volunteered for diving in 1961. Married and the father of three children, he is sandy-haired, blue-eyed and ruggedly handsome. He told his story with a fine sense of detail and irony, but with no hint of chest-thumping or false modesty.

Lafferty returned to Pollard Rock on April 24 in a helicopter, but the wind was too strong to permit it to winch down a man. The forward section of the wreck had sunk soon after the bombing. The afterpart had slipped backward, so that the '76' emblem on the funnel was under water. The forward end of the afterpart was sticking up at an angle, giving the aerial viewers a cross-section view of the tanks. The sea swished in them and spurted out through the bomb holes in the deck. Through the holes Lafferty could see the longitudinal stiffeners.

The entire diving team set out from HMS *Drake* on MFV (Motor Fishing Vessel) 1527 on June 4. Fog forced the sailors to wait at Hughtown, St Mary's, until June 7. That day high winds and a heavy sea defeated an attempt to reach the wreckage. The divers succeeded in locating it the next day, about 65 feet down. Luckily, extremely calm seas prevailed from June 8 through June 13, and the eight divers went down each day.

They found the bow had slid into a deep gully, folded up along its centre line to a 40-degree angle and split crosswise at several places. It lay perfectly still, a good thing for the divers. They worked in pairs, one making his way inside the wreckage, the other remaining on the upper deck tending his mate's lines. The danger that a man's lines would get fouled in the wreckage was compounded by the threat that the many jagged bits of metal would sever a line. The divers worked only during ebb tides, because the flood tides were too strong to swim against. Each man was limited to one 40-minute dive a day.

Up front, the divers found one compartment, the boatswain's store, relatively undamaged. Under it was a 'deep tank,' for bunkers, which Lafferty had been instructed to survey. He half expected to find oil in it. He opened the valve. No oil flowed out. Then Lafferty removed two deck inspection plates in the boatswain's store floor. Inside the deep tank there was only sea water.

Parts of the ship had been so fiercely bombed that they were unrecognisable. For example, it was impossible to follow the rearward starboard side. It just disappeared. The after superstructure, which had housed cabins, stores, laundry rooms, the mess and so on, was gone. From the deck the divers looked directly into the pump rooms.

'You couldn't tell you're on a ship between the superstructures. It was just jagged metal', Lafferty said. To orient himself, he sought out features which he could relate to the ship's plan, which he had studied.

For all the destruction, some things had remained intact: a rocking horse (presumably meant for some youngster in Italy), bed sheets, two of the three forward masts and a steaming light, the fixture and even the bulb. But the white bridge was identifiable only by its colour, not its shape.

EDWARD COWAN
Oil and Water
(1968), pp. 113–122

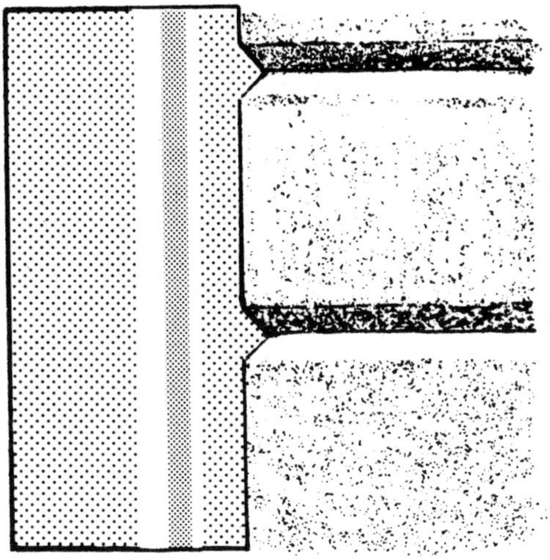

VIII
Individualists

1 Cuthbert Heath

Every generation has its special hazards and anxieties, and in the late August days of 1901 *The Times* reported 'a sudden increase' in the number of smallpox cases in the London area. The increase continued ominously through the first week of September, and as it went on, the more far-seeing tried to encourage vaccination. On 12 September a case was reported from a place called Five Oak Green, near Tonbridge: it was a hamlet famous for its hopfields, and the victim was one of the huge bands of East Enders who every autumn made the Kentish countryside the scene of a riproaring fiesta. In order to encourage vaccination, the resourceful curate of St Augustine's Church, Stepney, who was accompanying a party from his parish, organized what were called 'vaccination concerts' in a marquee on the village green, the idea being that people could be persuaded to get themselves vaccinated in special tents during the intervals. Probably such ideas did something to reduce the spread of infection, but it was not enough. By 17 September, 132 cases of smallpox were reported in the London area. By the end of October the total had steadied at around 200, but new cases were still being reported daily.

As usual, and especially because the outbreak had begun among East Enders, it was the poor who bore the brunt. For one case a day reported from Kensington, there were eight from Stepney. Soon special isolation hospitals had been set up at South Wharf, Rotherhithe, and in the grim setting of two isolation ships, the *Atlas* and *Endymion*, moored off Long Reach in the river.

Even so nobody could feel safe. The only way of preventing epidemics, proclaimed one advertisement for a firm in Long Acre, was to use 'Merryweather's Chlorus Distributor for disinfecting courts and alleys'. Another product, Merryweather's Hydraulic Sewer Flusher, would, it was claimed, clean drains with one-tenth of the water normally used for the purpose.

Such devices were candles in the wind. The grim roll-call climbed steadily through November and December, reaching 800 by early January. The thousand mark was reached before the end of the month. By March the total was 1,500, with upwards of forty new cases being reported daily.

Possibly Cuthbert recalled the cholera outbreak when he was seven, and how, even in such a safe zone as Leith Hill, the Heath children had been forbidden water and put on a gooseberry ration. Certainly he was quick to realize that at a time of anxiety, people needed some kind of talisman, and the talisman could be insurance. Like the curate of St Augustine's, he was a firm believer in vaccination, and before long he was insuring individuals against getting the disease at a rate of 2s. 6d. per cent, with the proviso that the assured must have been vaccinated. Thus anyone who paid £1 in premium would, if he got the disease, receive £800. 'News of this novel form of insurance,' said one observer,

reached the daily papers and immediately Lloyd's brokers were inundated with orders varying from amounts running into thousands of pounds to the humble £100 of the city clerk. So great was the rush that brokers sent juniors to keep a place in the queue at Mr Heath's box immediately Lloyd's opened, arriving later in the day with piles of 'slips' hastily prepared for the morning's orders. Mr Heath drafted every available clerk from his office into his box, with power to write without limit. If, however, the residence of the assured was in a locality from which a case of smallpox had been reported, the rate was increased to 3s. 9d. per cent, and if further cases were reported from that locality the rate rose to 5s. per cent.

Cuthbert made a small fortune from his smallpox underwriting. But there was a more important aspect. His insistence on vaccination sounded the first note of a new theme in insurance – the concept that what is good for the insurer is also good for the community in general. Years ahead of his time as usual, he was guiding the market towards the modern science of risk prevention.

ANTONY BROWN
Cuthbert Heath
(1980), pp. 88–90

2 *Samuel Plimsoll*

In 1928 a former sea captain who had earned for himself in a law court the description of 'the most dangerous man in Europe' – a testimonial in which he took a bitter relish – was groping about among the weed-grown graves in a churchyard at Sandgate, near Folkestone. From one of the stones he began to peel away the green moss, and found carved there a simple geometrical device familiar enough to seamen's eyes. His search was over. The device was the 'Plimsoll Line', and under that stone lay the body of Samuel Plimsoll, the 'Sailors' Friend'; a kindred spirit who, in his day, had been hailed as the most dangerous man in Britain.

The man who located the grave – he tells the story in his book *Seamen's Torch* – was Captain Edward Tupper, firebrand of the Seamen's Union, tactician of the historic Bristol Channel strike of 1911.

Tupper and his chief, J. Havelock Wilson ('ship's boy to Companion of Honour') determined to rescue from neglect the memory of the man who, in their eyes, had saved as many sailors' lives as Marconi, and whose only memorial thus far was a dockland street named after him. At their urging, the National Union of Seamen erected the present Plimsoll memorial on Thames Embankment. The man who unveiled it was a shipowner, Sir Walter (later Baron) Runciman, who had himself served as a seaman, long before the agitation by his friend Plimsoll, in what he has called 'days of aboriginal stupidity and sordid blood-sucking', when ships were 'scandalously unseaworthy, rotten, leaky, badly found, badly manned, abominably fed and always overloaded'.

In that month – August 1929 – Samuel Plimsoll had perhaps a better Press than ever he had received during his life or in the thirty years since his death. Even his obituary notices, in 1898, had lacked the flattery usually accorded to the newly-dead. *The Times*, while granting that he was a man of great sincerity, had described him as 'one whose sole stock-in-trade was an unrivalled capacity for becoming fervidly indignant upon hearsay evidence'. Of his famous pamphlet, *Our Seamen*, it said that 'the naked truth thrust itself through the cloak of exaggeration and ignorance'. The *Daily News* obituarist was more friendly, but said 'flattery itself could not have made of Samuel Plimsoll anything but a man of a very commonplace and ordinary type'.

Disraeli, in his day, had said harsh things about the propagandist of the loadline. Writing to Lady Bradford, in 1875, he described Plimsoll as 'a Moody and Sankey in politics, half rogue and half enthusiast – that is to say, one of those characters who live by pandering to passion and fall into an enthusiastic love and admiration of themselves'.

In Plimsoll's lifetime there were critics who denied that he had advanced by one iota the cause of the seaman, but held on the contrary that he had done it as much harm as he had wrought to the institution of Parliament. Even today historians are sometimes painfully cautious not to overpraise him. For example, in his well-known work, *British Shipping* (1939), R. H. Thornton says:

> Most of us have been brought up to believe that an enlightened and benevolent gentleman named Samuel Plimsoll fought a single-handed and triumphant battle with an industry ruthlessly exploited by human greed. . . . The facts are that throughout the whole period from 1850 to 1906 Parliament was actively concerned with the improvement of conditions in the Mercantile Marine and scarcely a year passed in which a Commission was not sitting or a Bill was not in course of preparation. The Plimsoll agitation was little more than an incident in that process. He was the sincere but hysterical member for Derby, a constituency as far removed from a British seaport as it is possible to be.

Plimsoll, says Thornton, adopted the familiar tactics of grossly overstating the case. This is Thornton's verdict:

> It is probable that on balance his efforts did more good than harm. But he was not a reformer. He was a propagandist and the famous 'Plimsoll Mark' indicating the maximum safe draught of a ship remained a valueless safeguard for no less than sixteen years after he secured it, for the simple reason that the selection of its position on the ship's side was left to the 'murderers' (i.e. the shipowners) themselves. . . .

The choice of an inland constituency – a point on which the member for Derby was frequently mocked – is explained by Dr A. H. Japp in his short sketch of Plimsoll in *Good Men and True*. Vested interests in the seaport towns, he says, were too strong for any candidate who let it be known that he aspired to clean up the shipping industry.

The first time Plimsoll contested Derby he was defeated, but he was elected as a Liberal Member in 1868, the year before the Suez Canal was opened. It was a period when British shipping, which carried more than half the world's maritime tonnage, was going through a change of life. For a generation sail had kept a long lead over steam, but now, with Holt liners steaming prodigious distances non-stop and the great ditch open at last, the sailing ship was doomed. Just as remorselessly, iron hulls were replacing wood.

Even those who most rejoiced in the ubiquity of the Red Ensign knew that there was a dark side to the picture. On the one side there were superb, arrogant East Indiamen, China Clippers of surpassing grace and speed, great vessels of which John Masefield (who served in them) wrote:

> They mark our passage as a race of men,
> Earth will not see such ships as those agen.

But on the other side of the picture were the coffin ships, the rogue ships, the spongy slums which had done so much over the centuries to foster the notion that it was part of a sailor's lot to be drowned; ships which even the most adventurous underwriter turned down, and which were 'insured' by the owners themselves in clubs which sometimes charged premiums as high as thirty per cent, on the theory that if one vessel in four sank there would still be a profit. . . .[1]

. . . Anyone could, as Plimsoll pointed out, build a ship to whatever specifications his caprice or greed might dictate, using insufficient strengthening timber or too-thin iron plates. He could superimpose poops and fo'c'sles and cattle decks until it appeared that he had built one ship on top of another. He could cut a vessel in two and lengthen it by fifty or seventy feet without strengthening it. He was under no obligation to have his vessel classed or surveyed. He could truss and patch and plug a hundred-year-old hulk, soft as a rotted pear, knowing that it had only to touch ground to disintegrate. Hardly ever was a ship broken up voluntarily; it was passed from owner to owner, in a way which reminded one Member of Parliament of the Irish girl who, finding that her fine dress was dragging her down to Satan, give it to her younger sister.

A shipowner could load a vessel until the deck was within a foot or two of the water and dispatch her into the forty-foot waves of the Bay of Biscay. He could put 786 tons of cargo into a ship of 550 tons register and send her, or try to send her, to New Orleans in December.[2] He could deck-load his vessel as he pleased (one owner said that the more bales of cotton on the decks the better the crew's chance of being saved if the ship went down). He could send steamers designed for lake and canal service across the Atlantic. He could load bulk grain in ships too weak, and inadequately equipped, to withstand its

1. Even more spectacular risks were accepted by some operators. Joseph Conrad tells of individuals who specialized in taking over the insurance, for a fat premium, of ships reported 'overdue' in the *Shipping Gazette*, in the hope that they would later turn up.

2. Case cited by Sir J. Pakington in House of Commons in 1873.

pressure (Plimsoll drew an analogy of crocuses and snowdrops moving flagstones, thanks to 'the vital forces which the spring sets in motion'). He could load a ship beyond the capacity of her engines. And he could insure both ship and cargo for a sum in excess of their real value, so that if the vessel foundered she would show a far more handsome profit than if she reached her destination. He could bully or dismiss those captains who refused to load heavily, and smile on those who did.

He could save money, again, by sending the vessel out undermanned, or manned only by the sweepings of the waterfront. By collusion with crimps and boarding-house keepers he could arrange to have men perpetually in his debt and thus always available for a voyage. And he could have the crews jailed for refusing to sail.

Plimsoll was never under the delusion that all these abuses could be cleared up immediately by one Act of Parliament. As it turned out, at least fifty Acts, all aimed at improving the sailor's lot, were passed between 1870 and 1900 – and even then men were still going down to the sea in slums. But Plimsoll did maintain that provision could be made to enforce the repair of all ships; that gross overloading could be prevented; that deck loading could be abolished, at all events in winter; and that grain ships could be loaded in such a way as to prevent them bursting apart.

The loadline, over which the major controversy was to rage, was not a new idea. Nearly a thousand years before, the Venetian and Sardinian sailors had a load mark – a disc very like what was later called the Plimsoll Line; so had the traders of the Hanseatic League. The British Navy found no difficulty in drawing up a loadline, based on fighting efficiency. Many chambers of commerce had petitioned for one to be imposed on merchant shipping. Admittedly, this was not the easiest matter on which to legislate. It was possible, at one stroke of the pen, to decree an arbitrary line for wooden ships and iron ships, sail ships and steam ships, of all dimensions, operating in all oceans and at all seasons. But if Plimsoll over-simplified the problem, his opponents zealously over-complicated it.

Samuel Plimsoll's first plea in Parliament for the British seaman was in 1870, when he brought forward a motion deploring the loss of life at sea, and urging his compulsory loadline. A Government Bill aimed at improving seamen's conditions was withdrawn that same year, owing to pressure of business. Next year, Plimsoll, having approached the trades unions for help, brought in a Bill of his own, but was persuaded to withdraw it in favour of a Government measure of seven hundred clauses, all of which the shipowners were prepared to contest indefinitely. If ever a Bill suffered from excessive deck loading, this was it. However, despite strong and sustained opposition, a few of the clauses were suffered to be passed that year. Shipowners were now compelled to mark draught scales on their vessels, and also to choose one name for a ship and – having marked it legibly on the hull – to stick to it. Applications to change a vessel's name were henceforth carefully vetted: the owners of a ship called *The Devil* had to fight hard to be allowed to re-christen it *The Printer's Boy*. The Act also allowed a crew to demand an investigation into a vessel which they believed to be unseaworthy, with the proviso that they should pay the cost of the examination if their allegations were unfounded – a stipulation well calculated to deter seamen from attaching too much value to their lives. It became a misdemeanour to send an unseaworthy vessel to sea.

Plimsoll made no secret of his disappointment. He decided it was time to rouse the indignation of the country. In 1872 he marshalled the facts for his celebrated exposure, *Our Seamen*, which was published at the beginning of the following year. It was not his first publication; he had already written unnoticed pamphlets on the coal trade, and one entitled *Plan to Have Fatherless and Motherless Children Cared For Instead of Being Consigned to the Workhouse*.

Our Seamen was described by its author, with more modesty than accuracy, as a pamphlet; in fact, it was a plump, well-illustrated volume. As time went on, it was to receive a good deal of re-editing, extending and expurgating. Those piquant passages which became the subject of legal proceedings were replaced by rows of asterisks. Soon after its publication, Plimsoll announced a fourpenny popular version of which he proposed to print a million copies, 750,000 of them for working men.

There was nothing cold and objective about Plimsoll's style – 'Oh, my God! What can I say, what can I write to make the people take thought on this terrible wrong?' Emotional as was the manner, however, the book was nevertheless a good job of exposition for the ordinary man, even though the experts were to quibble at his statistics and even more at the inferences he drew from them. A less impetuous man than Plimsoll would have taken the precaution of having the manuscript read by a lawyer and thus saved himself an immense amount of worry, besides strengthening his case.

Plimsoll's book began with photographic reproductions of some damaging passages from *The Lifeboat* and from the annual reports of the Board of Trade. In 1868 the officials of that department had noted that of the 2,000 vessels in the carrying trade which suffered wreck or casualty, 'half of the number is represented by the unseaworthy, overladen or ill-found vessels of the collier class chiefly employed in the coasting trade. For the six years ending 1868 the number is more than half.' Then, for the benefit of the man in the street, Plimsoll gave a detailed exposition of underwriting. He had a photograph of a typical insurance guarantee, in which dozens of underwriters, one after another, had contracted to cover £100 or so of a vessel's value. Plimsoll's point was that underwriters took a risk on a vessel which they had never seen, and of which they knew nothing. If the ship was sunk, it was easier to pay up without asking questions, however grave the suspicion that an over-insured vessel had been sent to her doom. To start an investigation would involve heavy expense in obtaining witnesses from overseas, and as often as not their evidence would be merely hearsay, the real witnesses being drowned. A spectator's statement that a vessel looked low in the water was no proof of overloading in a court of law. Underwriters, said Plimsoll, were perfectly aware that they were being defrauded. A Board of Trade official had written in the *Journal of the Society of Arts*: 'Let ships be lost and let cargoes be lost so long as underwriters are too sordid or too lazy to refuse payment of doubtful and fraudulent cases.' All that underwriters felt impelled to do was to form their own black list of flagrant and proved offenders. That was the reason why a cargo guarantee would sometimes read: 'Warranted not to be shipped in any vessels belonging to . . .' The Dutch, Plimsoll pointed out, had a rule that a vessel could be insured for no more than two-thirds of her value.

Our Seamen contained startling enough photographs of rotten beams and 'devil' bolts (sham bolts used by economical builders) which said more than words. The trouble was that the words said too much. One passage which was to involve Plimsoll in tiresome legal toils told how in 1870, when shipping legislation was before the House, he was approached by a certain member who said he would like to be present at the debate, but was unable to do so because of a dinner engagement. Said Plimsoll: 'I think you should not be absent.' When the member asked why, Plimsoll said it was because he might have to tell the House the name of a Member of Parliament 'notorious for excessive and habitual overloading and a reckless disregard for human life who had lost seven oceangoing steamers and drowned more than a hundred men in less than two years . . .'. The member who had accosted him, said Plimsoll, had put down an amendment to postpone the Bill for six months, but on hearing this warning he went silently away and withdrew his amendment, returning 'with a face like that of a dead man' to tell Plimsoll what he had done. Another member had threatened him with a libel action if he mentioned a certain sinking. Plimsoll said he refrained, in 1871, from revealing in Parliament the names of these two members, 'hoping to succeed without doing so'. They, however, spoke against his Bill, and by the rules of evidence he was unable to reply. But he warned: 'I recommend these gentlemen to be more discreet next session if they wish to preserve their incognito.'

It was an age when scores of excellent pamphlets, urging every variety of reform, were being printed at their authors' expense and hopefully circulated, only to be met with apathy and at once forgotten. *Our Seamen* was a dazzling exception. It received generous space in the newspapers and its charges became almost at once a national issue. Three hundred Members of Parliament wrote to Plimsoll, of whom ninety-seven asked that their names should be put on the back of his next Bill. As this was hardly feasible, he decided to select the first ten names. He was given leave to introduce his Bill, but the member for Kingston-upon-Hull, C. M. Norwood (of whom more was to be heard), said he hoped the House would suspend judgement as the book was an *ex parte* statement which could be satisfactorily answered.

In February 1873 Plimsoll sustained a succession of shocks resulting from *Our Seamen*. One of the sharpest was when the shipowner member for Tynemouth, Eustace Smith, complained that the book was a breach of the House's privilege. The Clerk read out the passages about the two Members of Parliament who were, by inference, guilty men; also the passage: 'Owing to the fact that two or three of what they call in the North "the greatest sinners in the trade" have got into the House, it is there and there only that opposition to reform is to be expected or is found.' This, coupled with Plimsoll's threat to disclose the identities of the two members if they took further part in debates, was, in the view of the member for Tynemouth, sufficient justification for condemning Plimsoll's conduct as 'highly reprehensible and injurious to the honour and dignity of this House'. Any motion of censure, the member for

Tynemouth pointed out, would be independent of legal proceedings which, he understood, the two members were taking against Plimsoll.

Plimsoll, taken by surprise, made 'the most ample apology in his power' for 'an inadvertent offence against the House' and then withdrew. As *The Times* later pointed out, the apology 'was carefully worded so as to appease the House itself, without making any *amende honorable* to individual members'. Fortunately for Plimsoll, the House was content with the terms of the apology.

In a month's time the number of legal actions against Plimsoll had increased to four. He wrote to *The Times* revealing the terms of a letter which solicitors acting for the owners of the *Parga* had sent him (this vessel had been stopped from going to sea by Board of Trade inspectors, acting on information from Plimsoll). The lawyers' letter ran:

> Sir. – A copy of your letter of the 19th of March addressed to the President or Secretary of the Board of Trade imputing utter unseaworthiness to our clients' vessel the *Parga* has been handed to us and we are instructed to demand the name of the person from whom you have received the intelligence and also to request an apology for injury sustained by our clients in consequence of your statement.

Plimsoll did not reveal the terms of his reply in *The Times* but it is on record in the *Nautical Magazine*:

> I will not give you the name of my informant. I will make no apology; and as to compensation, the only compensation due to your clients and all other shipowners who send unseaworthy vessels to sea with men a thousand times better than themselves on board is in my opinion a halter apiece and the offices of a hangman. Do your worst. [Signed] Samuel Plimsoll.

Also on record is the outcome of an appeal by the *Parga* owners; the vessel was ruled seaworthy, and heavy costs were awarded against the Board of Trade. It was not Plimsoll's most successful intervention.

There are few men who can go calmly about their day's work with a plurality of libel actions hanging over them. The strain and the excitement began to tell on Samuel Plimsoll. But his mail was not exclusively filled with threats and 'frighteners'. He received a large number of letters from seamen, and from wives and mothers of seamen, begging him not to let himself be discouraged by his initial setbacks. The man in the street was with him; the man in the street who cared not a straw for the feelings or dignity of Parliament, and who thought that a man who was not afraid to call shipowners villains and murderers was someone after his own heart, a man likely to achieve results.

From a ship's officer came a letter revealing the shocking overloading of ore ships from Spain. It ended: 'I dare not sign my name for I should never get a ship again.' The writer had no need to worry about getting another ship; he was drowned the day after he wrote the letter.

Wherever he spoke, and that was nearly everywhere, Plimsoll was greeted with a heady enthusiasm. At one meeting there was a shipowner in the audience with a legal document in his pocket, but he judged it expedient not to present it. Plimsoll's biggest personal success was probably at a crowded meeting at Exeter Hall – home of reformers' meetings – at which the audience stood cheering, waving hats and handkerchiefs, for some minutes. Plimsoll described the demonstration as 'like the sound of pipes to the beleaguered garrison at Lucknow'. He told this audience how he had been approached to limit the operation of his Bill for classifying all shipping to those vessels still unbuilt. A gentleman had said to him:

The people who own these ships will be put to a good deal of expense. Why, if they go to Lloyd's for survey some of these ships will have to be pulled to pieces (Voice: And a good job too!) and it won't do. These people will be conciliated if you let their ships go on as they are and apply your Bill to new ships. (Laughter).

The strongest words at this meeting were used, not by Plimsoll, but by the Earl of Shaftesbury, as president, who 'asked for no restraint of language and hardly for restraint of manners'. He spoke of the coffin ships traffic as 'one of the most terrrible, the most diabolical systems that ever desolated mankind.'.

In seaports Plimsoll was cheered and chaired; banners bore his name and bands preceded him. His own landlubber constituents of Derby endorsed his campaign with enthusiasm. A fighting fund was opened, to which Plimsoll himself contributed £1,000 and his wife £500. Yorkshire miners voted for a shilling levy and sent in £1,000, and a similar sum came from an engineers' union. Lloyd's also decided to contribute, with a strict proviso that their funds were not to be used to defray any libel damages. It was a notable gesture, considering that Plimsoll in *Our Seamen* had described underwriters as 'a weak body of men whom a shipowner can bully into an unjust settlement'. Probably the most encouraging event of this year for Plimsoll was the action of the Aberdeen White Star Line in christening their new wool clipper the *Samuel Plimsoll*, and even installing a frock-coated, top-hatted effigy of the member for Derby as a figurehead.

Plimsoll's earlier campaigns had been pooh-poohed by the shipowners on the grounds that an 'army' of inspectors would be needed to carry out surveys, and that the cost to the country would be £500,000, to which Plimsoll retorted that nineteen extra surveyors would be enough and that the State could even make a useful profit. With the publication of *Our Seamen* shipowners began to clutch to each and every argument against State interference. By tying up shipping in the ports, the Plimsoll plan would bring 'absolute and immediate ruin' to the industry, declared a Whitby shipowner. The *Shipping Gazette* said that his interference would cause a large percentage of collier vessels to be withdrawn from the coasting trade, 'to the benefit of inland carriers and to the interest of not a few of Mr Plimsoll's constituents'. It would be only a question of time, chorused the shipowners, before the Red Ensign was swept from the seas and the life of the great seaports was strangled. Those owners who wished to continue in business would have to sail their ships under a foreign flag. In Canada and elsewhere were found incredulous shipowners who threatened to boycott British ports, or who said they would demand to be treated as foreigners.

More cautious owners, not wanting to be accused of lack of solicitude for their seamen, contented themselves with deploring the idea of hasty legislation, or demanding that nothing should be done until a Royal Commission had reported, or (always a good delaying argument) until a measure of agreement had been achieved with other nations. Others argued that there was already an impossible amount of maritime legislation on the Statute Book; while yet others – the dewier innocents – thought that it was a 'dangerous precedent' for the Government to intervene in the shipping industry, and this after more than fifty years of State intervention in mill and factory.

One of the commonest arguments, to be repeated parrot-fashion for years, was that State inspection would destroy the owners' own responsibility to keep their vessels well found and manned; to which the quick answer was that the State could not destroy what in too many instances had never existed. More weighty was the fear voiced by Alfred Holt, who thought that the good owner, with standards far higher than those likely to be enforced by the State, might be tempted to lower those standards on seeing rival ships, approved by the Government, put to sea weighed down a foot deeper than his own. There was always a risk that certain owners might perform the minimum of maintenance in order to pass a survey, putting the blame for any subsequent mishap on the Government.

A powerful group of owners thought it wrong that the State should seek to delegate powers of survey to private organizations like Lloyd's and the rival classification societies, which might be tempted to compete for business by cutting each other's standards. It was even darkly hinted that Lloyd's were behind the whole campaign, being out for self-aggrandizement. The shipowning member for Tynemouth spoke of 'an irresponsible committee sitting in Cornhill', and the shipowning member for Kingston of Lloyd's 'hole and corner' constitution.

There was not such solidarity among the shipowners – including as they did rugged individualists of the most ruthless type – that they could not be divided among themselves. Even at their indignation meetings they were at loggerheads. Sometimes bad owners judged it expedient to give noisy support to Plimsoll, just as good owners, honestly convinced that his proposals were folly, took the risk of abusing him. The small owners waxed indignant when they found some of the big lines supporting Plimsoll (the naming of that clipper was hard to forgive) and even contributing to his funds; they smelled a conspiracy to put the small operator out of business. Loud were the moans of the men who operated the little ships. Were they not the nursery of Britain's merchant marine, and of her Navy too? Run them out of business, and commerce and defence alike were doomed. Unfortunately, with shipowners as with millowners, it was often the small operators who imposed the worst conditions on their servants. The man who had struggled up from the deck to the bridge and had finally saved enough to buy a decrepit old hulk could not afford to repair it – even if he had the urge to do so – until he had made a few successful voyages; and given keen competition, he could not make any successful voyages without overloading.

Into the controversy, too, was dragged Merchant Jack himself: an honest, loyal fellow, according to Plimsoll, a drunken incompetent according to the owners. Ships foundered, they argued, not because they were overloaded with cargo, but because their crews were overloaded with liquor. What was needed in the Merchant Marine was Navy discipline. In their low opinion of Merchant Jack, of his ability and his morals, the shipowners were supported by the Board of Trade. Cavendish Bentinck, secretary of that department, told Parliament that 'nobody would believe the sort of rubbish that was picked up to serve as seamen. Many of them did not know the meaning of starboard and port and could not be trusted at the helm.' And the Duke of Somerset told his fellow peers that the vessels in the Mersey and Thames were reduced to the status of hospitals in which drunken seamen, carried aboard by their lodging-house keepers, might recover from their 'crapulous imbecility'.

When all arguments were exhausted, it was an irresistible temptation to attack Plimsoll himself: Plimsoll the landlubber; Plimsoll the harebrained enthusiast; Plimsoll the notoriety hunter; Plimsoll the man who got the facts wrong; Plimsoll the man who did not apologize when he got the facts wrong; Plimsoll who spent thousands of pounds exposing scandals which could have been proved non-existent for the price of a shilling telegram; Plimsoll who sought to prohibit death by Act of Parliament; Plimsoll who had taken personal possession of a public cause and had let it take possession of him.

Certainly the maritime statistics of the period were a treacherous jungle for an unseasoned explorer. What safe deductions could be made from statistics of wrecks, at a time when the entire shipping industry was changing its character, when trade and the capacity of vessels were alike expanding, when scores of ships foundered from causes unknown, when savage winters upset the law of averages? Plimsoll's analyses of statistics were no doubt fallible. Accidents had a way of happening to classed ships as well as unclassed ones; to vessels which were uninsured as well as those which were fully insured. Each man could draw his own picture from the lists of casualties. Cavendish Bentinck, of the Board of Trade, sought to assure Parliament that few ships were in fact lost from the reasons which Plimsoll put forward, that 'the main causes of the loss of life at sea were collisions, strandings, fires, shipping heavy seas, forcing quick passages, bad seamanship, icebergs and floating wreck, none of which could be made subject to Act of Parliament'. He admitted that 'scores and hundreds of vessels had gone down in stress of weather simply because they had been built out of all reasonable proportion'. Moreover he thought that more ships were lost through being underloaded than overloaded (Joseph Conrad was critical of shipowners who advertised ships as being able to proceed without ballast). It was clear where Bentinck's sympathies lay when he said that, while he had no wish to discourage surveyors who might be appointed, he could not help thinking of the immense powers they would wield and of the enormous amount of capital over which they would exercise unlimited control if they were allowed on their own responsibility and judgement to stop a ship from going to sea.

Some of the misfortunes listed by Cavendish Bentinck – such as 'strandings' and 'shipping heavy seas' – could have been caused in part by overloading and other abuses, to which Plimsoll drew attention. When all the statistics had been bandied about, it was still clear enough to be unprejudiced that the causes which Plimsoll put forward contributed, singly or in combination, and to a culpable degree, to the deathroll on the high seas.

To say that a shipowner deliberately, and of malice aforethought, sent his over-insured vessels to sea in the hope that they would founder was a charge easy to make, almost impossible to prove. A man who burned down warehouses for insurance could, on occasions, be caught red-handed; a parent who killed an infant for its life insurance (a Victorian minor industry) could not always conceal the evidence of his sin. If arson and infanticide for insurance flourished, it may be that the murder of seamen for money also flourished. It is more probable, however, that the less scrupulous shipowners were actuated rather by the spirit of

> Thou shalt not kill, but needst not strive
> Officiously to keep alive.

The member for Tower Hamlets, J. Samuda, told Parliament of a shipowner who, towards the end of the Crimean War, invited tenders for building a new vessel. Estimates of £14,000 and £12,000 were submitted, and he accepted the lower. When the vessel sank, the builder who had tendered the £14,000 estimate said, 'You had better have had my ship.' Said the owner: 'Oh no, if I had it would never have gone to pieces; as it is I have the insurance on my ship and the insurance on my freight and I am better off than I should have been with yours.'

That was perhaps as near to murder as the more reckless shipowners approached; and it was quite near enough. No doubt, however, to a business man who practised such economics, and who salved his conscience by a generous contribution to lifeboat funds, it seemed iniquitous that a Newcastle paper should out-Plimsoll Plimsoll by talking of 'owners who regarded men as so much manure to force into enormous growth their private fortunes'. Some owners improved their standards as they improved their bank balances – but a man had to start somehow. After all, publishers of distinction had started by flooding the back streets with penny dreadfuls.

The popular indignation which had been aroused by *Our Seamen* had spurred the Liberal Government to appoint a Royal Commission, under the Duke of Somerset. Plimsoll was warned by *The Times* to curb his enthusiasm for legislation pending the Commission's report. The *Saturday Review* thought that perhaps he had succeeded in raising too much wind, and that the 'gusty vehemence of public opinion' might suffer a sudden reaction. The *Review* seemed pleased that Gustav Doré had snubbed Plimsoll by refusing to paint an epic canvas of a coffin ship foundering, and remarked that novelists had not yet taken up his theme. They had hardly had a chance as yet; in fact, several novels on the theme of coffin ships later appeared. To at least one of them – *A Voice from the Sea*, by the author of *Margery's Christmas Box* – Plimsoll contributed a foreword.

Meanwhile in the Queen's Bench the shipowner member for Kingston, C. M. Norwood, was seeking a criminal information for libel against Plimsoll. He had been accused by Plimsoll of sending a heavily overladen vessel, the *Livonia*, on a voyage to the Baltic after another shipowner had refused to touch the cargo. The *Livonia* had foundered a few miles from the English coast, and 'of course she was insured'. Norwood, owner of a dozen ships, said he had been in Egypt for the opening of the Suez Canal at the time of the *Livonia* episode so that he had had no personal hand in her loading. He had lost only one ship, and had never lost a seaman's life. The cause of the *Livonia* foundering, he said, was a breakdown in the engines which left her at the mercy of the sea. The Board of Trade had exonerated him, the underwriters had paid up their share of the loss; and his own loss had been £4,500. He never had a risk of less than £3,000 or £4,000 on each of his vessels.

The case of 'The Queen *v.* Plimsoll' occupied a great deal of space in the newspapers for several days. Ultimately after much learned wrangling it was cut short. Norwood lost his claim for a criminal information, as it was held that the *Livonia* had been overloaded. Two stevedores who helped store the cargo said, 'We would not have sailed three miles in the ship if we had to receive the whole ship and cargo as a present at the end of that distance.' But on the unfounded imputation that the *Livonia* had been hazarded in the hope of collecting insurance, Plimsoll was judicially reprimanded and ordered to pay his own very considerable costs. During the case the Attorney-General, Sir John Karslake, said that Plimsoll apparently imagined that 'so long as he had a laudable object in view he might say anything he pleased and make any accusation against whomsoever he chose'.

Not all the actions against Plimsoll came to judgement. According to Dr Japp there were as many as twelve against him at one period, but failure of the two principal ones caused the rest to be abandoned. Litigation only brought unfavourable publicity on the litigant. On the whole Plimsoll was lucky, for many of this statements had been undeniably reckless. He himself maintained, in letters to the newspapers and elsewhere, that he had been wrong in a negligible proportion of his statements, and that the only reason he did not defend himself in public against his accusers was that he did not wish to divert attention from the main issue.

Punch supported Plimsoll through thick and thin. Soon after *Our Seamen* appeared, it ran a full-page cartoon showing a seaman being embraced by his wife at the quayside. The sentiments expressed in the caption were a little premature:

> POLLY: O, dear Jack! I cannot help crying, but I am so happy to think you are not going in one of those *dreadful ships!*
> JACK: What, Davy Jones's Decoy Ducks! No, no, lass – never more! Thanks to our friend, Master Plimsoll, God bless him!

There was also a poem in praise of Plimsoll, to the air of 'Poor Jack', containing the lines:

> I call him the cherub who sits up aloft
> To keep watch for the life of Poor Jack.

The sometimes indiscriminate enthusiasm with which the Plimsoll campaign filled all manner of public bodies, from chambers of commerce to church assemblies, was a matter for great exasperation in the shipping Press. For example, the *Nautical Magazine*, which favoured reforms but not Plimsoll's reforms, was brought to a high state of indignation by a resolution of the Baptist Union, urging Parliament to enact that no vessels, overloaded, or undermanned, or in need of repair should be allowed to put to sea; not an unreasonable proposition, as it now appears. The *Nautical Magazine* decided to put the resolution on record 'in order that future readers may, in turning over our pages, be made aware of the extent to which unreason prevailed in 1873'.

> If 'little Bethel' would look after the 'spiritual and social' condition of the seamen, and of the Mollys of Wapping Old Stairs, and would endeavour to improve both, and would leave practical men to do the practical work of building and repairing ships, it would be better for all parties. . . . Would it not be better and wiser if 'little Bethel' were to petition Parliament to enact that all women shall be virtuous and all teachers of the people sensible?

Meanwhile the Royal Commission on Unseaworthy Ships was working its way through a mass of conflicting evidence. Charles MacIver, one of the founders of the Cunard Company, had no strong feelings about a compulsory loadline – 'it would not affect us one way or the other'. He agreed that there was extensive overloading of homeward-bound steamers from the Black Sea and Mediterranean, and concluded that the only reason that the more fortunate vessels survived the Bay of Biscay was that by this stage they had burned away some appreciable volume of their coal. If a Cunard captain brought home an over-heavy cargo, 'thinking to please', he was reprimanded for jeopardizing the ship. MacIver thought that all the ships should be classed, but was not in favour of breaking up old vessels. 'I would let [the foreigner] buy all our old ships just as the country sells old guns to Africans.'

Another leading shipowner, W. J. Lamport, was entirely against the loadline, as he thought it would encourage ingenious building to circumvent it, 'with the usual disastrous results of building with other objects than efficiency'. He considered that if the freeboard were marked it would be sufficient to allow a Board of Trade inspector to take action when he thought fit. Deck loading, he argued, was perfectly safe in summer, and 'it would not be suitable' to impose fines on owners of ships which arrived safely, deck-loaded, in stormy seasons. In fact, if all parties, including seamen, went into this matter with their eyes open, why should anyone object?

William Rundell, of the Liverpool Underwriters Association, said that his society had put 225 vessels on their blacklist in eleven years (one vessel, he admitted, had been on the list for eight years without disaster, though many others had gone down). The London underwriters had been offered this list, but had refused to give the necessary security guarantees. From Lloyd's secretary, Bernard Waymouth, came a curious sidelight on the inspection of ships. Once he had borrowed an engineer's overalls to crawl under a ship's boilers, where he found that the plates were badly wasted. At this point the owner arrived, indignantly refused to go on with the survey, and berated the engineer for lending his overalls and thus leading to embarrassing discoveries.

One merchant adventurer who had an uncomfortable passage before the Commission was the managing director of a Liverpool trading company owning twenty-three ships (the company turned out to be himself and his family). In his twenty-five years in the shipping trade, the witness had had an interest in seventy-three vessels, of which he usually insured the freights only. In the last ten years he had lost eighteen ships, some with all hands. The Commissioners took him remorselessly through his list of losses, which had been caused mostly, he claimed, by incompetence of the masters and crews. One vessel, the *Denmark*, formerly *The Great Republic*, which foundered in ballast *en route* to St John's had been described in this fashion by a member of the Commission, who reported on her:

She was trussed with transverse bars of iron, screwed up amidships like an old barn or church, before she started on this last voyage. That is to say, that the whole of the fastenings at the beam ends and knees were so rotten that there was no junction on the sides of the ship and this mode of fastening was introduced, and the only way of fastening the ship together was to introduce these enormous amounts of iron.

The witness said he had paid £3,500 for the ship and was then asked whether he had any reason to believe she was rotten. 'Not in the sense to make her unfit for her work,' was his cautious answer.

Do you think you have a right to expect a perfectly sound vessel at £1 a ton? – At that time there were a great many vessels in Liverpool and this vessel was not fitted for many trades but was fitted for the trade for which we bought her.

Another of the shipowner's lost vessels, the *Golden Fleece*, had been condemned as unseaworthy by two separate juries, in Liverpool and London, but the witness insisted that the cause of the ship's loss was negligence in closing a coal port.

What was the verdict? – It was against us.
Upon what ground? – I cannot tell the ground.
Do you mean to say that you do not know the ground upon which the jury found against you? – In both instances the verdict was found against us, and the point of unseaworthiness must have come before their minds.

Reducing the whole business to arithmetic, the witness pointed out that he had lost 139 men out of 10,928 employed, or only twelve per thousand, 'nearly half of them being lost by the captain's impropriety'. Of the balance, twenty-eight had been accounted for in one vessel, named, promisingly enough, the *Dawn of Hope*. The proportion of his losses, he said, was only six per cent in iron vessels and five per cent in wooden ones. And the witness stepped down, doubtless wishing that those who were so ready to criticize had the thankless job of selling off mishandled steamers in St Helena and arranging to bring the cargoes home piecemeal. For running ships on the cheap – apart from the ethics of the matter – must have been an accountant's nightmare.

To Plimsoll's chagrin, the Royal Commission did not favour a fixed loadline, still less Plimsoll's way of calculating one.[3] It decided that 'mismanagement and negligence of sailors is not less disastrous than carelessness of shipowners'; and in a later report it deplored insurance abuses. An Act was passed in 1873 to authorize Board of Trade surveyors to report overloaded ships, without however giving them any very useful guidance, and leaving a large loophole by which a master could put to sea while the surveyor was still awaiting a reply from the Board of Trade. Nevertheless, in the next two years 558 vessels were stopped from putting to sea, 515 of them being ruled unseaworthy, and 58 others had their cargoes lightened before they were allowed to proceed.

The Liberal Government fell early in 1874. As soon as Disraeli had taken over, Plimsoll introduced a new Bill to ban deck loading in winter and to force a survey of unclassed ships. He lost it by only three votes which, as *Punch* said, was tantamount in the circumstances to a victory. The Government introduced a new Merchant Shipping Bill, without giving it any exceptional facilities; and in the meantime Lloyd's and the Board of Trade endeavoured to draw up a system of buoyancy tables on which a scientific loadline could be calculated.

It was no sinecure being president or secretary of the Board of Trade at this period. Inevitably at times the occupants of these posts bridled at the constant jogging of their elbows, the allegations of complacency and inefficiency, not to mention manslaughter. Nor was it a sinecure being a doorkeeper at the Board of Trade, for Plimsoll was prepared to sweep into the Whitehall offices in the small hours of the morning to see that the department was on its toes. One day early in 1875 he tabled a Commons question asking Sir Charles Adderley whether he had an officer in attendance during the night to act on telegrams from surveyors reporting that unseaworthy ships were about to sail. Adderley replied that the porters had instructions to make contact with an appropriate official; whereupon Plimsoll said he had found telegrams at night at the Board of Trade which would not have been delivered but for his calling. Once, when Plimsoll asked about the overloading of the cable ship *International*, Adderley told the House that Plimsoll had drawn the attention of the assistant secretary of the Board of Trade to the case of the *International* at three o'clock in the morning. The House cheered, and Adderley hastily said, 'Yes, it was very much to the honourable member's credit'. In this instance, the port surveyor had already notified his department that the cable ship was overloaded, and she was lightened to the extent of one foot of freeboard. The same night, Adderley revealed, three other telegrams had been received alleging overloading of ships, one of which sailed before action could be taken. At this stage Adderley was promising a 'superior class of surveyors' who would be able to detain vessels on their own authority. The cavalier attitude of some shipowners towards port officials was revealed in another of Plimsoll's questions. What, he asked, did the Government propose to do in

3. Plimsoll's idea at first was to allow so many feet of freeboard to so many feet of hold, irrespective of the width of the ship. Technical experts favoured, but were slow to devise, a loadline based on 'reserve buoyancy', as calculated from 'the proportion which the capacity of the water-tight and solidly constructed part of the ship above the water bears to the capacity of the part immersed.'

the case of an official who was carried against his will to a Russian port? The House laughed, but Adderley said, 'I cannot see any cause for laughter – I think it is a most serious matter.' Then he announced that the master had been convicted under the 1873 Act and fined £5, the Court having decided that there were 'special reasons for inflicting a light penalty'.

Adderley did not like to see his department and his officials flouted; at the same time he was not a man to hurry the shipowners unnecessarily. Challenged over the case of the *Dania*, which left Shields for Malta with a clear side of fourteen inches on the port side and three feet one inch on the starboard, he said this was really only a question of list, and the mean of the two freeboards would be sufficient if the vessel were trimmed *en voyage*.

Plimsoll fumed increasingly at the delays of the Government Bill, and at the whittling down it sustained during debates. Even W. S. Lindsay, who was then writing his monumental *History of Merchant Shipping*, and whose sympathies were with the owners, admitted that much of the opposition to the Bill was frivolous. Adderley, who had charge of the Bill, was a 'weak vessel' (according to Disraeli), and at loggerheads with his colleagues. From time to time the Chancellor of the Exchequer, and even Disraeli, had to come to his rescue.

Once again Plimsoll had agreed to withdraw his own measure on the understanding that the Government Bill would be pushed forward and that he could move an amendment to it. Though he regarded this Bill as an 'atrocious sham' he still felt it could be improved in Committee. Frustration and delay continued to dog the Bill until, on 22 July 1875 – a memorable day in British Parliamentary history – Disraeli announced, 'with unfeigned and unaffected regret', that the Merchant Shipping Bill would be held over from that session, in order that the Agricultural Holdings Bill should go through. If both measures were debated, neither would be passed that session.

Plimsoll's demonstration of protest may or may not have been premeditated. In a state which the cautious *Hansard* describes as 'great excitement' – an unusual interpolation – he rose to move the adjournment of the House, urging his fellow members not to 'consign some thousands of living human beings to undeserved and miserable death'. The Shipping Bill, he said, had been so drawn as to afford 'unlimited facilities for death-dealing volubility and hypocritical amendments'. There were 'shipowners of murderous tendencies' outside the House, and they were 'immediately and amply represented inside the House' by men who talked to death every effort to provide a remedy.

In his excitement Plimsoll had forgotten that earlier occasion when he had challenged the honour of Parliament. The House was crying 'Name! Name!' and Plimsoll shouted, 'I will give names very soon.' He went on to talk of 'a few speculative scoundrels in whose hearts there is neither the love of God nor the fear of God'. Then, listing three 9,000-ton ships which had recently foundered, he said he would ask the President of the Board of Trade whether 'the registered owner of these ships, Edward Bates, is the member for Plymouth or if it is some other person of the same name'. Cries of 'Order' served to inflame him still further. According to the Parliamentary commentator, Sir H. W. Lucy, Plimsoll now advanced to the middle of the floor, opposite the Speaker, stamped his foot and shouted, 'I am determined to unmask the villains who send these men to their graves.' *Hansard* at this stage records 'Loud cries of "Order!" and much excitement'.

Mildly, in these circumstances, the Speaker said he trusted the word 'villains' was not intended to refer to any members of the House. Plimsoll assured him that it was, shook his fist at the imperturbable Disraeli and continued to declaim. Lucy says that at one stage he was eyeing the Mace as if contemplating making a clean sweep of the Treasury Bench with it. Twice he was invited to withdraw the expression 'villains', and twice he refused. Disraeli then rose to express regret that a member of the House should have conducted himself in a manner so unparalleled, at which Plimsoll retorted 'And so has the Government!' The Premier moved for a reprimand, whereupon Plimsoll withdrew, calling back as he left the chamber: 'Do you know that thousands are dying for this?'

Plimsoll's friend, A. M. Sullivan, member for Louth, rose to say that he knew Plimsoll to be 'extremely ill', and that the scene was the 'result of an overstrain acting upon a very sensitive temperament'. He suggested that after a few days' rest Plimsoll would be willing to apologize. Disraeli agreed to this course, and the motion of censure was put off for a week. There is no doubt that Plimsoll was lucky in the indulgences extended to him in Parliament.

Plimsoll's protest did him anything but harm in the country's eyes. The newspapers clicked their tongues at him, but they were very critical of Disraeli's decision to give preference to the Agricultural Bill – 'the greatest mistake the Government has yet made', said the *Morning Post*. It was not only the jubilant Liberals who suggested that Disraeli had misjudged the strength of national opinion. In his private correspondence with Lady Bradford, Disraeli recorded, half-contemptuously, the rumours that Plimsoll would arrive at the House defiant, 'with four brass bands, an open carriage with four white horses and 20,000 retainers', determined to get himself into the custody of the Serjeant-at-Arms.

To his credit, Plimsoll declined to become the central figure in a political stunt – if such a stunt were really contemplated. In a dignified speech to the Commons, he confessed that he had overstepped the limits, and apologized 'in no grudging or reluctant spirit, but frankly and sincerely'. Disraeli, showing more magnanimity in public than in private, said he would not have moved for a reprimand had he known that it was 'a case of over-strained sensibility in a man excited by his devotion to a cause'. The House was in a relieved, and hence forgiving mood, and the two members who rose to point out that Plimsoll had made no *amende* to Edward Bates received no noticeable support.

Bates went to some trouble to clear himself. He told the House that he had been unfortunate enough to lose six ships in three years, but all had been A1 iron ships and had been under-insured to a total of £41,285. 'All shipowners have not been blessed with the world's gear to the extent that I have been', he said, in explanation of his continued solvency. The House accepted his explanation; but Plimsoll held his peace.

Even before Plimsoll apologized to Parliament, a new Merchant Shipping Bill, containing an assortment of clauses skimmed from the longer Bill, was rushed before the House. The day after Plimsoll's apology it received its second reading. New powers were given to the Board of Trade to detain any vessel deemed unsafe through defective hull, machinery or equipment, or improper loading or overloading, and officers were empowered to act without reference to Whitehall. The Act even contained provisions for a loadline, but it was a loadline to be fixed where the owner thought fit. To this extent the Bill was a triumph for Plimsoll's old adversary Norwood. At least, it was argued by Norwood and his supporters, a loadline of this type would enable seamen and shipping agents to see how far in the water it was proposed to immerse a vessel, and a master would be discouraged from shipping those last few tons at the last minute. Charles MacIver protested at the physical disfiguring of merchant vessels by the new device, which was only a temporary measure. The best criticism of this so-called 'Plimsoll Line' – more correctly the Norwood Line – came from a whimsical Cardiff captain, who inscribed the device on his funnel.

This temporary Act was confirmed and extended in 1876. The Commons had even agreed to ban deck loading, but the Lords, under 'the malign and homicidal influence' of Lord Carlingford (Plimsoll's phrase) altered the Bill to allow three feet of deck loading. A limit was also set on the amount of grain which could be carried in bulk.

This rush of legislation drew acid comment from the anti-Plimsoll party. After the big scene, the writer of a letter in the *Shipping Gazette* (which itself had preferred Plimsoll's own Bill to that of the Government) had written:

> Plimsollism is founded on the false basis that every man but a Plimsollite is a rogue and every ship is a dangerous coffin. . . . Plimsollism is another word for terrorism. The present Bill is 'Plimsollism in a panic'. It will place the whole shipping interests in the country under Board of Trade beadles. It is a revival of 'parochial bumbledom' in its worst form. It will give every one of those Board of Trade beadles power to detain any ship he may see and it will encourage tips to the beadles not to see.
>
> Mr Plimsoll's eccentricities the other night were expressly excused by his friend on the ground that he was so excited as not to be responsible, and yet in shipping matters Plimsollism endeavours to secure safety and sanity by taking away responsibility. The one system treats the nation as an honest nation and an Englishman as an honest and brave man; the other (Plimsollism) treats the nation, Parliament and Government as dishonest and Englishmen as rogues and fools of an emasculated race.

Vanity Fair complained that 'the assembly which practically rules us has neither ability nor courage to resist the most insane and fatal propositions, if only they are presented with sufficient violence and clamour'. The new legislation meant the death of the small adventurers, said *Vanity Fair* – the kind of men who took their wives to sea with them. Hundreds of little craft had been broken up, and in every Continental port could be seen the humiliating spectacle of British vessels with British crews sailing under Belgian colours 'because they have been driven out of their nationality by [Plimsoll's] ridiculous and vexatious interference'.

These vessels, said *Vanity Fair*, were 'perfectly good for the trade in which they are employed; but even if it were not so there can be no right in a free country to forbid men from earning their living by sailing in them. The captain certainly knows the ship and the crew are not forced to join her unless they please to do so, any more than the captain.'

The British sailor will soon be found walking about our ports with his hands in his pockets wondering why it is he cannot obtain employment and when he finds it becomes more and more difficult haply he may become aware that his friend Plimsoll has brought about this himself out of pure affection for him.

Vanity Fair had it that since 1873 some 875 British ships had transferred to foreign flags, not because they were unseaworthy but because the owners disliked 'interference'. Plimsoll in one of the later editions of *Our Seamen* said that of fifty-nine vessels which had transferred to the Belgian flag in eighteen months, twenty-one had since been wrecked and six were missing. There is independent evidence that the Belgian Government failed to show a proper gratitude for this influx of disreputable tonnage. Edward Matthews, who was sailors' chaplain at Antwerp, put in on record that one English owner was sent to jail and another fled over the border in the nick of time. . . .

The loadline which is Plimsoll's monument has suffered many adjustments, in peace and war. When it was raised in 1906 H. M. Hyndman used Plimsollian language in his pamphlet of protest entitled *The Murder of British Seamen by Mr Lloyd George, the Liberal Cabinet and the Board of Trade*. Subsequent statistics tended to show that his fears were unfounded.

As for deck loading – a problem which in its day vexed the ancient Greeks – it would have distressed the shade of Samuel Plimsoll to have listened to the debates on the Merchant Shipping Bill in the spring of 1949. The measure aimed, *inter alia*, at providing better radar equipment of merchant ships. Mr William Keenan, a Liverpool member, said:

I have very frequently seen very high deck cargoes coming into Liverpool, and no doubt they come into other ports as well. Sometimes the cargo has been lost overboard, or a ship comes into port with half the cargo over the side instead of on the deck.

And Mr S. Awbery, member for Bristol (Plimsoll's birthplace), said: 'I have seen a ship coming up the Bristol Channel with a deck cargo of twelve feet of timber and with a cable round the ship and the cargo to keep the cargo from moving.'

E. S. TURNER
Roads to Ruin
(1966), pp. 157–190, 200–201

3 Cornelius Walford

Even though most fields of human endeavour have an all-embracing work of reference in the English language, insurance is one area which seems to be peculiarly resistant to the encyclopaedic approach. Even in recent times, publishers eager to branch out into the buoyant sector of financial services publishing will investigate why there is no insurance encyclopaedia available to guide the industry and to serve as a ready reference of first resort. After all, each field has a Diderot of its own to build upon, lawyers have their *Halsbury's*, historians their Cambridge standard histories and so forth: The answer to the investigations as to why insurance has no such literary monument is provided by the awful example of the work of Cornelius Walford (1827–1885) and his *Insurance Cyclopaedia* which to this day exists in manuscript form in the archives of the Chartered Insurance Institute and in five stillborn 600-page bound volumes ending haphazardly with the first instalment of a sixth volume whose final pages comprise an article on hereditary diseases.

Walford, according to the entry in the *Dictionary of National Biography*, was something of a self-made man: solicitor's clerk at 15, inevitably, one supposes, a shorthand writer, a minor functionary for insurance and building society interests, followed by elevation as an actuary; later called to the Bar. His earliest success came with an *Insurance Guide and Handbook* in 1857 which possibly gave him the impetus to start a grander work. The *Handbook* enjoyed much greater success in the United States than at home – a persistent feature of Walford's life.

When Walford decided to proceed with his *Insurance Cyclopaedia* he did so – somewhat recklessly one feels – at his own expense; in this venture he lost several thousand pounds, a considerable sum of money in the 1870s. The preface to the work speaks volumes. Compilers, editors and authors of large reference works will know Walford's feelings:

> I cannot tell how far the work may even be welcomed in a popular sense here – the depressed state of our Insurance interests I confess causes me some misgivings. But I have one abiding consolation; and that is that every page of it will receive a hearty welcome on the other side of the Atlantic. There, it is an axiom of the business that knowledge is power; and in that spirit every word written either upon the former history or present practice of Insurance finds in the great body of Insurance officials, agents and canvassers countless thousands of readers. I must own (and without intending the smallest disrespect to Insurance interests here) that the recognition of this fact has had a sustaining influence upon me; it has often flashed across me in the dreary hours of the night imparting a ray of hope to the heart and renewed power to the pen.

Walford clearly had the instincts and attributes of an encyclopaedist. He appears to have excluded nothing from his gigantic work, he laboured mightily and worthily (as only a good Victorian could) over all manner of subjects of any conceivable insurance interest. The passage reproduced below, the entry on gluttons, will have to serve as a sample of the vast and rambling whole.

GLUTTON, GLUTTONY (from the Latin glutio, *I swallow*). – One who eats voraciously or to excess; one who stuffs or gluts himself with food; a gormandizer. The act or practice of a glutton. The words have other and more diffuse significations. The question has often been raised as to what effect gluttony has upon the human system? This point is too technical for discussion here; but what follows will throw some light upon it.

England has often been pronounced to be a nation of gluttons, and there is prob. too much truth in this impeachment. Dr Thomas Wilson [Dr of Civil Laws], in his *Discourse upon Usurie*, pub 1572, speaking of the characteristics of the different nations of Europe, says the charge against the Englishman is 'gluttonie in steade of hospitalitie;' and many other authors speak in the same sense – except that we are not in later times usually charged with want of hospitality.

Sir John Sinclair, in his well-known *Code of Health and Longevity*, first published in 1807, says: 'every one is aware that good health depends on a proper quantity of food, and a just proportion of solids and fluids. In polished nations, men commonly eat at least double the quantity of food necessary, and often four or five times more than they ought to do; and it cannot be doubted, that among the higher orders of society, *almost all the chronic diseases*, and many of the infirmities of old age, as well as the shortness of life in general, are owing to repletion.'

The subject will receive further elucidation under LONGEVITY.

Dr Farr says (32nd Rep. of Reg.-Gen.): 'Refined gluttony is as fatal as intoxicating drink.' And he asks, 'When will the culinary art be kept within its due limits, by simple elegant means please the taste, satisfy appetite, and sustain health. Who will take the lead in this cultivated temperance, and make an effort to put a stop to the ann. sacrifice of so many precious lives?' He is here referring to the increasing proportion of deaths from *Gout* [GOUT.]

It is very customary to associate (perhaps more by way of joke than in earnest) the Aldermen of the City of London with gluttony, very much on account of the number of public dinners their official life calls upon them to attend. This is only one of many vulgar errors. Mr J. J. Mechi, the well-known agriculturist, and himself for some few years an Alderman of the City, writing to the *City Press*, 18 Sept 1878, says: 'our City Aldermen are good living men, but temperate, and their minds are generally fully and variously occupied. During my aldermanship not one of our twenty-six had the gout, except friend . . . who was a most abstemious man, but I believe that he inherited it. Many of them have served the office from 15 to 34 years, and, as a body, their ages are, I am told, above the average.'

There are also cross-references to Abstinence, Food, Gormand, Gout, Intemperance, Longevity and Starvation.

The published volumes appeared between 1871 and 1878 though they do not seem to have occupied more than a part of Walford's busy life for he continued as the European manager of the New York Insurance Company, as an author of many varied works on such topics as decimal coinage, the Hanseatic League, guilds and fairs and a large number of articles on insurance topics. He was also a leading luminary of the Shorthand Society. Reading the scattered references to Walford in the insurance publications of his day, one recognises that the New World was far more impressed with Walford than his own countrymen. The American references to him dwell upon his great library and erudition, his prodigal labour (in addition to everything else he sired nine children by two different women and was married altogether three times). The DNB entry duly sets out his literary career, but refers perhaps slightly sneeringly to his 'short time at Felstead School', his residences in 'two adjoining houses in Belsize Park Gardens' and his interment at Woking Cemetery. Perhaps it is not so surprising that the only substantial scholarly work on Walford's work is a thesis by Humbert Q. Nelli of Georgia State University entitled *Index and Guide to Walford's Insurance Cyclopedia* (1976).

Closer to home, the remaining function of Walford's great inchoate work seems to be to act as a warning to publishers not to contemplate lightly or hastily the undertaking of such a project in the modern age as an encyclopaedia of insurance. So do the twentieth-century citizens of London continue to live in the houses and on the precedents laid down by their Victorian ancestors.

JONATHAN S. IGNARSKI

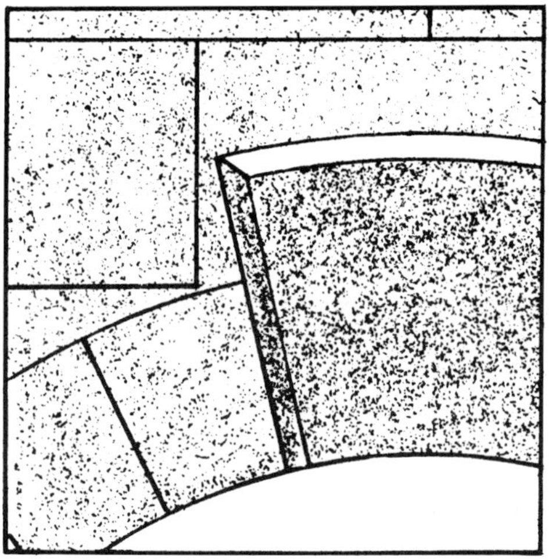

IX
Requirements of the Profession

1 The Right Type

A job in the Eastern Staff of the Union [Insurance Society of Canton, Ltd] usually started with an interview in London. The interview seems to have been rather cursory, with the Society looking for young men of that curious British classification, 'the right type'.

No precise definition exists of 'the right type', but it seems to have been a combination of an acceptable educational background, games aptitude, self-confidence and sociability.

Some candidates may have had some family connection with the East, though not necessarily in the Society. This is, perhaps, an indication of the status of the Society as an employer in the East as seen by others.

However, most candidates seem to have been motivated by romantic notions of Asia and a sense of adventure.

Before acceptance, the candidate had to pass a medical examination, which also seems to have been somewhat cursory.

Gus Caddick remembers his own medical in 1938 by an elderly doctor who had retired from the East, and whose practice in the City of London seemed to consist of medically examining candidates for the big British companies of Asia.

'The medical examination took place in a very small dark room, the walls covered with faded photographs of the Bund in Shanghai, the Peak in Hong Kong and similar', Caddick recalls. 'After the examination, the doctor looked me in the eye and said: "Going to the East for the first time, my boy? There is a lot of drinking in the East. There is nothing wrong with drinking. It is all that standing at bars which is bad for the heart." Armed with this advice, Caddick claims to have used bar stools ever since.

After acceptance, the candidate was on probation for six months in London, without pay, according to Roy Davidge, who joined in 1924. During this period, the candidate was supposed to learn the rudiments of insurance, and attend the School of Oriental Languages to learn Mandarin.

'It was said that acquiring this knowledge had little bearing on your future', says Davidge, 'except that it was likely to ensure that you were not sent to a place where it was spoken.' Davidge spent the early years of his service in Japan where he became proficient in Japanese.

ALAN CHALKLEY
Adventures and Perils
(1985), p. 18

2 The Right Place

Friday, offices of Hook Line & Sinker Re

A momentous day in the life of F. Rote! Robespierre Stanislav Jenkins, Chief Executive of Hook Line & Sinker Re ordered me to go to the Monte Carlo Rendez-vous which to the uninitiated is a more important conference for reinsurance than all the other hundreds of important conferences held throughout the year that reinsurers are forced to spend their time attending. Until now, my key role has been holding the fort back home but on account of Damian Ffanshawe falling off his polo pony and cracking three ribs, there was a vacant place to fill. I immediately thought of a hitch and explained that I had allowed my passport to lapse after an unfortunate holiday in Lanzarote when Mother got bitten by a waiter but RSJ went his usual dark purple (a typical type A, I fear) and told me to consult with Radcliffe Smith Fetlock, his PA, on the details. Mr Fetlock is going to Monte Carlo as is Miss Charlene Leotard, an ex-night club hostess whom RSJ very kindly is giving a chance to break into the reinsurance business. Think I will splash out and buy one of those executive briefcases with combination locks and built in bottle opener. Have a feeling that Mother isn't going to approve of the location particularly in view of her strong feelings about gambling.

Saturday, Hotel de Highrise

Staying in a pleasant hotel equipped with such necessities as a fridge bar, electrically operated curtains, an interesting device which if you put money in it makes the bed rock (unfortunately broken), a Bible (Mother please note) and dozens of colourful placards advertising the Lotus Eater Grill Room and Jimmy's Pad 'an exotic Mecca for the sophisticated set with cozy dining alcoves etc'. They brighten up the room no end. You can even see the sea if you peep round the tall block of holiday flatlets being built in front of the hotel. I definitely prefer it to Charlene's place, a huge American Hotel with its own casino in very vulgar colours and as for RSJ and Radcliffe I think they have got a very raw deal. A shabby looking place with few facilities apart from bidets, which Radcliffe told me with a ghastly snigger was specially built for the ladies in waiting for Edward VII.

I enjoyed the flight down and had a very pleasant light snack provided by British Airways. Probably the last decent meal I will have for some time. I always feel safe with Cling Film. I will draw a veil over the goings on of the rest of the passengers, most of whom I regret to say were of the same profession as myself. They were drinking gin and whiskies at 9 o'clock in the morning. Perhaps it was nerves. Charlene was certainly scared of flying and RSJ showed an unexpected kindly side to his nature plying her with brandies and patting her hand. He soon reverted when she was sick all over him. It was then he decided she would be more comfortable in the American Hotel and that he and Radcliffe should stay at this other curious place.

After we had arrived RSJ gave me the important job of registration. I collected a file with details of who is staying where and with whom. I wonder what sort of hotel the Residence Privee is? Some delegates are so hard up they have to live on a boat. I admire their determination to attend at whatever personal cost. Delegates from the Third World favour Nice – perhaps they feel more at home in an old British Colony. Went back to RSJ's hotel to find that he and Radcliffe had gone to meet an important client and in an emergency could be contacted at the Casino. Given up on getting the cocoa I ordered and will have to make do with the two boiled sweets I found tucked into my pyjamas.

Sunday, back at the Hotel

Reported for duty at 9 am prompt. RSJ came to the door of his room looking terrible. 'What the Hell, do you want, Rot?' he growled ungraciously. Do wish he would get my name right. I explained how keen I was to get cracking but he told me that the most useful thing I could do was to lie on the beach. 'Stop you looking like death warmed up', he bellowed. Thought it best to take him at his word and discovered a useful little mini bus just like the one that takes Mother to the Cherry Club. After parting with lots of cash to sulky young men and with very little on, I was soon esconced by a huge swimming pool surrounded by young ladies quite a few of whom were T*pl*ss! Passed a pleasant day plunging into the pool now and then to cool off. I overdid the sun a bit and by the time I returned to the hotel had to use a whole tin of Germolene Mother had thoughtfully provided. A brief message from RSJ to say that he and Radcliffe had an important meeting with our French counterparts SAVOIR FAI RE and in an emergency could be contacted at the Casino. I was to report at 8.45 sharp in the lobby of some hotel or other. Ate my boiled sweets and turned in early.

Monday

Put on my best dark suit, white shirt and Lloyd's Budgerigar Breeders' tie. As I approached the hotel I could hear the most extraordinary din coming from the lobby. Surrounded by thousands of people dressed in short sleeved shirts and light coloured trousers all laughing like banshees and clapping each other on the back. I assumed that RSJ had got the wrong hotel and instead of being at the Rendez-vous I had somehow got caught up in a get together of Cross Channel Ferry Stewards. Was astonished, therefore, to see RSJ dressed in the same fashion with his arm round someone's shoulder. 'Good Heavens' Rale!' he said breezily, 'I should think you're a bit warm in that get up aren't you? Meet Horacio Benvenuto.' With that Mr Benvenuto took me into his arms. I froze and winced at the same time on account of the sunburn and replied coldly when he asked for a meeting later in the day that I had come to a conference and there wouldn't be time for idle chat. RSJ went such a dark purple I was convinced the executive coronary had begun. 'You will meet Mr Benvenuto at the Cafe at 11' he commanded 'You don't come to a conference to attend the conference, you fool!' Decided that if I was required to sit around in cafes all day then so be it. Soon entered into the spirit of the thing and made several appointments in my Boots Nature Lovers Diary. Found the

Cafe quite disappointing, dirty tablecloths, tin ashtrays and gawping Italian day trippers. Mingling with them were lots of insurance men talking softly to each other over cups of coffee looking at the rest of the occupants of the cafe as though they would rather be with them. Caught sight of Mr Benvenuto with broker from LUSH PATSY & SCAPEGOAT. 'Room for a little one?' I said and drew up a chair. The man from LP&S choked and stormed off. Some people are odd. Benvenuto looked a little taken aback but suddenly slapped me on the back and said. 'I like you style, let's do some business.'

Back to the hotel in plenty of time to change into slacks and my Billericay Badminton Club blazer ready for the cocktail party. Proved to be disappointing. Considering how much we paid to be invited I think it a bit off to hold it in the municipal car park. Soon saw several old friends from other companies I have worked for before they were taken over and was chatting away happily until Radcliffe came up to me and hissed 'Don't let the old boy see you talking to friends – mingle.' It put me off my stride completely. I tried saying 'Hello there. Frederick Rote of HOOK LINE & SINKER here', but no one seemed interested. I saw Benvenuto but he was being looked after most solicitously by Charlene. RSJ and Fetlock were talking to two lovely young ladies who turned our to be our French counterparts. Life is full of surprises. RSJ seemed to have recovered his temper and was quite expansive. 'Neddy, old lad,' he boomed, 'we have one or two knotty problems to untangle with our French counterparts, why don't you and Charlene go and have dinner somewhere? Put it down on expenses.'

Tuesday, or should I say early Wednesday

Dinner party for our most important clients. We chose a little known but completely authentic bistro patronised by real French families and their dogs. After a long climb, through building sites and other authentic aspects of old Monaco we reached our destination. And what a time was had! Some of the other guests had been to a cocktail party which had been doling out vodka so we spent some time in the cordial way the Scandinavians have of toasting each other. Fortunately I am one of those people who can hold their drink and my trick with the disappearing coin went down particularly well. Charlene gave us her old night club act but as she said it is not quite the same without the python. Then we organised a race for the ladies round the streets of Monte Carlo. They entered into the spirit of things and disappeared into the night. Charlene won hands down but Mrs Benvenuto, a nice lady rather like Mother, only covered in diamonds, didn't return. Mr Benvenuto didn't seem to notice being busy congratulating Charlene. Altogether a very successful evening.

Wednesday

Dear Mother, just to let you know all is well. The sun is shining, how are things in Billericay? I am wearing my sun hat so no need to worry. Working very hard all day and most of the night. I had my first decent breakfast today at some do organised by a magazine called RENEW or something. It was nice to have eggs and bacon for a change although I had to ask for toast. They had some lovely sparkly orange juice as well. I wonder if you can get it at Safeways? I've switched off the air conditioning because of Legionnaires Disease and I am not letting any of the water pass my lips. See you Saturday. Don't forget Icarus's cuttlefish. Freddy.

Much later on

Had a meeting today with a very important client in a tent on a beach. Found it hard to concentrate talking business with scantily clad colleagues. After a nice dinner at which I entertained some clients by explaining the rules of cricket, one of the wives woke up and demanded to be taken to The Room. I pointed out the 'ladies' but apparently The Room is some sort of nightclub. The place was in darkness with loud music playing. Suddenly there was a roll on the synthesizer and a large lady appeared wearing a silver breast plate and began singing 'I Did It My Way' when from out of the darkness came leaping hundreds of people I recognised. There was old Turnups from CANDLEWICKS, Dave from WALLIES, FIBBER and Barry from FLOG, ROB & RUN like a Dantes Inferno in Lime Street. I left them to it but when I arrived back at the hotel there was a message from Radcliffe saying 'Come to the Casino. Urgent and bring some readies.' What a disappointment. Full of fruit machines and people in shorts with polythene cups of coins. Found RSJ looking harassed in the end rooms where you can only be admitted if you are in possession of a gold card which fortunately I had remembered. 'Where the Hell have you been?', he shrieked and snatched the cash from me. 'Here you are Vladi, old boy' he cried to his companion, a grim looking Slav, 'try your luck with that'. Mr Vladivostock kissed him rather extravagantly and blew the last of the petty cash on number 19. Suddenly felt very tired and missed Billericay.

Friday, 3 a.m.

Another full day of meetings, lunches, post lunch drinks, pre tea drinks, post tea drinks, pre cocktail parties, cocktail parties etc. RSJ was in generous mood and gave me two tickets for the Gala on condition I took Charlene. Unfortunately, he and Fetlock were going to be tied up all evening with our troublesome French colleagues again. Well I didn't need any urging. Charlene looked stunning in a gold lame jumpsuit with matching leg warmers and headband. After an excellent dinner the roof rolled back and on came the star turn, no less than Rick York, that wonderful singer from the 50's all in black leather slashed to the waist showing a gold medallion. We put our hands together for his wonderful band, his wonderful arranger and his wonderful new wife and then sang 'I Did It My Way' to rapturous applause. Charlene shattered the dream by saying she had had enough and wanted to go home. I noticed the Benvenutos leaving at the same time, Mrs B weighed down by jewellery and furs and looking grim. Watched the fireworks and looked in on the Casino at the American Hotel. Came across Mrs Benvenuto doing the Mexican Hat Dance in the middle of a fascinated audience. Not to put too fine a point on it she was completely whistled. Tried to restrain her but to no avail. This calls for a woman's touch I thought and immediately sought out

Charlene. Ran up to her room and knocked urgently on the door. Charlene answered in a fetching pink negligee trimmed with swansdown. To my surprise also saw Mr Benvenuto. 'Just the chap I wanted to see', I said cheerily. 'Your wife is feeling a little emotional, shall I tell her you're here?' Mr B gave a shriek and disappeared beneath the sheets and Charlene said 'Look you little twerp. Mr B and I are in conference right now. The air conditioning has failed, that is why we have taken extreme measures to keep cool. Go down to Mrs Benvenuto and if you value your job, keep your trap shut, OK?' Felt sure Mrs Benvenuto would understand when I explained about the air conditioning but when I returned found she had passed out cold, then Benvenuto arrived picking bits of swansdown off his jacket. 'Most grateful to you, my boy', he said 'Horacio Benvenuto knows how to repay a debt. I will be in touch.' He gave a hideous wink, put one finger to his lips and then began slapping his wife's face. Enough excitement for one evening.

Friday

Barely awake when a message came that a car was waiting down below. It was Benvenuto's Rolls-Royce which whisked me to a luxury villa in the hills. Round a swimming pool and consulting frequently on a white telephone Benvenuto promised me not only a share of his business but 100%. He repeatedly gave that hideous wink putting his finger to his lips and nodding in the direction of Mrs Benvenuto who, clad in a pair of dark glasses, swung in a hammock, moaning softly. 'Mamma's the word, eh!' he said. Quite frankly I would say anything he wanted for the enormous amount of busines he had just put my way. RSJ couldn't believe it when I told him the good news. 'You and I will have to do some talking, Fred old chap.' he said. 'Oh, by the way, Forelock, make sure Mr Rote and I are sitting together on the flight back will you?' Radcliffe went a pale purple.

Saturday. Acacia Avenue, Billericay

A successful first conference I think. Robespierre and I had a useful talk on the flight home and decided there was a lot of dead wood in the company and some harsh decisions would have to be made. The only blot on the horizon was a most vulgar note from Charlene saying she had decided to pack in reinsurance and had joined the crew of the Sun Goddess and that RSJ could take a running jump or words to that effect. Mother was glad to see me and I was glad to see her but have a feeling that Acacia Ave won't be quite the same. Still only a few more weeks until Baden Baden.

ANNE SWAIN
The Review (3 September 1984)

3 *The Right Time*

The most important work of the newly constructed [Antony Gibbs & Sons'] Insurance Department in the early nineteen twenties was the placing of Nitrate Insurances and at that time many Nitrate Cargoes were carried in Sailing Ships. The famous Laeisz Clippers, the 'Flying P Line', were chartered for many consecutive years as were the great French Barques of Ant. Dom. Bordes et fils, and many of the most famous British Sailers. One of the most interesting placements of the Insurance Department at that time concerned two well-known Sailing Ships, *Bellco* and *Milverton*. Both Ships were bound for France; one for La Pallice and the other for Dunkirk. According to prevailing delivery commitments it was necessary for the ships to be 'safely anchored within the Port' by the 30th June of the year in question. With about a month to go before the salient date both ships (some 70 days out from Chile) were unreported and unspoken. These vessels did not at that time carry long range wireless, and it was decided to obtain quotations for Policies to pay a Total Loss in event of the ships failing to arrive at their destinations by 30th June. The Underwriter first approached on the risk was Captain F. G. Povah, the last remaining Master Mariner to be an active Underwriting Member of Lloyd's. After looking up the voyage records of the ships and the personal records of their Masters in the archives of Lloyd's, Captain Povah rated the risks at 25 guineas per cent and instructions were given for £50,000 to be insured at this rate in respect of each vessel. Captain Povah led the risk with only £100 liability on each vessel but such was the respect in which he was held in regard to Sailing Ship matters the whole of the required amounts were covered on the terms he quoted.

The close of the adventure was dramatic in the extreme. Both Ships were 'spoken' off the Azores with about three weeks to go and both arrived off the Lizard with a very narrow margin of time and in unfavourable weather. There was a feeling amongst some of the Underwriters that fast and powerful tugs should be sent out to pull the Ships in but this was sternly negatived by Captain Povah who said a bargain was a bargain and he would see the venture through. One Ship reached La Pallice with 36 hours in hand and the other got into Dunkirk less than twelve hours before expiry of the period. The Underwriters interested sent messages of congratulation to the Masters and provided suitable gifts and gratuities for the Officers and Crews.

WILFRED MAUD
Antony Gibbs and Sons Ltd, Merchants and Bankers
(1958), p. 71

4 A Good Claims Department

When I got back to the office I found Keyes had been looking for me. Keyes is head of the Claim Department, and the most tiresome man to do business with in the whole world. You can't even say to-day is Tuesday without he has to look on the calendar, and then check if it's this year's calendar or last year's calendar, and then find out what company printed the calendar, and then find out if their calendar checks with the World Almanac calendar. That amount of useless work you'd think would keep down his weight, but it don't. He gets fatter every year, and more peevish, and he's always in some kind of a feud with other departments of the company, and does nothing but sit with his collar open, and sweat, and quarrel, and argue, until your head begins spinning around just to be in the same room with him. But he's a wolf on a phoney claim.

When I got in there he got up and began to roar. It was a truck policy I had written about six months before, and the fellow had burned his truck up and tried to collect. I cut in on him pretty quick.

'What are you beefing to me for? I remember that case. And I distinctly remember that I clipped a memo to that application when I sent it through that I thought that fellow ought to be thoroughly investigated before we accepted the risk. I didn't like his looks, and I won't——'

'Walter, I'm not beefing to you. I know you said he ought to be investigated. I've got your memo right here on my desk. That's what I wanted to tell you. If other departments in this company would show half the sense that you show——'

'Oh.'

That would be like Keyes, that even when he wanted to say something nice to you, he had to make you sore first.

'And get this, Walter. Even after they issued the policy, in plain disregard of the warning on your memo, and even with that warning still looking them in the face, day before yesterday when the truck burned – they'd have paid that claim if I hadn't sent a tow-car up there this afternoon, pulled the truck out, and found a pile of shavings under the engine, that proved it up on him that he started the fire himself.'

'Have you got him?'

'Oh, he confessed. He's taking a plea to-morrow morning, and that ends it. But my point is, that if you, just by looking at that man, could have your suspicions, why couldn't they? Oh, well, what's the use? I just wanted you to know it. I'm sending a memo to Norton about it. I think the whole thing is something the president of this company might very well look into. Though if you ask me, if the president of this company had more . . .'

He stopped and I didn't jog him. Keyes was one of the holdovers from the time of Old Man Norton, the founder of the company, and he didn't think much of young Norton, that took over the job when his father died. The way he told it, young Norton never did anything right, and the whole place was always worried for fear he'd pull them in on the feud. If young Norton was the man we had to do business with, then he was the man we had to do business with, and there was no sense letting Keyes get us in dutch with him. I gave Keyes' crack a dead pan. I didn't even know what he was talking about.

JAMES M. CAIN
Double Indemnity
(1936), pp. 6–7

5 A Good Pen

The annual report of the Accident Institute for the year 1909 contains an article which I am giving below which Kafka wrote as a clerk of the office. Naturally, Kafka is not mentioned by name in the report itself. But I remember exactly Kafka bringing me the annual report that year, and telling me this article was his work. His boss had corrected his draft, but Kafka's style can be seen unmistakably in passages here and there even in this technical work. The high official who was kind enough to see me also pointed out the passage, as well as another one in the annual report for 1910, and told me they were Franz Kafka's work.

Here is an extract from this document which is interesting in more respects than one:

Our illustrations show the difference between square spindles and cylindrical spindles as it affects the technique for the prevention of accidents. The cutters of the square spindle are connected by means of screws direct to the spindle and rotate with exposed cutting edges at speeds of 380 to 400 revolutions per minute. The dangers to the operator, presented by the large space between the cutter spindle and the surface of the table, are obvious. Such spindles were used either because the danger was not recognised, which may incidentally have increased the danger, or with a knowledge of the presence of a permanent danger which could not be avoided. Although an extremely cautious operator could take care not to allow any joint of his fingers to project from the timber when guiding it over the cutter head, the main danger defied all caution. The hand of even the most cautious operator was bound to be drawn into the cutter space if it slipped, particularly when, as often happened, the timber was hurled back (by the cutter block) while the operator was pressing the article to be planed against the table with one hand and feeding it to the cutter spindle with the other. This lifting and recoiling of the timber could not be anticipated nor prevented as it may have been due to gnarls or knots in the timber, to an insufficiently high cutting-speed, to warped cutters, or to uneven pressure of the operator's hands on the article. In such accidents usually several joints, and even whole fingers, were severed. Not only every precaution but also all protecting devices seemed to fail in the face of this danger, as they either proved to be totally inadequate or, whereas they reduced the danger on the one hand (automatic covering of the cutter slot by a protecting slide, or by reducing the width of the cutter space), they increased it on the other by not allowing the chippings sufficient space to leave the machine, which resulted in choked cutter spaces and in injured fingers when the operator attempted to clear the slot of chippings.

By turning back the spindle according to Schrader's patent and flattening it in a gentle slope right up to the cutters [i.e. by making it, eccentric – TRANSLATOR], clogging up of the cutter block will be avoided, whereby easy feeding of the timber to the cutter spindle and sufficient space for the chippings to leave the machine will also be effected.

The most important point in this connection, however, from the point of view of the prevention of accidents is that only the cutting edges of the cutters should be permitted to project, and that these cutters, forming as it were an integral part of the spindle, can be very thin without danger of fracture.

MAX BROD
The Biography of Franz Kafka
(1947), pp. 66–67

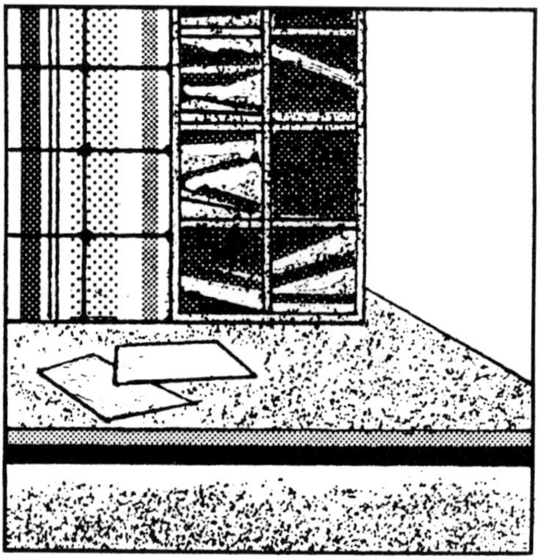

X
A Bad End

1 Walter Huff

I gulped down some orange juice and coffee, and then went up in the bedroom with the paper. I was afraid to open it in front of the Filipino. Sure enough, there it was, on Page 1.

OIL MAN, ON WAY TO JUNE RALLY, DIES IN TRAIN FALL

H. S. Nirdlinger, Petroleum Pioneer, Killed In Plunge from Express En route to Reunion At Leland Stanford.

With injuries about the head and neck, the body of H. S. Nirdlinger, Los Angeles representative of the Western Pipe and Supply Company and for a number of years prominently identified with the oil industry here, was found on the railroad tracks about two miles north of this city shortly before midnight last night. Mr Nirdlinger had departed on a northbound train earlier in the evening to attend his class reunion at Leland Stanford University, and it is believed he fell from the train. Police point out he had fractured his leg some weeks ago, and believe his unfamiliarity with crutches may have caused him to lose his balance on the observation platform, where he was last seen alive.

Mr Nirdlinger was 44 years old. Born in Fresno, he attended Leland Stanford, and on graduation, entered the oil business, becoming one of the pioneers in the opening of the field at Long Beach. Later he was active at Signal Hill. For the last three years he had been in charge of the local office of the Western Pipe and Supply Company.

Surviving are a widow, formerly Miss Phyllis Beldon of Mannerheim, and a daughter, Miss Lola Nirdlinger. Mrs Nirdlinger, before her marriage, was head nurse of the Verdugo Health Institute here.

Twenty minutes to nine, Nettie called. She said Mr Norton wanted to see me, as soon as I could possibly get down. That meant they had already had it, and I wouldn't have to put on any act, going in there with my paper and saying this is the guy I sold an accident policy to last winter. I said I knew what it was, and I was right on my way.

I got through the day somehow. I think I told you about Norton and Keyes. Norton is president of the company. He's a short, stocky man about thirty-five, that got the job when his father died and he's so busy trying to act like his father he doesn't seem to have time for much else. Keyes is head of the Claim Department, a holdover from the old regime, and the way he tells it young Norton never does anything right. He's big and fat and peevish, and on top of that he's a theorist, and it makes your head ache to be around him, but he's the best claim man on the Coast, and he was the one I was afraid of.

First I had to face Norton, and tell him what I knew, or anyway what I was supposed to know. I told him how I propositioned Nirdlinger about the accident policy, and how his wife and daughter opposed it, and how I dropped it that night but went over to his office a couple of days later to give him another whirl. That would check with what the secretary saw. I told him how I sold him, then, but only after I promised not to say anything to the wife and daughter about it. I told how I took his application, then when the policy came through, delivered it, and got his cheque. Then we went down in Keyes' office and we went all over it again. It took all morning, you understand. All while we were taking phone calls and telegrams kept coming in, from San Francisco, where Keyes had our investigators interviewing people that were on the train, from the police, from the secretary, from Lola, after they got her on the phone to find out what she knew. They tried to get Phyllis, but she had strict instructions from me not to come to the phone, so she didn't. They got hold of the coroner, and arranged for an autopsy. There's generally a hook-up between insurance companies and coroners, so they can get an autopsy if they want it. They could demand it, under a clause in their policy, but that would mean going to court for an order, and would tip it that the deceased was insured, and that's bad all the way round. They get it on the quiet, and in this case they had to have it. Because if Nirdlinger died of apoplexy, or heart failure, and fell off the train, then it wouldn't any longer be accident, but death from natural causes, and they wouldn't be liable. About the middle of the afternoon they got the medical report. Death was from a broken neck. When they heard that they got the inquest postponed two days.

By four o'clock, the memos and telegrams were piled on Keyes' desk so he had to put a weight on top of them to keep them from falling over, and he was mopping his brow and so peevish nobody could talk to him. But Norton was getting more cheerful by the minute. He took a San Francisco call from somebody named Jackson, and I could tell from what he said that it was this guy I had got rid of on the observation platform before I dropped off. When he hung up he put one more memo on top of the others and turned to Keyes. 'Clear case of suicide.'

If it was suicide, you see, the company wouldn't be liable either. This policy only covered accident.

'Yeah?'

'All right, watch me while I check it over. First, he took out this policy. He took it out in secret. He didn't tell his wife, he didn't tell his daughter, he didn't tell his secretary, he didn't tell anybody. If Huff here, had been on the job, he might have known——'

'Known what?'

'No need to get sore, Huff. But you've got to admit it looked funny.'

'It didn't look funny at all. It happens every day. Now if *they* had tried to insure *him*, without *him* knowing, *that* would have looked funny.'

'That's right. Leave Huff out of it.'

'All I'm saying, Keyes, is that——'

'Huff's record shows that if there had been anything funny, he'd have noted it and we'd have known it. You better find out something about your own agents.'

'All right, skip it. He takes out this policy in absolute secrecy. Why? Because he knew that if his family knew what he had done, they would know what he was up to. They knew what was on his mind, we can depend on that, and when we go into his books and his history, we'll find out what the trouble was. All right, next point, he fractured his leg, but he didn't put a claim in. Why? That looks funny, don't it, that a man had an accident policy, and didn't put a claim in for a broken leg? *Because he knew he was going to do this, and he was afraid if he put a claim in the family would find out about this policy and block him off.*'

'How?'

'If they called us up, we'd cancel on him wouldn't we? You bet we would. We'd return his unused premium so fast you couldn't see our dust, and he knew it. Oh no, he wasn't taking a chance on our doctor going out there to look at his leg and tipping things off. That's a big point.'

'Go on.'

'All right, he figures an excuse to take a train. He takes his wife with him to the station, he gets on the train, he gets rid of her. She goes. He's ready to do it. But he runs into trouble. There's a guy out there, on the observation platform, and for this he don't want any company. You bet he doesn't. So what does he do? He gets rid of him, by putting up some kind of a story about not having his ticket, and leaving it in his briefcase, and as soon as this guy goes, he takes his dive. That was the guy I just talked to, a man by the name of Jackson that went up to Frisco on a business trip and is coming back to-morrow. He says there's no question about it, he had the feeling even when he offered to get Nirdlinger's briefcase for him that he was trying to get rid of him, but he didn't quite have the heart to say no to a cripple. In my mind, that clinches it. It's a clear case of suicide. You can't take any other view of it.'

'So what?'

'Our next step is the inquest. We can't appear there, of course, because if a jury finds out a dead man is insured they'll murder us. We can send an investigator or two, perhaps, to sit in there, but nothing more than this. But Jackson says he'll be glad to appear and tell what he knows, and there's a chance, just a chance, but still a chance, that we may get a suicide verdict anyway. If we do, we're in. If we don't, then we've got to consider what we do. However, one thing at a time. The inquest first, and you can't tell what the police may find out; we may win right in the first round.'

Keyes mopped his head some more. He was so fat he really suffered in the heat. He lit a cigarette. He drooped down and looked away from Norton like it was some schoolboy and he didn't want to show his disgust. Then he spoke. 'It was not suicide.'

'What are you talking about? It's a clear case.'

'It was not suicide.'

He opened his bookcase and began throwing thick books on the table. 'Mr Norton, here's what the actuaries have to say about suicide. You study them, you might find out something about the insurance business.'

'I was raised in the insurance business, Keyes.'

'You were raised in private schools, Groton, and Harvard. While you were learning how to pull bow oars there, I was studying these tables. Take a look at them. Here's suicide by race, by colour, by occupation, by sex, by locality, by seasons of the year, by the time of day when committed. Here's suicide by method of accomplishment. Here's method of accomplishment subdivided by poisons, by fire-arms, by gas, by drowning, by leaps. Here's suicide by poisons subdivided by sex, by race, by age, by time of day. Here's suicide by poisons subdivided by cyanide, by mercury, by strychnine, by thirty-eight other poisons, sixteen of them no longer procurable at prescription pharmacies. And here – here, Mr Norton – are leaps subdivided by leaps from high places, under wheels of moving trains, under wheels of trucks, under the feet of horses, from steamboats. *But there's not one case out of all these millions of cases of a leap from the rear end of a moving train.* That's just one way they don't do it.'

'They could.'

'Could they? That train, at the point where the body was found, moves at a maximum of fifteen miles an hour. Could any man jump off there with any real expectation of killing himself?'

'He might dive off. This man had a broken neck.'

'Don't trifle with me. He wasn't an acrobat.'

'Then what are you trying to tell me? That it was on the up-and-up?'

'Listen, Mr Norton. When a man takes out an insurance policy, an insurance policy that's worth $50,000 if he's killed in a railroad accident, and then three months later he *is* killed in a railroad accident, it's not on the up-and-up. It can't be. If the train got wrecked it might be, but even then it would be a mighty suspicious coincidence. A *mighty* suspicious coincidence. No, it's not on the up-and-up. But it's not suicide.'

'Then what do you mean?'

'You know what I mean.'

'. . . Murder?'

'I mean murder.'

'Well wait a minute, Keyes, wait a minute. Wait till I catch up with you. What have you got to go on?'

'Nothing.'

'You must have *something*.'

'I said nothing. Whoever did this did a perfect job. There's nothing to go on. Just the same, it's murder.'

'Do you suspect anybody?'

'The beneficiary of such a policy, so far as I am concerned, is automatically under suspicion.'

'You mean the wife?'

'I mean the wife.'

'She wasn't even on the train.'

'Then somebody else was.'

'Have you any idea who?'

'None at all.'

'And this is all you have to go on?'

'I told you, I have nothing to go on. Nothing but those tables and my own hunch, instinct, and experience. It's a slick job, but it's no accident, and it's no suicide.'

'Then what are we going to do?'

'I don't know. Give me a minute to think.'

He took a half hour to think. Norton and I, we sat there and smoked. After a while, Keyes began to bump the desk with the palm of his hand. He knew what he meant, you could see that.

'Mr Norton.'

'Yes, Keyes.'

'There's only one thing for you to do. It's against practice, and in some other case I'd oppose it. But not in this. There's a couple of things about this that make me think that practice is one of the things they're going to count on, and take advantage of. Practice in a case like this is to wait, and make them come to you, isn't it? I advise against that. I advise jumping in there at once, to-night if possible, and if not to-night, then certainly on the day of that inquest, and filing a complaint against that woman. I advise filing an information of suspected murder against her, and smashing at her as hard and as quick as we can. I advise that we demand her arrest, and her detention, too, for the full forty-eight hours incommunicado that the law allows in a case of this kind. I advise sweating her with everything the police have got. I particularly advise separating her from this accomplice, whoever he is, or she is, so we get the full value of surprise, and prevent their conferring on future plans. Do that, and mark my words you're going to find out things that'll amaze you.'

'But – *on what*?'

'On nothing.'

'But, Keyes, we can't do a thing like that. Suppose we don't find out anything. Suppose we sweat her and get nothing. Suppose it *is* on the up-and-up. Look where that puts us. Holy smoke, she could murder us in a civil suit, and a jury would give her every nickel she asks for. I'm not sure they couldn't get us for *criminal* libel. And then look at the other side of it. We've got an advertising budget of $100,000 a year. We describe ourselves as the friend of the widow and orphan. We spend all that for goodwill, and then what? We lay ourselves open to the charge that we'd accuse a woman of *murder* even, rather than pay a just claim.'

'It's not a just claim.'

'It will be, unless we prove different.'

'All right. What you say is true. I told you it's against practice. But let me tell you this, Mr Norton, and tell you right now: Whoever pulled this was no punk. He, or she, or maybe the both of them, or the three of them or however many it took – knew what they were doing. They're not going to be caught just by your sitting around and hoping for clues. They thought of clues. There aren't any. The only way you're going to catch them is to move against *them*. I don't care if it's a battle or a murder case, or whatever it is, surprise is a weapon that *can* work. I don't say it will work. But I say it can work. And I say nothing else is going to work.'

'But, Keyes, we can't do things like that.'

'Why not?'

'Keyes, we've been over that a million times, every insurance company has been over it a million times. We have our practice, and you can't beat it. These things are a matter for the police. We can help the police, if we've got something to help with. If we discover information, we can turn it over to them. If we have our suspicions, we can communicate them to them. We can take any lawful, legitimate step – but as for this——'

He stopped. Keyes waited, and he didn't finish.

'What's unlawful about this, Mr Norton?'

'Nothing. It's lawful enough – but it's wrong. It puts us out in the open. It leaves us with *no* defences – in case we miss on it. I never heard of a thing like that. It's – tactically wrong, that's what I'm trying to say.'

'But strategically right.'

'We've got our strategy. We've got our ancient strategy, and you can't beat it. Listen, it *can* be suicide. We can affirm our belief that it's suicide, at the proper time, and we're safe. The burden of proof is on her. That's what I'm trying to say. Believe me, on a keg of dynamite like this, I don't want to get myself in the position where the burden of proof is on us.'

'You're not going to move against her?'

'Not yet, Keyes, not yet. Maybe later, I don't know. But so long as we can do the conservative, safe thing, I don't get mixed up with the other kind.'

'Your father——'

'Would have done the same thing. I'm thinking of him.'

'He would not. Old Man Norton could take a chance.'

'Well, I'm not my father!'

'It's your responsibility.'

I didn't go to the inquest, Norton didn't, and Keyes didn't. No insurance company can afford to let a jury know, whether it's a coroner's jury or any other kind of jury, that a dead man is insured. It just gets murdered if that comes out. Two investigators were sent over, guys that look like everybody else and sit with the newspaper men. We got what happened from them. They all identified the body and told their story, Phyllis, the two conductors, the red-cap, the porter, a couple of passengers, the police, and especially this guy Jackson, that pounded it in that I tried to get rid of him. The jury brought in a verdict 'that the said Herbert S. Nirdlinger came to his death by a broken neck received in a fall from a railroad train at or about ten o'clock on the night of June 3rd in a manner unknown to this jury'. It took Norton by surprise. He really hoped for a suicide verdict. It didn't me. The most important person at that inquest never said a word, and I had beat it into Phyllis's head long before that he had to be there, because I had figured on this suicide stuff, and we had to be ready for it. That was the minister that she asked to come with her, to confer with the undertaker on arrangements for the funeral. Once a coroner's jury sees that it's a question of burial in consecrated ground, the guy could take poison, cut his throat, and jump off the end of a dock, and they would still give a verdict, 'in a manner unknown to this jury'.

After the investigators told their story, we sat around again. Norton, Keyes, and myself, in Norton's office this time. It was about five o'clock in the afternoon. Keyes was sore. Norton was disappointed, but still trying to make it look like he had done the right thing. 'Well, Keyes, we're no worse off.'

'You're no better off.'

'Anyway, we haven't done anything foolish.'

'What now?'

'Now? I follow practice. I wait her out. I deny liability, on the ground that accident is not proved, and I make her sue. When she sues, then we'll see what we see.'

'You're sunk.'

'I know I'm sunk, but that's what I'm going to do.'

'What do you mean you know you're sunk?'

'Well, I've been talking to the police about this. I told them we suspect murder. They said they did too, at first, but they've given up that idea. They've gone into it. They've got their books, too, Keyes. They know how people commit murder, and how they don't. They say they never heard of a case where murder was committed, or even attempted, by pushing a man off the rear end of a slow-moving train. They say the same thing about it you say. How could a murderer, assuming there was one, be sure the man would die? Suppose he only got hurt? Then where would they be? No, they assure me it's on the up-and-up. It's just one of those freak things, that's all.'

'Did they cover everybody that was on that train? Did they find out whether there was a single one of them that was acquainted with this wife? Holy smoke, Mr Norton, don't tell me they gave up without going into that part. *I tell you, there was somebody else on that train!*'

'They did better than that. They covered the observation car steward. He took a seat right by the door, to mark up his slips for the beginning of the trip, and he's certain nobody was out there with Nirdlinger, because if anybody had passed him he would have had to move. He remembers Jackson going out there, about ten minutes before the train pulled out. He remembers the cripple going by. He remembers Jackson coming back. He remembers Jackson going out there again with the briefcase, and Jackson coming back, the second time. Jackson didn't report the disappearance right away. He just figured Nirdlinger went in a washroom or something, and as a matter of fact it wasn't till midnight, when he wanted to go to bed and he still had the briefcase that he supposed had Nirdlinger's ticket in it, that he said anything to the conductor about it. Five minutes after that, at Santa Barbara, was where the Los Angeles yardmaster caught the conductor with a wire and he impounded Nirdlinger's baggage and began taking names. There was nobody out there. This guy fell off, that's all. We're sunk. It's on the up-and-up.'

'If it's on the up-and-up, why don't you pay her?'

'Well wait a minute. That's what I think. That's what the police think. But there's still considerable evidence of suicide——'

'Not a scrap.'

'Enough, Keyes, that I owe it to my stockholders to throw the thing into court, and let a jury decide. I may be wrong. The police may be wrong. Before that suit comes to trial, we may be able to turn up plenty. That's all I'm going to do. Let a jury decide, and if it decides we're liable, then I pay her, and do it cheerfully. But I can't just make her a present of the money.'

'That's what you'll be doing, if you allege suicide.'

'We'll see.'

'Yeah, we'll see.'

I walked back with Keyes to his office. He snapped on the lights.

'He'll see. I've handled too many cases, Huff. When you've handled a million of them, you know, and you don't even know how you know. This is murder. . . . So they covered the porter, did they. Nobody went out there. How do they know somebody didn't swing aboard from the outside? How do they know——'

He stopped, looked at me, and then he began to curse and rave like a maniac. 'Didn't I tell him? Didn't I tell him to drive at her right from the start? Didn't I tell him to have her put under arrest, without waiting for this inquest? Didn't I tell him——'

'What do you mean, Keyes?' My heart was pounding, plenty.

'He was never on the train!'

He was yelling now, and pounding the desk. 'He was never on the train at all! Somebody took his crutches and went on the train for him! Of course that guy had to get rid of Jackson! He couldn't be seen alive beyond the point where that body was to be put! And now we've got all those sworn identifications against us——'

'Those what?' I knew what he meant. Those identifications at the inquest were something I had figured on from the start, and that was why I took such care that nobody on that train got a good look at me. I figured the crutches, the foot, the glasses, the cigar, and imagination would be enough.

'At the inquest! How well did any of those witnesses see this man? Just a few seconds, in the dark, three or four days ago. Then the coroner lifts a sheet on a dead man, the widow says yes, that's him, of course they all say the same thing. And now look at us! If Norton had thrown the gaff into her, all those identifications and everything else about it could have been challenged, the police would have waked up, and we might be somewhere. But now—— So he's going to let her sue! And just let him try, now, to break down those identifications. It'll be impossible. Any lawyer can crucify those witnesses if they change their story now. So that's being conservative! That's playing it safe! That's doing what the old man would have done! Why, Huff, Old Man Norton would have had a confession out of that woman by now. He'd have had a plea of guilty out of her, and already on her way to do a life stretch in Folsom. And now look at us. Just look at us. The very crux of the thing is over already, and we've lost it. We've lost it. . . . Let me tell you something. If that guy keeps on trying to run this company, the company's sunk. You can't take many body blows like this and last. Holy smoke. Fifty thousand bucks, and all from dumbness. Just sheer, wilful stupidity!'

The lights began to look funny in front of my eyes. He started up again, checking over how Nirdlinger got knocked off. He said this guy, whoever he was, had left his car at Burbank, and dropped off the train there. He said she met him there, and they drove down in separate cars, with the corpse in one of them, to the place where they put the body on the track. He figured it up that she would have time to get to Burbank, and then get back in time to buy a pint of ice cream at the drugstore at 10.20, when she showed up there. He even had that. He was all wrong on how it was done, but he was so near right it made my lips turn numb just to listen to him.

'Well, Keyes, what are you going to do?'

'. . . All right, he wants to wait her out, make her sue – that suits me. He's going to cover the dead man, find out what he can about why he maybe committed suicide. That suits me. I'm going to cover *her*. Every move she makes, everything she does, I'm going to know about it. Sooner or later, Huff, that guy's got to show. They'll have to see each other. And as soon as I know who he is, then watch me. Sure, let her sue. And when she goes on the witness stand, believe me, Huff, Norton's going to eat it. He's going to eat every word he's said, and the police may do some eating, too. Oh no. I'm not through yet.'

He had me, and I knew it. If she sued, and lost her head on the witness stand, God knows what might happen. If she didn't sue, that would be still worse. Her not trying to collect on that policy, that would look so bad it might even pull the police in. I didn't dare call her up, because for all I knew even now her wires might be tapped. I did that night what I had done the other two nights, while I was waiting on the inquest. I got stinko, or tried to. I knocked off a quart of cognac, but it didn't have any effect. My legs felt funny, and my ears rang, but my eyes kept staring at the dark, and my mind kept pounding on it, what I was going to do. I didn't know. I couldn't sleep, I couldn't eat, I couldn't even get drunk.

JAMES M. CAIN
Double Indemnity
(1936), pp. 55–70

2 *Dr Savundra*

'People in Britain probably knew a bit about the good Dr Savundra', commented *The Economist* wryly, 'so why did 400,000 car drivers not get to hear of it?' Was it something to do with a tradition in British business circles which said: 'Don't tell anyone, least of all the papers?' Or was it due to the tradition in British newspaper offices which said: 'Don't print a word, he's got a good lawyer?'

In the House of Commons Mrs Barbara Castle, the then Minister of Transport, warned motorists insured by FAM [Fire, Auto and Marine] that they must immediately take out new policies. Many, however, were unaware that they were no longer covered. As a demonstration of judicial sympathy, one offender was let off with the nominal fine of 5s. The crash came in the middle of the holiday period when many policyholders were abroad and not in touch with the daily news. Others had effected their insurance through garages or brokers and were in many cases unaware of the name of their company.

When an insurance company failed at that time there was no redress for the customers. Unlike a member of the public who suffers loss through the professional negligence of, say, a solicitor, there was no corporate body to take over the responsibility. The Motor Insurers Bureau, which is jointly financed by all motor insurance companies, would pay out claims to third parties injured by an uninsured driver – but the driver himself had no cover. . . .

Outside Jacqueline House there were extraordinary scenes as crowds of angry motorists besieged the building demanding to have their claims paid or their money back. Security men on the double doors had to struggle to keep them out. One woman, mother of two Mrs Mary Wightman from Essex, managed to slip through the cordon and stage a six-hour sit-in protest. . . .

Gradually some of the facts became clear. FAM had a total deficit of almost £3m, out of which £300,000 was owed to the 43,000 policyholders who had outstanding claims. The exact figure FAM was owed was to take a long time to establish as the accounts, mainly because of the computer, were in a chaotic state. The estimated figure of £1,500,000 due from brokers turned out to be a wildly optimistic figure: what had happened was that many brokers had been sent incorrect statements. Because of the computer's incapacity to handle changes, some of these demanded money for policies which had been cancelled – one broker's statement showed £600 as owing instead of the correct figure of £20; in another case a demand for nearly £400 was eventually withdrawn and £10 accepted as settlement.

Some accounts sent to the larger brokerages revealed even more serious exaggerations – in one case £13,000 instead of £5,000. One top broker, Frank Briscoe, reflected the general feeling among the more established firms when he criticised FAM for the way its accounts contained duplications and charges for policies which had been cancelled and which often did not include credits due. . . .

The man at the centre of the storm was still in Ceylon but less than a month after the completion of the Cheek report he was on his way back to England. He had decided to return.

For many, his action of voluntarily stepping into the lion's den poses an insoluble puzzle. True, he would shortly have had to leave Ceylon with the expiry of his temporary visa, but there are various countries in South America which do not have extradition treaties with Britain where he could have found refuge. So *why* did he come back?

Some say the clue is to be found in his vanity. Yet the reasons go deeper than that. Savundra was a gambler who always believed he would win – whatever the odds. Who was to say he could not do it again?

To stay away from Britain might have been prudent. But to return was the ultimate challenge, and in his eyes not to return would have been an admission of guilt and weakness. He had fooled governments before. And after all he had opted out of FAM *before* the crash. Things had only gone wrong after the hand-over. So back he came.

One problem he did not have to anticipate on his return, incidentally, was that of personal re-insurance. Emil Savundra was not himself one of the 400,000 policyholders of Fire, Auto and Marine. The certificate for his maroon-coloured Rolls-Royce was in the name of Co-operative Insurance Company.

Typically, his return was far from a straightforward operation.

He had prefaced it some time earlier with a letter to the Official Receiver, the main purpose of which seems to have been to demonstrate that some of the world's most eminent doctors had insisted he be treated lightly. The letter said:

> I confirm to you officially that I suffered a coronary thrombosis in May this year, confirmed by Dr Samuel Oram, Chief Cardiologist, King's College Hospital, London, Dr Alec Wingfield, Chief Cardiologist, Willesden General Hospital, Dr Charles Friedberg, Chief Cardiologist, Mount Sinai Hospital, New York, Dr Edward Partinope, Chief Cardiologist, New Jersey Hospital, and various other eminent cardiologists, every one of whom has confirmed the diagnosis categorically by reason of the electrocardiograph and other findings. The result is that *I am suffering from severe angina pectoris* which will be no doubt vastly aggravated by cold, strain, effort and anxiety.

Despite these health problems, Savundra, immaculately dressed in a dark suit, white shirt and blue tie, boarded an Air Ceylon VC-10 at Colombo airport bound for London, via Karachi and Rome. He told reporters: 'I have an appointment I intend to keep.'

The appointment with Mr Cheek was fixed for 9th January, 1967.

Savundra spent two nights in Rome at the Lux Hotel, a second-class establishment near the railway station, and then vanished. He left the hotel without breakfast, announcing that he was going to the City Air Terminal, but the airport had no record of a departing passenger called Savundra.

Reporters were convinced that his return to England was a hoax. However, he reappeared two days later in a small hotel near St. Peter's. On 17th December he drove to the air terminal, not to resume his journey, but to meet his family whom he had asked to join him in Rome.

White-haired and with a pronounced limp, he was unusually amiable towards the reporters who surrounded him. In his hand was the inevitable small attaché case. 'This is not full of money, you know. It contains winter woollies for the children. I myself have not got a penny. All I got out of the insurance business was a heart attack.'

Clearly he felt no apprehension about his appointment with Mr Cheek. His spell in Ceylon had completely re-established his old self-confidence.

'I will conduct a symphony orchestra', he declared. 'I will write the score and the authorities in Britain will have to play under my baton.'

Then he announced he had decided to stay in Rome over Christmas with his family. 'They are more important to me than the whole British public. We will go to London in the New Year. We will stay together now and only force will part us.'

The date of his appointment, 9th January, passed, however, and still he lingered on in his small forty-shillings-a-night *pension*. His heart was playing him up again. Visitors were shown copies of his cardiograph and hospital bills as 'proof' that his condition was genuine. A new appointment was fixed for 23rd January.

Surrounded by his usual battery of pill bottles Savundra now issued a challenge to the BBC. He would, he claimed, appear before a television 'jury' to explain his actions. His fee would be £100 per second and with an hour's programme earning £360,000, he would donate the proceeds to FAM to pay out to disappointed creditors.

'A hundred pounds a second' became the cry whenever he was asked any question regarding FAM, although he would talk as freely as ever on his two pet subjects – his health and the obnoxiousness of the Press.

Then, to everybody's surprise, he stepped out of his *pension* one morning and caught the plane to London. It is a measure of the close surveillance under which he had been kept that the fact that he was heading for London became known and such a large crowd was waiting for him at Heathrow that the police had to escort him through the barriers.

Peter Earle of the *News of the World* was one of the journalists to meet him. They were old acquaintances.

Dressed in a Savile Row suit and carrying a rolled umbrella, Savundra strutted across the tarmac towards the airport bus. 'I am poor as a church mouse now', he proclaimed, 'and I wish to demonstrate my poverty by riding on humble public transport.'

'My dear Doctor', said Earle, 'you have really torn the seat out of it this time. Not even you can beat this rap, and you have beaten some in your time.'

'Nonsense', snapped Savundra, 'I am like General MacArthur. He said: "I shall return" when the Japs drove him out of the Pacific. And I, the great Savundra, am returning in likewise fashion.' Then he smiled. 'I've had fifteen pills already today. They are nitroglycerine, you know. I feel I am going to explode at any moment.'

As usual he was vociferous on the subject of the Press. Asked why he thought the Press had been persistent, he replied by pulling up his coat sleeve to expose his coloured skin. 'That is why', he said. 'Why else would they have hounded me so much? There have been other insurance scandals recently and they have not received the same treatment.'

One thing he was determined to demonstrate was the fact that he was broke. 'If I cannot get a job', he declared, 'I shall demand my rights as an Englishman who has paid his taxes and demand national assistance for my wife and five children.'

He was as good as his word. After a day at White Walls in a state of siege, with the wrought-iron gates barred and his faithful gardener on guard, the man who one year before had been living like a millionaire emerged at 10 a.m. on Monday, 16th January, got into a friend's car and was driven to the Labour Exchange in Regent's Park Road.

The spectacle of Dr Emil Savundra painfully climbing the stairs, followed by a crowd of photographers, to the yellow-painted vacancy section on the first floor was described by one newspaper as 'the oddest sight of the year so far'.

Savundra found himself sixth in the queue. 'It's nothing to wait three hours', a fellow unfortunate told him, but he was lucky. The manageress of the Employment Exchange accorded him VIP treatment. As he was ushered down the corridor to her private office he walked past posters urging him to

'Drive a London ambulance', take 'a secure job as a postman', even, ironically, 'Enjoy a brighter future with the Prison Service'.

His visit did something to restore his faith in Britain. The interview lasted seventy minutes. Afterwards he said:

> They could see the impossible situation I was in and went out of their way to be kind. They took my coat, gave me a cup of tea and offered me a cigarette.
>
> I told them that I could not dig roads but my doctors say that I am fit for light sedentary work. Perhaps with my experience I can be of some use to the country's export trade. They filled in the necessary forms for me and promised to make all the arrangements.
>
> Damn it, this is the only civilised way to behave. This is cricket. This is what the Union Jack is all about.

As he passed the queue of fellow applicants on his way out, one of them stood up respectfully. It was his former gardener at White Walls. And in the crowd outside one woman who had been a policyholder with FAM said: 'I know him. He was such a nice gentleman. I do hope he gets a good job.'

Another bystander was less sympathetic. Taking off his hat with a sweep, he shouted sarcastically: 'Let's have a whip round for poor Mr Savundra.'

Determined to demonstrate his poverty, Savundra walked from the Exchange to Regent's Park, stopping to buy a sandwich on the way ('My wife gave me £3 this morning for small expenses'), which he proceeded to eat sitting on a park bench, feeding the crumbs to the pigeons. It made wonderful press material.

Making his way back to White Walls on foot, however, he met an old acquaintance to whom he confided the real humiliation he felt at having to 'sign on'. He spoke of his loyal wife and wonderful children.

> I used to have many friends, but not one has come near since my return. In a situation like this you find out who are your fair weather friends and who are your foul weather friends. Last year I got 650 Christmas cards. This year I had two. They were waiting for me when I came home. One from my gardener and one from the man who holds the burglar alarm keys.

JON CONNELL AND DOUGLAS SUTHERLAND
Fraud – The Amazing Career of Dr Savunda
(1978), pp. 182–190

Epilogue

The final chapter of *The Underwriter's Bedside Book* is hardly the final word on how insurance permeates the lives of everyone.

Insurance is one protection against the grimmer faces of Fate; it must be unsurprising that the tales told of it so often concern the catastrophes of life or the worst sides of our natures. Equally insurance is a people business with more than its fair share of lighter moments.

Perhaps what *The Underwriter's Bedside Book* indicates most clearly is that, in good times or in bad, the lifeline of the insurance industry is communication. Which leads us to end on a story told to us in our search for material for this anthology, the favourite, and allegedly true, tale of a Suffolk broker who received a telephone call from an agitated lady in her later middle years. Though his firm had dealt with the family for some time it had never received a claim and he was eager to be helpful until he was told: 'The cat is dead!'

'We cannot insure pets against death', he explained gently, understanding the natural grief. 'Cats are so vulnerable.'

'But you must', she said.

'I am so very, very sorry', he said.

He heard no more. Premiums on the various policies the family held continued to be paid. Then, three months later, he decided to call upon them to discuss the possible diversion of moneys into a new form of equity fund. To his astonishment the house was surrounded by scaffold and builders. The gardens were a sea of mud, bricks and cement. A cheerful client invited him into a section of the house which seemed barely to have survived a bomb blast.

'What happened?', he asked.

'You know that dreadful storm we had last July,' said the client. 'I'm afraid we were struck by lightning. Terrible fire, most of the house gone, nearly all our possessions. Dreadful.'

The bemused broker could only stutter, 'B-b-but you never even made a claim. It must be costing you thousands'.

'But we did', replied a puzzled client. 'You said we weren't covered. Sorry business, all told. Wife very upset. Loved that animal. All I can say is it's lucky the cat was the only one in the house!'

Bibliography

M. E. Barlen, M. P. Stambach & D. P. C. Stileman, *Bedford School and the Great Fire*; London: Quiller Press Ltd (1984)

William Bolitho, *Murder for Profit*; London: Dennis Dobson Ltd (1953)

Max Brod, *The Biography of Franz Kafka*; London: Secker & Warburg (1947)

Antony Brown, *Cuthbert Heath*; Newton Abbot & London: David & Charles (1980)

James M. Cain, *Double Indemnity*; London: Robert Hale Ltd (1936)

Erskine Caldwell, *The Complete Stories of Erskine Caldwell*; London: Lawrence Pollinger Ltd

William H. A. Carr, *Perils Named and Unnamed*; New York: McGraw Hill (1967)

Alan Chalkley, *Adventures and Perils*; Ogilvy & Mather Public Relations (Aus) Ltd (1985)

Jon Connell & Douglas Sutherland, *Fraud – The Amazing Career of Dr Savundra*; London: Hodder & Stoughton Ltd (1978)

Joseph Conrad, *Youth* (1902)

Edward Cowan, *Oil and Water*; London: William Kimber & Co (1968)

William Charles Crocker, *Far from Humdrum*; London: Hutchinson & Co (1967)

Raymond Flower & Michael Wynn Jones, *Lloyd's of London*; Lloyd's of London Press Ltd (1981)

D. E. W. Gibb, *Lloyd's of London*; London: Macmillan & Co Ltd (1957)

John E. N. Hearsey, *London and the Great Fire*; London: John Murray Ltd (1965)

A. P. Herbert, *Uncommon Law*; London: Eyre Methuen Ltd (1935)

David Keir, *The Bowring Story*; London: The Bodley Head (1962)

Rudyard Kipling, *Definitive Edition of Rudyard Kipling's Verse*; London: Hodder & Stoughton Ltd (1940)

Frank Ledwith, *Ships Afloat in the City*; London: Robert Hale Ltd (1977)

Frank Ledwith, *Ships that go Bump in the Night*; London: Robert Hale Ltd (1974)

E. P. Leigh-Bennett, *On This Evidence*; London: The Baynard Press (1936)

F. J. Maclean, *The Human Side of Insurance*; Sampson Low, Marston & Co Ltd (1931)

Wilfred Maud, *Antony Gibbs and Sons Limited – Merchants and Bankers* (1958)

R. E. Megarry, *A Second Miscellany-at-Law*; London: Stevens & Sons Ltd (1973)

Stephen Pile, *The Book of Heroic Failures*; London: Routledge & Kegan Paul (1979)

J. M. Ramsden, *The Safe Airline*; London: Macdonald & Jane's (1979)

Alexander Roda Roda, *Die Versicherung*; Vienna & Hamburg: Paul Zsolnay Verlag (1905)

L. T. C. Rolt, *Red for Danger*; London: The Bodley Head (1955)

Lionel Rose, *The Massacre of the Innocents*; London: Routledge & Kegan Paul (1986)

A. W. Brian Simpson, *Cannibalism and the Common Law*; Chicago and London: University of Chicago Press (1984)

Frank C. Spooner, *Risks at Sea*; Cambridge University Press (1983)

Anne Swain, *The Secret Diary of Frederick Hole, Aged about 39*: The Review (1984)

E. S. Turner, *Roads to Ruin*; London: Penguin Books in association with Michael Joseph (1966)

Tony Waltham, *Catastrophe – The Violent Earth*; London: Macmillan & Co Ltd (1978)

Charles Wright & C. Ernest Fayle, *A History of Lloyd's*; London: Macmillan & Co Ltd (1878)

Index

[*Authors of and titles of contributions to this book are indexed to the first page of the extract*]